THE
AGITATOR
& THE
POLITICIAN

Printed in the United States of America.

ISBN: 978-1-63385-349-2
Library of Congress Control Number: 2020901296

Layout and Design by Jason Price

Published by
Word Association Publishers
205 Fifth Avenue
Tarentum, Pennsylvania 15084

www.wordassociation.com
1.800.827.7903

THE
AGITATOR
& THE
POLITICIAN

SECOND EDITION

WILLIAM LLOYD GARRISON, ABRAHAM LINCOLN
AND THE EMANCIPATION OF THE SLAVES

ROBERT MacDOUGALL

WORD ASSOCIATION PUBLISHERS
www.wordassociation.com
1.800.827.7903

Contents

Preface

I love reading biographies. They are personal stories and they make me think: What would I have done if I had been in the same circumstances as the person I'm reading about? They take me back to different eras and offer insights into the way life was lived: How did most people get their news back then and how might events have been different if news traveled as fast as it does today? And, most significantly, biographies offer "on-ramps" to understanding the major events in history: How did this person's actions and thoughts influence the events of the Civil War . . . and how did the war influence him?

When I was in high school, abolitionist William Lloyd Garrison caught my attention. I was a lukewarm history student, but I was fascinated by a man who was willing to live in poverty for his whole life for the sake of an oppressed race. Garrison endured outrageous abuse by angry people wherever he spoke, yet he soldiered on for over thirty-five years until, almost miraculously, he witnessed the success of his long and often frustrating crusade. He lived to see the emancipation of the four million enslaved African-Americans in the United States.

Garrison's story so fascinated me that I developed a love for history. After years of seeing history as a long list of boring facts, I finally realized that there are hundreds of interesting people whose *life* stories make up the fabric of our *nation's* story, and *that* revelation made history came alive for me. I went from enduring the subject as a graduation requirement, to eagerly reading everything I could about it. I pursued my passion for history through college, and then began a forty-nine year career of working to pass on my enthusiasm for history to resistant students . . . and sometimes succeeding.

In the late 1960's, at the height of the civil rights movement, I decided to write a book about my hero William Lloyd Garrison, the man who had lived the principles of non-violent, yet uncompromising protest that were being practiced in my time by Dr. Martin Luther King, Jr., and his followers. As I researched and began writing, I noticed a parallel between what was happening in the 1960's and what had happened in Garrison's day:

Dr. King's crusade was partly propelled forward by the repugnant reactions of the racists in the country who persecuted him and his followers. The fire hoses, the church bombings, the police beatings, and the racial slurs all aroused sympathy for his cause. Likewise, William Lloyd Garrison was aided by the over-reactions to his efforts by Southerners and pro-slavery people in the North.

Ultimately, Dr. King's movement would not have achieved the success that it did without the political skills of President

Lyndon Johnson. Similarly, William Lloyd Garrison would never have seen the slaves throw off their shackles without the adroit maneuvering of President Abraham Lincoln.

Because of these parallels, I realized a radical would fail without the help (perhaps reluctant help!) of a skilled politician. Therefore, I decided my biography should focus on Garrison *and* Abraham Lincoln. As I researched and wrote, I realized how much each man's life experiences prepared him for the role he was to play in the dramatic abolition of slavery in the United States. Neither man would have accomplished what he did without the other, even though they were very far apart in their philosophies of life and their political positions during most of their lives. The evolution of the views of these men as they reached the point where they stood together is the major theme of this book.

Over the last fifty years, *The Agitator and the Politician* has had a long and somewhat tortured history. I completed the original manuscript in the early 1970's. Then, because of my teaching, coaching and family responsibilities, it sat gathering dust for thirty years. Finally, I dug it up, polished it and published it in 2005. But, in the years since then, I have decided the original work had some gaps that needed to be filled, and some flaws that needed correcting. Consequently, I am producing this "second edition" which does more justice to the fascinating stories of these two very consequential men than the original edition did.

My absorption in the endeavor has occupied much of my energy and time. For her encouragement in this, I owe a great debt of gratitude to my wife, Diane, who has prodded me on and encouraged me when I was tired and on the verge of quitting. For fifty years she has been my inspiration, and also my best proof-reader!

I am also indebted to two of my former colleagues at Central Catholic High School in Lawrence, Massachusetts. Fellow history teacher, Denise Horan, read the manuscript and offered many helpful suggestions for making it a more enjoyable read. English teacher, Katherine Coyne, read through to find grammatical and typographical mistakes that I had overlooked.

Introduction

In the year 1831, a mighty effort to remove African slavery from the United States began in earnest. On New Year's Day, William Lloyd Garrison put out the first edition of his abolitionist newspaper *The Liberator*. Occupying more radical ground than all of the anti-slavery advocates before him, Garrison called for the *immediate* emancipation of the slaves without compensation to the slave owners and without any attempt to colonize the freed black people outside of the country. Eight months after Garrison launched his paper, a slave named Nat Turner led a bloody rebellion in Virginia. He and his followers killed fifty-seven white people in their nighttime rampage before all of them were killed or captured. Turner himself was eventually apprehended and sent to the gallows, but his rebellion sent shock waves across the South and seriously undermined the fiction that the slaves were content with their lives.

In response to Garrison's publication and the Turner revolt, white Southerners began to harden their support for slavery.

Having long believed that slavery was an evil — but a *"necessary evil"* — they now began to follow the lead of Vice-President John C. Calhoun of South Carolina who argued that slavery was not an evil but a *positive good* for both races and should be preserved in perpetuity. Calhoun argued that all of the great cultures in history — Egypt, Greece, Rome — rested on slavery. Slavery put the burden of manual labor where it belonged — on the backs of the lower forms of human life — and thereby freed the more intelligent people to create great cultures. American slaves also benefitted, Calhoun continued, because slavery provided them with a civilized life far better than what they, in their benighted condition, could provide for themselves. After 1831, the concept that slavery was a positive good for both races took hold across the South, and most white people, rich and poor, subscribed to it.

Clearly, in 1831 the battle lines for an epic struggle over slavery were drawn.

In the three decades that followed, it seemed that Garrison and his tiny coterie of followers would lose the struggle and were doomed to die as failures. The South and its slave system seemed to be grasping the country with a vise-like grip:

- All of the presidents, from Andrew Jackson in 1831 to James Buchanan in 1860 were either slaveholders themselves or Northerners who sympathized with the South's view of the "peculiar institution."
- In 1837 the House of Representatives imposed a "Gag Rule" on any petitions or resolutions regarding slavery; all such documents were to be tabled. Only Herculean efforts by Representative John Quincy Adams got the obnoxious rule repealed in 1844 so that the subject could at least be discussed.
- In 1845 Congress nearly doubled the territory in which slavery was legal by adding Texas to the Union as a slave state.

- In 1850 Congress passed the Fugitive Slave Act that required all people, Northerners included, to return runaway slaves to their "rightful owners."
- In 1854 Congress passed the Kansas-Nebraska Act opening those two territories to slavery for the first time.
- In 1857, the Supreme Court ruled that Congress could not ban slavery from any territory owned by the United States because such a ban would conflict with the Constitution's protections of private property. If the Court was prohibiting Kansas Territory from banning slavery, many people asked, could a prohibition on all "free states" doing so be far behind?

By 1860 some observers believed the United States was on the brink of becoming a slave republic.

In the face of all this, where was the abolitionist movement that William Lloyd Garrison and others had started with such energy in 1831? Through the 1830's, *The Liberator* came out every week, anti-slavery meetings were held, and speakers fanned out across the North to address people wherever they could find a hall or an audience. Most Americans branded the abolitionists as hotheaded, fanatical incendiaries, and either ignored them or violently attacked them. Gradually, however, a climate change did occur. The abolitionists gained a small following, and by the 1840's soil had been broken so that seeds of new thought began to sprout. Some people now respected the abolitionist speakers. By the 1850's a growing number of Northerners were beginning to think that slavery was anathema to American values and should at least be restricted to the states where it already existed. Abraham Lincoln emerged as one of the leading proponents of that point of view.

Still, as the presidential election of 1860 approached, public opinion polls — had they existed at that time — would have shown almost *no* support for the immediate emancipation of the slaves, and even less support for emancipation without financial compensation to the owners and a colonization plan to send the freed African-Americans out of the country.

Yet, within three years, immediate emancipation without compensation or colonization *did* occur. William Lloyd Garrison, once the scourge of civilized Boston, became the toast of the town and Abraham Lincoln became known as the "Great Emancipator." The fascinating story of how this truly convulsive change in American society came about so abruptly unfolds in the pages that follow. The remarkable irony of the story is the key role played by Abraham Lincoln who, in 1831 and even as late as 1860, would have called Garrison a dangerous lunatic. Lincoln was a very conservative politician — pro-business and anti-social change. Garrison once wrote that Lincoln had no more anti-slavery feelings than a wet rag. And yet, without Lincoln, slavery would not have ended when it did and William Lloyd Garrison would probably have died an unknown failure.

This is the story of two men who, in 1831, were worlds apart, yet came to stand together in 1863 on the same ground fighting for the most fundamental change in the United States since the founding of the nation. The two roads to emancipation these men followed wound through many dramatic turns and climaxed with an ironic twist that was breathtaking in its magnitude.

CHAPTER ONE

Two Young Americans In 1831

Abraham Lincoln and William Lloyd Garrison were in very different places in the summer of 1831. Both were in their early twenties, but Lincoln was exploring life on the frontier and Garrison had already committed himself to the life of an anti-slavery agitator.

1. THE YOUNG FRONTIERSMAN

Men wearing buckskin boots and sweaty shirts and children in homespun came down to the water's edge from the village of New Salem, Illinois, to watch. Out on the Sangamon River was an eighty-foot-long flatboat loaded with barrels of pork, corn and many large, grunting hogs. The bow was sticking up over a milldam; a corner of the stern was submerged and rapidly taking water; barrels were sliding and hogs were running about. On board was a tall, long-armed man shouting instructions to his companions and grabbing barrels as they slid.

Abraham Lincoln wrestled with his problem as townspeople came and went. Some offered encouragement or advice. Others shook their heads and wandered off. Finally, Lincoln told his companions, John Hanks and John Johnston, to unload part of the cargo onto the riverbank. When the load was lighter, they lifted the stern while Lincoln jumped into the water and bore a hole in the bottom to let the water run out. Then, they plugged the hole, eased the boat over the dam into the water on the other side, re-loaded the cargo and resumed their trip. The villagers went back to their business talking with admiration of the young man's cool head and competence. In a wilderness settlement such as New Salem, people respected a man who could handle adversity so well.

New Salem was in the middle of the great American frontier. Although Illinois had been a state for thirteen years, most of it was still sparsely settled. The Native Americans had only recently left and they would be back. Travel was difficult over rough dirt roads or down narrow twisting rivers such as the Sangamon. People were arriving every day from the East — Kentucky or Indiana, or even as far away as Virginia. Some were settling in the tiny villages such as New Salem; others were pushing on across the Mississippi River to the fertile lands of "Unorganized Territory."

Guiding his craft skillfully through the channels of the Sangamon, Abe Lincoln was every inch a man of the frontier. He was twenty-two and striking out on his own in the rugged country carrying a load of produce down to New Orleans for a man named Denton Offutt, a New Salem merchant. The year before, young Abe had come to Illinois from Indiana and had helped his father and stepmother make it through a snowy Illinois winter in a rough lean-to. Before Indiana, he had lived as a young boy in Kentucky. His life had been one of enduring lonely winters in log cabins, clearing land, and suffering the deaths of loved ones who succumbed to the hardships of the wilderness. He had learned how to read and write with less than a year's formal schooling. He had learned to love people. On the boat he laughed and swapped stories with Hanks and Johnston and rejoiced in the warmth of companionship.

After navigating the Illinois River and gliding out onto the broad Mississippi, the young men saw a shoreline that was largely uninhabited. Lincoln looked west into the slave state of Missouri. Illinois did not allow slavery, so the river was the boundary line between slave territory and free. Occasionally, he saw villages along the river, but mostly he saw rolling hills, forests and grassy prairie.

St. Louis was a bustling town of nearly six thousand souls and Lincoln walked its muddy streets and watched wagons loaded with families and their household goods rumble past. He had heard of "opening the west," the Great Plains and Texas. It seemed that the West must be rapidly filling up with people, and indeed it was. Settlers were heading out from St. Louis to the interior of the state, and a few were talking about pushing on across the plains and the mountains to the lush Willamette Valley of Oregon. St. Louis was becoming the gateway to the West.

Further down the river Lincoln passed Arkansas Territory, an area quickly being settled by people from the South and destined to become a slave state. On the east bank was Tennessee, home state of the president, Andrew Jackson, the first Westerner in the Executive Mansion and a symbol to the nation of the growth and political importance of the West. Jackson was talking about cutting the eastern bankers down to size and giving the common man a larger voice in government.

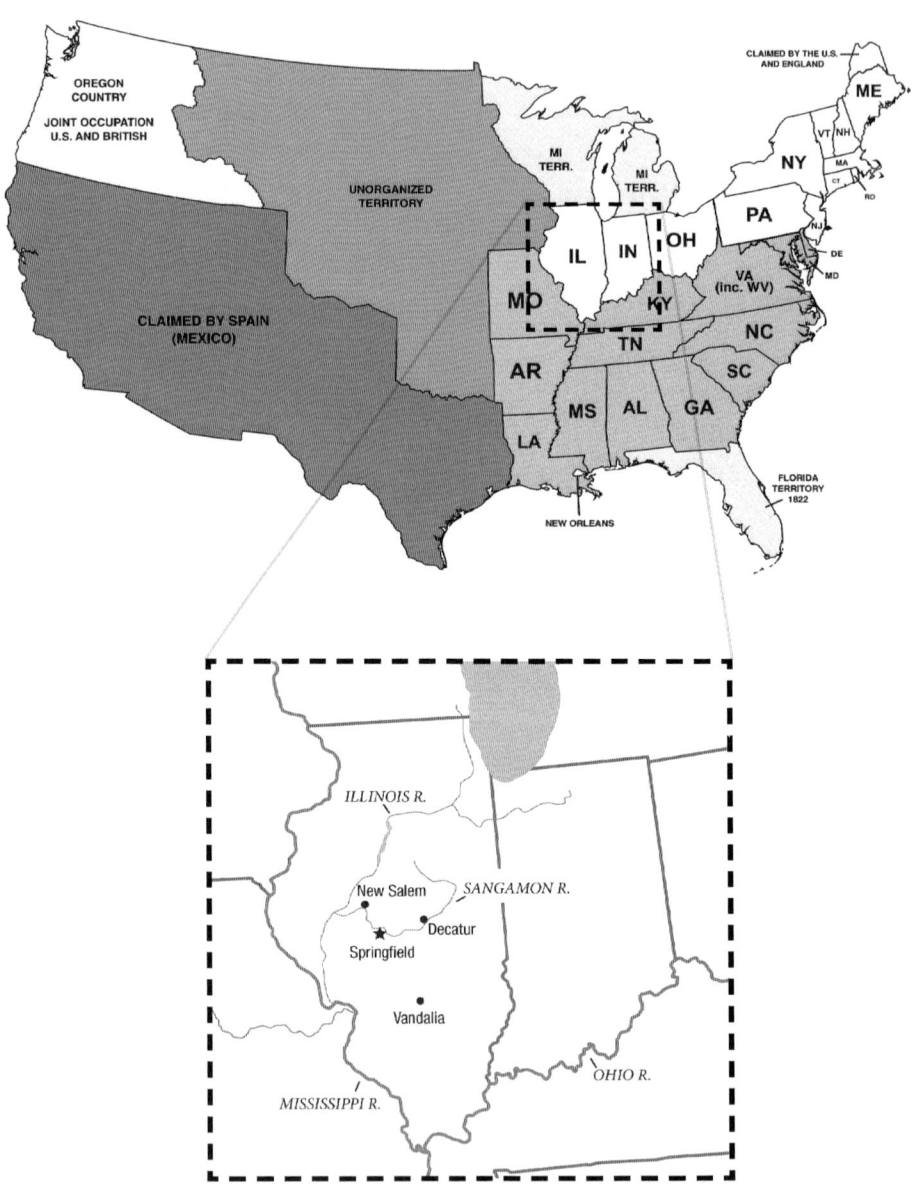

Below Tennessee there was Louisiana on the west side and Mississippi on the east. Lincoln was now in the Deep South.

When he finally reached New Orleans, summer's oppressive heat was settling in on the historic old city. Lincoln had been there before on another flatboat trip, but the size of it and the swarms of humanity still amazed him. The city was built on a crescent in the Mississippi and its curved shoreline was gorged with boats of all descriptions. There were hundreds of flatboats laden with farm produce from the Northwest, and there were sailing vessels taking on bales of cotton produced on the great plantations of the South.

Along the narrow cobblestone streets Lincoln saw every sort of human being imaginable. There were drunken flatboat men, beggars, prostitutes, wealthy businessmen and plantation owners. And there were slaves. New Orleans was a center of commerce for the South, and one very important item of trade was the "Negro." Lincoln read signs offering "Negroes of all descriptions." He stood near a trading block to watch men who smoked long cigars inspect the mouths and buttocks of the naked and chained captives and then make bids to the auctioneer.

No doubt Lincoln was repulsed by what he saw for he knew the slaves in New Orleans were just a tiny corner of the slave empire that stretched from the Gulf States all the way up to Missouri, Kentucky and Maryland. He had heard tales of excessive cruelty, especially on the large cotton plantations of the Deep South. In these stories, slaves were often under the supervision of a white "overseer" who was responsible for production quotas and who hated the "niggers" — the only people on earth he could look down upon. White men drove slaves from sunrise to sunset, whipped them severely for "laziness" or "ineptitude," "sheltered" them in rude cabins with leaking roofs and dirt floors, and fed them only bread and salt pork. When slaves tried to escape, they were hunted down by bloodhounds, whipped until they were near death, and clamped in painful leg irons.

There were other versions of slavery, promoted especially by the planters, which minimized the number of bad plantations. According to these stories, most slaves were happy and lived side-by-side with their masters in mutually beneficial relationships. They were given easily accomplished tasks that they often finished early enough in the day to spend the afternoon fishing or tending their own gardens. In return for their labor, they received agreeable living quarters, adequate clothing and food, and medical care. Moreover, they were given spiritual guidance, often by the master's wife, who taught them Christianity and good manners. Lincoln was inclined to think that perhaps a few of these plantations did exist, but to him the fact that any people could be denied the basic right of freedom and could be subject to the whims of "masters" made slavery an immoral and disgusting institution.

There had been some limited opposition to slavery in the United States, particularly at the time of the revolution from Britain. Jefferson had even wanted to include a condemnation of the system in the Declaration of Independence, an idea that was rejected by his fellow Southerners. By the time Lincoln visited New Orleans, Southerners were promulgating the idea that slavery was a "blessing" to both races. It was not a "necessary evil," as they had once thought, but rather a "positive good." Slavery, the argument went, enabled the South to produce cotton, tobacco, rice and other crops cheaply; it provided a social structure in which blacks and whites had clearly defined positions and were not in competition with each other; it provided the "Negro," who Southerners insisted was inferior, with a civilized, productive life he would never be able to arrange for himself; and it kept the black man — always a potential danger — under strict control.

The few Southerners who did object to slavery felt that the only way to deal with it was to deport "Negroes" — but only those whose masters had willingly freed them. Any plan of emancipation that left "Negroes" in the country would be economically and socially unacceptable. In 1817 men who wished to send freed "Negroes" to Africa organized the American Colonization Society, established a colony on the west coast of Africa named Liberia, and began sending small numbers of African-Americans to inhabit it.

If Lincoln had any thoughts about the Colonization Society or about slavery itself he did not express them while he was in New Orleans. Many years later John Hanks claimed that Lincoln cursed under his breath at the sight of the slave auctions and said, "If ever I get a chance to hit that thing . . . I'll hit it hard." (1) This story makes an excellent bit of foreshadowing but, since Hanks had left the boat in St. Louis and was not with Lincoln in New Orleans, it is most likely a fabrication. For the next five years Lincoln said hardly a word about slavery. His look at the institution had probably left an impression on his mind that was to last, but it had not moved him to action.

However, in the summer of 1831, as Lincoln boarded a steamboat to go back to New Salem, another young man in Massachusetts was already making a career of hitting that thing and hitting it hard.

2. THE YOUNG FIREBRAND

William Lloyd Garrison was first awakened to the plight of the slaves by a soft-spoken Quaker named Benjamin Lundy. In 1828 Garrison was editing a small newspaper in Boston and living at the boardinghouse of Reverend William Collier. One evening he sat with eight clergymen in Collier's living room to hear Lundy ask them to form an anti-slavery society in Boston. For over an hour, Lundy described with deep feeling the terrible plight of the slaves and begged his listeners to take action. One would expect that "men of the cloth" would be deeply moved and stirred to do something on behalf of fellow human beings who were suffering.

"He might as well have urged the stones in the streets to cry out in behalf of the perishing captives," Garrison later recalled. "Every soul in the room was heartily opposed to slavery, BUT – It would terribly alarm and enrage the South to know that an anti-slavery society existed in Boston! BUT – It would do harm, rather than good, openly to agitate the subject! BUT – We had nothing to do with the subject and the less we meddled with it, the better." (2)

Yet, Garrison was impressed with Lundy's plea. He admired this man who walked all over the country speaking to small groups and who carried a knapsack full of type on his back so he could publish his anti-slavery newspaper, the *Genius of Universal Emancipation*, wherever he went. He sympathized with Lundy's tale of how, as a young man, he had seen chained slaves in Virginia and had become an angry opponent of slavery. "I heard the wail of the captive," Lundy recalled, "I felt the pang of his distress, and the iron entered my soul." (3)

As the clergymen were putting on their coats to leave, Garrison went up to Lundy and asked for more information about slavery. Flushed with excitement, Garrison avowed he would like to help crusade against slavery if he knew more about it. Recognizing an eager convert in this young man with thinning hair and metal spectacles, Lundy promised to send more materials and to keep in touch.

A few months later Garrison had taken a job editing *The Journal of the Times* in Bennington, Vermont, and was writing editorials against slavery. Lundy, perhaps to challenge Garrison, wrote in the *Genius*:

> There are many who are ready to acknowledge – O yes, they will *acknowledge* (good honest souls!) . . . *that something should be done* for the abolition of slavery. They will, also, pen a paragraph - - perhaps an article or so — and then — the subject is EXHAUST-ED! They cannot for the lives of them discover how the condition of the colored race can be meliorated by *their* exertions. . . . We will not, however, pursue this part of the subject lest our friend Garrison may think we are about to insinuate a voice of censure against *him*, in anticipation! In truth, *we do hope* he will remain *true to the cause.* (4)

Startled that Lundy would question his dedication, Garrison responded in *The Journal*:

> (We assure the editor) that our zeal in the cause of emancipation suffers no diminution. Before God and our country we give our pledge that the liberation of the enslaved Africans will always be uppermost in our pursuits. The people of New England are inter-ested in this matter, and they must be aroused from their lethar-gy as by a trumpet call. They shall not quietly slumber while we have the management of a press, or strength to hold a pen. (5)

Convinced now that the anti-slavery effort had, indeed, a zealous crusader, Lundy walked from Baltimore to Bennington (nearly 400 miles!) to see his convert. He offered Garrison joint editorship of the *Genius of Universal Emancipation*, which they would publish on a weekly basis in Baltimore. Garrison, excited at the prospect of becoming a full-fledged anti-slavery agitator, immediately accepted. A few weeks later he wrote in his farewell editorial to the people of Bennington, "I trust in God that I may be the humble instrument of breaking at least one chain, and restoring at least one captive to liberty. It will amply repay a life of severe toil." (6)

Before going to Baltimore to join Lundy, Garrison spent a few months back in Boston. Anxious to make some sort of anti-slavery mark on the city, he accepted an invitation from the congregational societies of Boston to deliver a Fourth of July address at the Park Street Church on behalf of the American Colonization Society. As the Fourth drew near, however, he grew increasingly anxious and wondered what he had gotten himself into. "My very knees knock together at the thought of speaking before so large a concourse," he wrote a friend. (7) And so, he carefully prepared his speech and practiced delivering it many times, sometimes going off into the woods to try it out on the trees and squirrels.

On the Fourth of July, the weather was unusually cool and damp as a large crowd filed into the brick church with its white steeple next to the Common. When his time came to speak, Lloyd stood in the pulpit his face flush with self-consciousness. He began shakily, but gradually he gained confidence and soon he was speaking with the soft-spoken certainty that would mark his public addresses for the rest of his life.

His words were stronger than the American Colonization Society was accustomed to hearing. We in the free states share the guilt of slavery, he told the audience, for we are part of the country that allows it to exist and we are liable to be called upon, through our service in the armed forces, to put down slave rebellions. It is our right, it is our duty, to demand a gradual elimination of slavery.

Then he chided those who said there were constitutional limitations to what could be done about slavery. "Suppose that, by a miracle, the slaves should suddenly become white," he proposed. "Would you shut your eyes upon their suffering and calmly talk of constitutional limitations? No, your voice would peal in the ears of the taskmasters like deep thunder; you would carry the constitution by force, if it could not be taken by treaty; patriotic assemblies would congregate at the corners of every street. . . . You would say that it is enough that they are white, and in bondage, and they ought immediately to be set free." (8)

As some in the audience squirmed in their seats, he warned that there would be a great resistance to the abolition of slavery. "We shall have to contend with insolence and pride, and self-ishness of many a heartless being," he predicted. He expressed confidence, however, that "heartless beings" would be overcome by "meekness, perseverance and prayer." (9) Slavery could not be abolished immediately, he concluded, but would have to be taken down brick-by-brick so it would not bury the nation in its ruins.

The crowd gave Garrison tepid applause. Many of the people were annoyed at his attempt to make them feel guilty about slavery; they believed they were dealing with a thorny problem in a sensible way and they expected him to give them credit for it. Also, they were disturbed that Garrison had emphasized emancipation with hardly a word about colonization. Was this young man suggesting the abolition of slavery with no provisions for getting the freed black people out of the country? If so, he was very radical! They would have been appalled to know that they had just heard the most moderate speech William Lloyd Garrison would ever make in his anti-slavery career!

A few weeks later when Garrison met Lundy in Baltimore, he was already regretting that he had talked of *gradual* emancipation at the Park Street Church and that he had, by not speaking directly enough on the subject, condoned the idea of colonization. He could not admit that slaveholders had any right to own slaves for a few years or even a few hours, he told Lundy, for that implied they had the right to own them forever. As for sending the freed Negroes out of the country, very few black people wanted to leave and, moreover, since they were born in the United States and were the equals of white people, they had every right to stay.

Lundy had always believed that, although slavery was dreadfully wrong, emancipation could only come about gradually. As for colonization he was so enthused about it that he was trying to organize a colony for ex-slaves in Haiti. Thus, he could not agree with his new partner's more radical views, but he still wanted to go ahead with the joint editorship of the *Genius*. "Thee may put thy initials to thy articles, and I will put my initials to mine," he suggested. Garrison replied, "That will answer, and I shall be able to free my soul." (10)

The two men began issuing the *Genius of Universal Emancipation* in the late summer of 1829. In his first editorial, Garrison immediately went on the offensive. He denounced colonization as a trick played by Southerners to convince Northerners that slavery was being dismantled, whereas nothing of the sort was happening. He renounced his statements at the Park Street church on gradual abolition and announced his conviction that black people were the full equals of whites and should be allowed to remain in this country as free men.

These thoughts, and many that followed in subsequent editorials, were too much for many of the *Genius's* subscribers. They began cancelling in droves, often accompanying their cancellation with angry letters to Lundy chastising him for taking on a firebrand. For every new subscriber Lundy could find, Garrison would scare away ten.

A slave trader named Austin Woolfolk, who had once beaten Lundy almost to death, took offense at an editorial on slave trading in the *Genius* and wrote a letter threatening him again. Garrison replied in the paper that it was *he* who had written the offensive editorial and said of Woolfolk, "If he wishes to discuss slavery, or to complain of the slander of his character, I shall be happy to see him at my boarding house, no. 135 Market Street, where I shall endeavor to convince him that he is pursuing a wicked traffic. . . . " (11) Woolfolk never came.

It was a wonder, however, that others like him did not attack the two editors. Publishing an anti-slavery newspaper in the middle of a slave state was very dangerous business. But, since Lundy and Garrison were probably two of a very few abolitionists Baltimore had ever heard of, perhaps they were simply passed off as harmless cranks and mostly ignored.

An advantage of being in Baltimore was the opportunity Garrison and Lundy had to observe slavery first hand. One Sunday afternoon, a slave came to the two men and showed them his back. Aghast at what he saw, Garrison counted thirty-seven painful lashes oozing blood. The man had not unloaded a wagon fast enough to suit his overseer and had received this terrible beating as his punishment.

Garrison and Lundy printed this slave's story in "the Black List," a special column of the paper devoted to stories of slavery's atrocities. Garrison's favorite items for the "Black List" were details of the slave trade, some of which he could see from the windows of the *Genius*'s office as slaves in chains were marched down the street. On November 13, 1829, he included in the list a description of a sailing ship from Newburyport, Massachusetts owned by Francis Todd that was taking seventy-five slaves for sale in the Deep South. In the next *Genius* Garrison wrote that slave traders should be "sentenced to solitary confinement for life; they are the enemies of their own species — highway robbers and murderers." (12) Todd, outraged at this attack on his good name, sued for liable and won his case against Garrison in court. The fine was $100, which Garrison could not — and would not — pay. And so, on April 17, 1830, the co-editor of the *Genius of Universal Emancipation* went to jail. As he walked into the dingy, gray building, the veteran inmates shouted "fresh fish!"

In many ways Garrison welcomed imprisonment. It brought publicity to the cause and gave him the chance to play the role of martyr. Sympathetic letters came to him from all over the country. "Up to that period," he later wrote, "no single incident connected with the subject of slavery had ever elicited so much attention, or excited such a spontaneous burst of general indignation." (13)

From his cell, Garrison wrote letters to newspapers and to well-known people throughout the country asking what had happened to freedom of the press when he could be jailed for merely telling the truth about Todd. He declared he would continue to point the finger at slave traders either in the *Genius* or in any other paper he might edit. He wrote poems on his cell walls and pronounced that the city of Baltimore could imprison his body, but it could never imprison his mind.

Finally, forty-nine days after Garrison began his sentence, Arthur Tappan, a wealthy New York businessman who had adopted abolitionism, sent the one hundred dollars to pay the fine. Garrison left jail almost reluctantly; it had served as an excellent platform for anti-slavery agitation. He would not forget the sympathy for the cause he had achieved while he was a victim of the system.

By the time Garrison was a free man again, Lundy had about given up hope of continuing the *Genius* as a weekly paper. Like most journals of an unpopular cause, the *Genius* was in deep financial trouble. Moreover, Lundy felt it would be increasingly difficult to continue putting out the paper with his very radical friend. Garrison had reached the same conclusion and had decided to publish a paper of his own. Although they were still friends, the two men parted company, each to promote the anti-slavery cause in his own way.

Garrison planned to call his paper the *Public Liberator and Journal of the Times.* He printed a prospectus telling potential donors that he would publish the paper in Washington, D.C., the capital of the nation and the one place in the South where Congress could abolish slavery immediately without regard for state laws. Because truth "is best discovered by plain words," he proposed to use "great plainness of speech." (14)

To raise money for his venture, Garrison decided to travel through the North, speaking to groups wherever he could find a hall. Once he had raised sufficient funds, he would go to Washington to begin publication. No one in Baltimore would permit him to speak in any building, which did not surprise him in a city with such a heavy interest in slavery. In Philadelphia, however, he was able to secure the Philadelphia Institute, where he spoke to a group of free African-Americans and Quakers. Although they had long opposed slavery, most of the Quakers thought his language was too severe and his demands too radical. He did not get much money from them. The free African-Americans gave him support, but they were very poor and could give him very little but words of encouragement. His fund-raising was off to a slow and discouraging start.

In New York he spoke at Broadway Hall where Arthur Tappan, the man who had sent the money for the fine, attended. Tappan never forgot his surprise upon meeting the man who had written such fiery words in the *Genius*. Garrison, in person, was very quiet and almost shy. Heartily approving of the young editor and his cause, Tappan gave him a blank check for the new paper. Thus began a relationship that lasted several years in which Tappan was Garrison's chief benefactor and patron.

When he finally got to Massachusetts, Garrison decided to give Newburyport — his birth place and boyhood home — the honor of hosting his first antislavery address in the state. He soon discovered that the town did not consider hosting such a speech to be an "honor." Only the minister of the Presbyterian Church would allow him to hold a meeting. Happy to have any place, and hopeful of drawing a large crowd, Garrison put up posters and distributed handbills announcing his event. But, when a small crowd gathered at the church door on the evening of the meeting, they found the door locked. The Board of Trustees, fearful of violence, had overruled the pastor and refused to allow its church to be used by such a radical speaker.

The trouble Garrison was having finding a place to speak illustrated a fact he had known for a long time — certainly since the evening he first heard Lundy speak at the Reverend Collier's house. The people of the North supported slavery almost as much as the South did, and even when Northerners disapproved of it, they were anxious not to offend the South by speaking their minds — or letting anyone else do so. This attitude prevailed for a number of reasons. Northern merchants traded with the South, sometimes transporting slaves, as evidenced by Francis Todd. Northern textile factories, such as those in many of the towns around Boston, depended on southern cotton. Senator Charles Sumner of Massachusetts would one day refer to the agreement on slavery between plantation owners and textile producers as an unholy alliance between the "lords of the lash and the lords of the loom."

More important than any of these economic reasons was an emotional one. Northerners – even the hundreds of thousands who worked small farms and had no contact with slavery — had an irrational and ignorant hatred of African-Americans and were anxious to "keep them in their place." Garrison had already commented on this at the Park Street Church, and he referred to it again in a letter he wrote to the Newburyport *Herald* after he had been shut out of the Presbyterian Church. "If I had visited Newburyport to plead the cause of twenty white men in chains," he wrote, "every hall and every meeting house would have been thrown open. . . . The fact that two millions of colored beings are groaning in bondage, in this land of liberty, excites no interest or pity!" (15)

Disgusted with Newburyport, Garrison went to Boston and published a notice in the Boston *Courier* asking for a hall. If he found none, he told readers, he planned to address the people of Boston on the Common. For a while it seemed as if he might have to speak outdoors, but finally a man named Abner Kneeland, leader of a religious sect called "The First Society of Free Enquirers," offered him the use of Julien Hall.

On the sixteenth of October, 1830, Garrison spoke to a small group gathered in the hall. He delivered what he thought was his best anti-slavery speech ever, but when he finished, most people left without saying a word. Sitting in the front row, however, were two men who reacted favorably to his denunciation of slavery and colonization. One was Samuel May, a small and gentle man who was a Unitarian minister in Brooklyn, Connecticut. The other was Samuel Sewall, a Boston lawyer and a descendant of Judge Samuel Sewall who, in 1700, had been one of the first Americans to advocate the abolition of slavery. As the people filed out and Garrison stood alone on the platform, May said to Sewall, "This is a providential man; he is a prophet; he will shake our nation to its center, but he will shake slavery out of it. We ought to know him; we ought to help him." (16) They went up to shake Garrison's hand and offer their support.

Partially because May and Sewall offered such enthusiastic help, Garrison began to consider publishing his paper in Boston rather than in Washington. It had once seemed that he ought to challenge slavery on its own ground, but judging from the reception he had received in Massachusetts, it was clear that there was as much anti-slavery work to be done in the North as there was in the South. When May and Sewall said they would find subscribers for the paper, Garrison made his decision. He would publish his anti-slavery newspaper in Boston, the birthplace of the American Revolution and the "cradle of liberty."

Through the fall of 1830, Garrison had long conversations with his new friends and the few other Bostonians they could enlist for the cause. They knew they were a tiny group surrounded by thousands of people who were hostile to their thinking but, as they discussed the horror of slavery, they took comfort in the belief that they were right and that the country would one day face up to its crime.

When they talked of a name for the paper Sewall suggested something unlikely to arouse peoples' fears, such as the *Safety Lamp*. But Garrison would have none of it. His original idea had been the *Public Liberator and Journal of the Times*, but now he proposed to make it more blunt and to the point. It would be called *The Liberator*.

On January 1, 1831, William Lloyd Garrison printed the first edition of his paper. He had convinced an old friend from Newburyport, Isaac Knapp, to be his partner and the two of them had stayed up all New Year's Eve printing *The Liberator* with type they had borrowed from another newspaper. Their first edition had four pages, but the type was skillfully composed and neatly arranged. Since it had only a few subscribers, Lloyd sent many of the four hundred copies to newspapers around the country hoping that editors would reprint some of the material or comment on it.

In his introductory editorial, Garrison apologized for speaking of gradual emancipation in his Park Street Church address two years earlier. Then he left no doubt about where he stood on the slavery issue and how determined he was to fight the vile institution:

> I found contempt in New England more bitter, opposition more active, detraction more relentless, prejudice more stubborn and apathy more frozen, than among the slaveholders themselves. . . . This state of things afflicted but did not dishearten me. I determined, at every hazard, to lift up the standard of emancipation in the eyes of the nation, within sight of Bunker Hill and in the birthplace of liberty. . . . Let Southern oppressors tremble – let their secret abettors tremble – let their northern apologists tremble – let all the enemies of the persecuted blacks tremble. . . . I am aware of the severity of my language; but is there not cause for severity? I *will be* as harsh as truth, and as uncompromising as justice. On this subject I do not wish to think, speak or write with moderation. . . . I am in earnest — I will not equivocate — I will not excuse — I will not retreat a single inch — AND I WILL BE HEARD! (17)

In the spring of 1831, While Abraham Lincoln was traveling the Mississippi, William Lloyd Garrison was publishing *The Liberator* once a week. He and Knapp were living in a boarding house and printing the paper in a dingy room in Merchants Hall. The room was littered with paper. In one corner stood an old bed, in another a printing press and type case, both secondhand. The windows were splattered with printer's ink, allowing only gray light to filter through. Often, with little money coming in from subscribers who were mostly free but poor African-Americans unable to pay the two dollars annual fee, Garrison and Knapp ate only bread and water. They were prisoners to the cause, but their spirits were high. In the first edition Garrison wrote: "The publishers of *The Liberator* (are determined) to print the paper as long as they can subsist upon bread and water or their hands obtain employment. The friends of the cause may therefore take courage; its enemies — may surrender at discretion." (18)

CHAPTER TWO

The Prairie Politician

1831-1844

Abraham Lincoln's childhood and early experiences brought him into close touch with people and their complexities. His understanding of human nature and his love for people led him into a career in law and politics. As he ran for political office in Illinois and joined the Whig Party, he learned the art of deal making, compromise, and the importance of following the law and legal procedures.

1. EARLY STRUGGLES

When Abraham Lincoln went to live in New Salem in the summer of 1831, he had no idea what occupation he would pursue. He had agreed to operate a general store for Denton Offutt, a quirky and rather feckless character, but only a small thinker would envision himself clerking for the rest of his life, and Lincoln was not a small thinker. Within a half year he was announcing his intention to run for public office. In a handbill distributed to the voters of New Salem, he declared himself a candidate for a seat in the state legislature. He put forth, as his major objective, a widening of the Sangamon River to improve navigation and trade — an objective surely inspired by his own boating difficulties. He explained to the voters why, at the age of twenty-three, he was running for public office: "Every man is said to have his peculiar ambition. . . . I can say, for one, that I have no other so great as that of being truly esteemed by my fellow men, by rendering myself worthy of their esteem." (1)

Of course, a man who wants to be thought well of by people does not necessarily have to solicit their votes. The reasons Lincoln became a politician lay in his past, in his relationship with the frontier and the people who lived there. He honed the skills necessary for political life on the land and among the people of rural America.

Abraham Lincoln spent his growing up years on small farms, first on the one that his father, Thomas Lincoln, carved out of the woods on Knob Creek in Kentucky. Later he spent his teenage years on a hardscrabble farm that he and his father carved out of the woods on Pigeon Creek in Indiana. Abraham lived as one with the seasons. The snows of winter locked him into the rude cabin where he slept on a bed of cornhusks and ate potatoes, cornmeal and pork, when times were good. Spring brought new awakenings, the fresh scent of wet earth, the sounds of his father's axe and his own hacking away stubborn stumps so more land could be cultivated. Summer came with long, hot afternoons and a boy's natural desire to sneak off from work in the dusty fields to run through tall grass and splash in the cool waters of the creek. Fall's colors meant hard work storing up food and wood, and listening to somber talk among grownups about the coming winter. The frontier did not co-operate with its human intruders, and Lincoln learned that a man must live with nature or be conquered by it. He learned that the land changes to man's will, but only slowly, and that man hurries the process at his peril. The old farmer's adage went: Don't till new fields while weeds are snuffing the life out of the corn in the old fields.

Frontier life was lonely. Days went by when Abe would talk to no one except his taciturn father as they swung their hoes or struggled to make an ox pull a plow. Visits by traveling preachers, salesmen with farm implements, or just folks moving west were always welcome. Welcome, also, were trips to town and the chance to sit around the general store and talk with the men about local events. They always took up important issues, such as which man in the area could lift the heaviest cider keg. In all these encounters, Abe learned to love people, and they learned to love him. His friendly manner, his way of walking up to a man and saying "hiya" as he offered a firm handshake, his willingness to go out of his way to help people — all of these things made him a very popular young man in Indiana. It may have been his own peculiar response to the loneliness of frontier life that made Abe Lincoln so warm with the people he met, but very likely it was a character trait he was born with or developed at an early age from his loving and affectionate mother.

Abe's mother was Nancy Hanks Lincoln. She was a dark haired, gentle woman who possessed a deep faith in God and was happy to have a husband, children, and a log cabin roof over her head. In the evenings, by the light of the fire, she would read the Bible to Abraham and his older sister, Sarah, and then send them to their beds with a good night kiss. The passages she read were about kindness and understanding, about Jesus protecting the fallen woman, and welcoming lepers and hated tax collectors into his presence.

For the first nine years of his life Abraham Lincoln felt loved and cared for by his mother, Nancy. But Nancy fell sick with a severe fever and her tongue took on the terrible white coating characteristic of the deadly "milk sickness," a disease brought on by drinking the milk of cows that had eaten the poisonous snakeroot. She sank slowly towards death and Abe wept on his mother's bed as she passed away. He was losing the one person in his life who comforted him and encouraged his passion for learning.

Not long afterward, Thomas Lincoln left Abe and Sarah with Hanks relatives and went back to Kentucky. Months passed, and then he returned in a wagon loaded with furniture and a new mother for his children.

Sarah Bush Johnston was different from Nancy Hanks. She seemed stronger and less likely to suffer. But her touch was just as warm and Abe soon learned to love her and to feel good about the world again. Sarah cleaned the cabin and brought in a chest of drawers, a bed for Abe to sleep in, and other furniture and utensils. She also brought three children from her first marriage. The Lincoln cabin became a crowded yet happy place.

As Abe became a teenager, he occasionally heard his father or other relatives talk about Nancy Hanks and her mother, Lucy Hanks. It seemed that Lucy had given birth to Nancy out of wedlock and was generally known to be a woman of loose morals. There was something evil about all of this, and the evil seemed to hang about Nancy as well as her mother. Abe could never quite understand. His mother had been to him a glowing example of the goodness in the human heart. He must have wondered if judgments about people were always fair.

Abe saw the difficulties in judging people in other ways. Men who were thought to be upstanding Christians would refuse to help a neighbor in trouble, but a wandering derelict, dismissed by everyone as "no good," would stop to help a man pull a wagon out of the mud. A man who did not pay his debts was sometimes not lazy or delinquent, but rather a victim of hard luck. Abe began to feel that it was wrong to judge anyone. The Bible said, "Judge not, and ye shall not be judged.' (*Luke* 6:37), and he felt that was good advice.

When Abe and some friends were going home one night, they came upon a drunk passed out in a mud puddle. The others were for passing the man by and went on, but Abe was afraid the poor fellow might freeze to death in the cold night air. He carried him home to a warm fire. It was a scene straight from the "Good Samaritan" in the Bible. Such was the concern for humanity — regardless of its failures — imbedded deep in the soul of Abraham Lincoln. (2)

Lincoln found that people not only warmed to him as a friend, but also looked to him for leadership. This was partly due to his great physical ability. From age eleven on, young Abe could handle an axe with skill and strength, and he could always run faster and wrestle better than anyone his age. Men talked about how far he could sink an axe into a tree and how, when he was in the woods chopping, the trees fell so fast a man would swear there were three men at work. By the time he was eighteen he stood six feet four inches tall, he could lift a corncrib singlehandedly, and he could lick any challenger at whatever the upstart dared to propose. In a land where survival often depended on physical strength, such a man was respected and admired.

Another ability Lincoln had was even more respected. In a place where books were almost unknown, Abe could read and write. With the warm encouragement of both of his mothers and the grudging consent of his father, he had occasionally walked several miles to school. One of his early schools was called a "blab school" because the children read their lessons aloud to assure the teacher they were doing their work. In such classrooms, Lincoln learned his simple ABC's and arithmetic, and developed his life-long preference for reading out loud so that his brain heard the information as well as saw it.

Since his total schooling added up to less than a year, much of what Lincoln knew he taught himself. He borrowed every book he could find from miles around and read constantly, much to the bewilderment of his father, stepbrothers, sister and cousins. He practiced writing with charcoal on a wooden shovel. By the time he was fifteen, men were coming to the Lincoln farm to ask the boy to "write up something" for them. He would carefully open his bottle of ink made from crushed berries and write what they said in a ponderous yet legible scrawl.

A final talent that secured Lincoln's leadership credentials on the frontier where entertainment was scarce, was his knack for telling an amusing story. He listened intently to the yarns spun by the old men in the general store; he drew passersby into conversations and heard of their experiences; he read *Aesop's Fables* and made up a few fables of his own. When he met new people, he could tell the stories he had heard with a casual drawl, a cunning glint in his eye, and a keen sense of timing that would leave the listener doubled up with laughter.

Armed with his skills and attractive personality, Lincoln won quick acceptance and admiration wherever he traveled. When the Lincoln family moved to New Salem, Illinois, he made many friends during his first week in town. There was a need for a man who could write and record the votes of the villagers in a local election. Lincoln admitted to being able to make a few "rabbit tracks," and so he was set at a table to write down the vote of each man who came up to announce his choice. (In 1830 there was no secret ballot.) Lincoln met all the men in town that day as he wrote down their names. He joked with them and held story telling sessions with those who spent the whole day gathered at the polling place. The men liked this newcomer who listened to them and made them laugh.

Within a few months Lincoln and Offutt had built a log cabin general store. Abe was behind the counter telling more stories and making more friends as he measured flour and counted change. People came into the store just to talk with young Lincoln, to hear the one about the preacher and the lizard one more time, or to discover other treasures in the young man's bulging storehouse of yarns.

Men also began to appraise the newcomer's physical strength. In Clary's Grove, a settlement near New Salem, the champion wrestler was Jack Armstrong. Could Lincoln beat him in a fair match? A meeting was arranged and people came to Offutt's store from miles around to witness the great event. Armstrong was much shorter than Lincoln, but folks thought he might be more powerful. When the fight began, Lincoln was not about to let his opponent get in close where his power could count. So, with long arms, he held Armstrong off, wearing him down and frustrating him. Finally, Lincoln threw the weary champion of Clary's Grove to the ground and pinned his shoulders. Several young men from Clary's Grove began shouting that Abe had cheated and moved toward him menacingly. But, as Lincoln backed up to the wall of the store ready to take on all comers, Armstrong broke through the crowd, took Lincoln's hand and announced that Lincoln had won fairly and was "the best fella that ever broke into this settlement." (3) From that day on, Lincoln was known as the man who had beaten Jack Armstrong and he was respected as most likely the strongest man in the area. Characteristically, Lincoln befriended Armstrong and they remained friends for as long as Lincoln was in New Salem.

By the winter of 1832, as Lincoln slept in a back room of Offutt's store and tended counter during the day, he had become a popular man in New Salem and the surrounding settlements. Men asked him to judge horse races and wrestling matches and to settle their disputes. Sometime during that cold, closed-in winter when there was not much to do but sit around the stove, a few of Abe's friends suggested he should run for the state legislature. It couldn't hurt, they reasoned, and it might give him a start that could lead to other things. Lincoln listened. He realized he had many friends and that people looked up to him. He enjoyed people, always looked for the good in them and cultivated new friends while he remained loyal to the old. He wanted to help make things better for his fellow men. He felt he knew what was needed in New Salem and across the prairies of Illinois. He understood the importance of roads and rivers to communities of hard working people. He knew he had communication skills; he could write and put what people thought and felt into words. All of these qualities seemed to make politics a natural field for him.

And, there was another quality that a few who knew him had already seen. He was ambitious. His father had been interested only in making a go of a small farm and staying out of debt. Lincoln did not want to be like him. He wanted to learn and expand his horizons beyond New Salem. He wanted to make a mark. Perhaps his ambition came from a critical examination of his father's life, or perhaps it came from the books he devoured such as Parson Weems's *Life of Washington*. Wherever it came from, it was there and it was strong. As a future law partner of Lincoln's was to write, "His ambition was a little engine that knew no rest."

Ambition made Lincoln say "yes" to his friends' idea. He would enter politics. He would enjoy helping people and working to solve the problems of Illinois society. If it went well, he would be "esteemed by his fellow men" and ride on their shoulders to success and recognition.

2. POLITICAL APPRENTICE

Lincoln's first experiences in politics were dreary with failure. However, he learned new things, won more new friends, and laid the groundwork for future success.

He had hardly declared his candidacy for the legislature in March, 1832, when news came to New Salem of the return of Chief Black Hawk and his warriors. Black Hawk had left Illinois a few years before after signing treaties with the white men, but now he was announcing that the land could not be sold and that his tribe was going to plant corn on its old soil. Volunteers were needed to drive Black Hawk and his people back across the Mississippi. So, Lincoln signed up, along with many friends and neighbors, including Jack Armstrong and the boys from Clary's Grove. As a sign of their respect, Armstrong and his friends voted Lincoln captain of their company.

As Lincoln was to write years later, his experience as a captain in the Black Hawk War consisted mostly of marching, sleeping on wet ground, and wondering where the Indians were. What fighting there was, Lincoln only heard about or arrived at after it was over. His men respected him as their captain although he was anything but a military genius and had little real authority over his company. Sometimes his troops would ignore his commands or say "Awe, Abe," and talk him into changing his mind. An amusing test of his ability to command occurred when his company came to a gate. He had no idea how to order them to march through it two-by-two. Befuddled only momentarily, he ordered the men to take a two-minute break and regroup on the other side of the gate when the break was over. (4)

Black Hawk was finally driven north to Michigan Territory and captured by regular army troops. After eighty days at war, Lincoln returned to New Salem as a military veteran and a man wiser to the ways and thinking of army volunteers — a wisdom that would serve him well when the time came for him to be commander-in-chief of the largest American army ever assembled.

After his months of soldiering, Lincoln had only three weeks to campaign for the election. Making the most of his short time, he traveled all over Sangamon County speaking to small groups of villagers, helping farmers with their chores as he talked with them about the advantages of improving the river, and obliging the local wrestlers who wanted to have a go at him. It was politics in its purest form, and Lincoln was a natural. On Election Day he placed only eighth out of thirteen candidates (The top four would go to the Illinois State House.), but in New Salem he received 277 of the 300 votes cast.

Largely because of the intemperate drinking habits of Denton Offutt, the store failed while Lincoln was away. And so, after his defeat at the polls, Lincoln was a man without an occupation. In a fix, he decided to buy out Rowan Herndon's half of a store he owned with William F. Berry and go into another business enterprise. But no two business partners were more destined to fail than Lincoln and Berry. Berry ignored the place altogether and Lincoln, when he did open for business, spent most of his time day-dreaming and engaging the few customers who dropped by in long-winded conversations.

In the fall Abe had a new interest that put the store even further from his thoughts. He was learning the law. Day after day, as the leaves turned color and cool breezes began blowing them off the trees, New Salemites saw him sprawled on a hillside reading *Blackstone's Commentaries*, the first book for all would-be lawyers at the time. Hour after hour he poured over the tiny print, learning the details of common law. People asked what he was doing, and he would be so absorbed he would not answer. New Salem gradually became aware that Abe Lincoln intended to become a lawyer.

The practical problem of earning a living and keeping financially afloat kept interfering with Abe's serious study of the law. In 1833, the Lincoln-Berry store finally "winked out," leaving Lincoln saddled with debts. Slight help came in May when he was appointed postmaster of New Salem, a small job that involved meeting the mail when it arrived. Twice a week he distributed it to the people who called at the mail counter in Hill's Store. The pay was fifty dollars a year, but the job brought Lincoln once more into contact with the people. It also gave him the opportunity to read the newspapers that came, and he began the practice of devouring papers from other cities, a habit he continued for the rest of his life. Disturbingly careless about his postal duties, Lincoln often left the mail unattended and went off to study his law books or earn a few dollars doing odd jobs for people in the district.

In the fall of 1833, a new opportunity arose to learn more about the land and to meet more people. The surveyor of Sangamon County offered to give Lincoln surveying jobs in his part of the county if Lincoln would learn how to survey. For six weeks Abe stayed up nights, sometimes until dawn, studying Gibson's *Theory and Practice of Surveying*. He wore himself to exhaustion, but at last he was ready to buy a horse, a saddle and surveying instruments (thus going more deeply into debt). He began to travel about surveying property and roads. This work, his job as postmaster, and various odd jobs kept him alive and enabled him to make a small dent in the amount of money he owed.

In the two years after his 1832 defeat, Abe made some important contacts that were to prove essential to getting his political ambitions off the ground. Attorney Bowling Green, a jovial, big-bellied man, was justice of the peace. During long, comfortable evenings in the Green home, Abe discussed Illinois law with the noted lawyer. Occasionally, when Green held court, he allowed Abe to try small cases. Green was a loyal follower of President Andrew Jackson, a Democrat. Lincoln admired Henry Clay, Jackson's bitter enemy and leader of the Whigs, the anti-Jackson party. Yet, as the election of 1834 approached, Green urged his fellow Democrats to support Lincoln, whom he had come to admire as a man of integrity.

Besides the backing of Green and his friends, Lincoln had the help of John T. Stuart, a lawyer in the nearby town of Springfield and leader of the Sangamon Whig Party. Lincoln had met Stuart during the Black Hawk War and had made friends with him on the basis of their mutual admiration for Henry Clay. Their friendship was strengthened by Lincoln's desire to learn the law that Stuart practiced so successfully.

Stuart was a crafty strategist. He told Lincoln to make the most of his chances to get Democratic votes by speaking very little about the issues and simply making himself visible. Abe followed that advice and showed up at picnics and corn- huskings, but made very few speeches. On Election Day, he was second in the field. He would go to the State House as a representative from Sangamon County — his first political office. He had won it by gaining the friendship and confidence of the people, and by playing careful politics to ensure drawing support from both sides. At the capital, he would learn more of the politician's craft from Stuart and other masters.

3. A POLITICAL MAN

As the time approached when the legislature would convene, Lincoln borrowed more money from a friend and bought himself a tailored suit. It would not do for a man in his position to represent Sangamon County wearing his customary denim shirt. In November, with his few possessions under his arm and his coat hanging loosely over his boney shoulders, he boarded the crowded, horse-drawn stagecoach to Springfield. Arriving there after a bumpy twelve-mile ride, he met Stuart and the other two representatives from Sangamon — William Carpenter and John Dawson. Together, the four men took the stage to Vandalia, capital of Illinois.

Vandalia was a rough-hewn town of wooden, two story frame buildings even smaller than Springfield. Lincoln was not impressed. Nevertheless, he was a bit awed by the legislators, judges and other powerful people he saw on the streets and in the hotel lobbies. Then, too, there were the ladies — dressed in fine dresses and fashionable bonnets — who had accompanied their husbands to the legislative session. Their presence prompted an air of refinement in the otherwise crude politicians. Getting about in this society would take some skill. Lincoln was glad he had Stuart, the acknowledged Whig leader, to introduce him to people and explain to him some of the rules of parliamentary procedure.

The room where the House of Representatives met was as run-down as the town. Members sat three abreast at long tables, spat into spittoons, and dodged plaster that sometimes fell from the ceiling as they spoke. Most of the men looked impressive in their black coats and white collars, but an air of casualness prevailed as they sat listening to the debates with their muddy boots propped up on the tables.

Lincoln kept mostly to himself during the first session, watching Stuart and the other leaders manipulate votes and carry the debates. He did rise on a few occasions to introduce minor bills and, since Stuart was often attending to committee work, Lincoln kept him informed of the latest developments on the floor and passed on messages from Stuart to other Whigs. By the time the session had ended, Lincoln had seen bad laws passed because certain men supported them, and good bills die from inept management. He had learned that very few legislative measures succeeded on their own merits alone; they had to be pushed to success by men who knew what to do and when to do it.

Returning to New Salem in the winter of 1835, Abe resumed the study of law. He was encouraged by Stuart who was acting as though Abe were the number two Whig in the legislature. It was hard work studying law on his own but, as he later told a young man interested in a law career, "If you are resolutely determined to make a lawyer of yourself, the thing is more than half done already." (5) Lincoln was certainly resolutely determined. In the late summer of 1836 he easily passed the bar exam and received his license to practice law on September 9, 1836.

That same year, Lincoln ran for re-election to the legislature. Confident that he was a leading Whig and could win on his own without Democratic support, Lincoln declared himself a Whig candidate, thus beginning a firm connection to that party that he would, one day, find difficult to break. He won the election handily, and so did all the other Whigs in the county. Thus, Sangamon was to be represented by seven Whig representatives and two Whig senators. Since all of the men, like Lincoln, were very tall, they came to be called the "Long Nine."

When the "Long Nine" went to Vandalia, Lincoln was emerging as their leader. They had very definite ideas, ideas that were becoming the bedrock of the Whig philosophy. Like the national leader of the party, Henry Clay, they favored a national bank. In their own state, they wanted "internal improvements" — roads, canals, bridges and even railroads — to be built at public expense so that Illinois could grow. Also, they wanted the capital moved from Vandalia to Springfield. Springfield was a larger town, far more refined than Vandalia, more centrally located . . . and, part of Sangamon County. Employing political shrewdness and driving hard bargains, the "Long Nine" would get most of what they wanted.

Providentially, a group of Illinois businessmen and bankers was in Vandalia at the start of the legislative session. Meeting in what they called an "Internal Improvement Convention," they recommended to the legislature a program of multi-million dollar construction of roads, railroads and canals crisscrossing the state. This was all to be done with money raised by the sale of state bonds. A more golden opportunity could not have been handed to Lincoln and the "Long Nine." They met constantly in taverns and hotel rooms with fellow legislators who were anxious that their districts be included in the internal improvement plans. "We'll vote for the bridge being proposed in your area if you'll support Springfield as the capital," Lincoln might say to one. "The railroad through your town will get our vote if you will stand by Springfield," he might say to another. Every man who agreed got a warm clap on the back and a firm handshake closing the deal. It was legislative "logrolling" — I'll help you roll your log up the hill if you'll help me roll mine — at its best, and Lincoln soon had enough votes lined up to make Springfield the capital.

Opponents of the move said that Lincoln was a corrupt bargainer, that he would sell his soul for a Springfield vote. Lincoln's friends knew it was not so. He could make a hard bargain when both issues at stake had his approval, or when he could trade his vote on an insignificant bill for a vote on an important one. But, he drew the line at voting against his principles. One evening the "Long Nine" were meeting late into the night trying to convince Lincoln to vote for a bill he disliked in order to secure a block of votes for Springfield. As the oil lamps were burning low, Lincoln told the dimly lit faces, "You may burn my body to ashes and scatter them to the winds of heaven; you may drag my soul down to the regions of darkness and despair to be tormented forever;

but you will never get me to support a measure which I believe to be wrong, although by doing so I may accomplish that which I believe to be right." (6)

When the massive internal improvements bill had passed, and the "Long Nine" had upheld their parts of several bargains by voting for it, the way was open for passage of a bill moving the capital to Springfield. However, several stumbling blocks appeared. The first had nothing to do with the capital — or even the state of Illinois to any great degree — but it had the potential of creating a storm of controversy if Lincoln carelessly spoke his mind.

Governor Duncan told the legislature that some southern states had demanded that the northern states suppress the growing number of abolitionists, and stop the flow of abolitionist mail to the South. In the Illinois legislature there were fifty-eight members who had come to the state from south of the Ohio River, and only four who had come from New England. Thus, the overwhelming majority sympathized with the South and passed a resolution saying, in part: "We highly disapprove of the formation of abolition societies; . . . the right of property in slaves is sacred to the slaveholding states by the Federal Constitution and . . . they cannot be deprived of that right without their consent . . . ." (7)

Lincoln could not join this unequivocal support of slavery, so he was one of only six who voted "nay" on the resolution. He and Dan Stone, another "Long Niner," prepared their own resolution protesting abolitionism AND *slavery*. Rather than disrupt the legislature, antagonize the members and possibly jeopardize the Springfield bill, Lincoln waited until the end of the session, when all his bills were safely enacted, before introducing the Lincoln-Stone Resolution.

Another stumbling block in front of the passage of the Springfield bill was the fanatical opposition of the representatives from the Vandalia area, particularly John Dement. This short, bombastic man tried every political trick he knew to turn back the Springfield tide. His last, desperate ploy was to move postponement of the matter until July fourth, a date well after the scheduled adjournment of the legislature. The postponement passed by one vote, and it appeared that Lincoln had been stopped short at victory's gate. However, he was not to be thwarted by so narrow a margin. Immediately after the postponement vote, he began collaring legislators in the halls to remind them of the votes he had cast for their internal improvements. He gave each of the "Long Nine" a list of legislators to seek out and pressure into changing their votes.

The next day, with several minds converted, the Springfield bill was voted back onto the floor. There was no stopping the measure now. By a vote of 73 to 50, the state capital of Illinois was moved to where it is today. Springfield became the capital in 1837 not so much because it was the best city available, but because Lincoln and his allies fought for it with their persuasive powers and political bargains.

4. A MAN OF THE LAW

The capital was not all that moved to Springfield in 1837. Abe Lincoln decided that New Salem, despite all it had given him in friends, memorable experiences – and votes – was no longer big enough for him. He would go to Springfield, become a law partner with John Stuart, and be an important part of the fast-moving political world of the new capital. He had established himself as a political force in the state. Now, in the law office of Stuart, the Whig leader, perhaps he could extend his influence even further.

It was a lucky break for Lincoln as a fledgling lawyer to team up with Stuart, for Stuart had the most successful law practice in Springfield. They shared a second floor office from which Lincoln could look down onto the muddy streets of the city and watch humanity pass by. There were dignitaries, particularly after the capital was officially moved to Springfield in 1839. There were also farmers, some of them tending pigs that roamed at will through the mud, and there were drunks who stumbled out of the several saloons. Every day, some of these people came into the office seeking assistance. Lincoln handled property disputes, breech of promise cases, cases involving destruction of crops by wandering farm animals, and even a few murders.

The courts in Springfield were in session only a few weeks of the year, so Abe often "rode the circuit," traveling around the twelve thousand square miles of the Illinois Eighth Judicial Circuit to wherever the judges were holding court. For weeks at a time he would be gone, riding the lonely roads on horseback with law books and a change of clothes in his saddlebags. To get to the next court on time, he might have to ride through drenching prairie rainstorms. At night he put up in taverns that had little more to offer than a warm fire and a lumpy bed — which he sometimes shared with several other lawyers. Life on the circuit was not easy in the 1830's!

Occasionally judges would hold court at a table in the general store. In these makeshift settings, Lincoln learned even more about people and further developed his close contact with the common man. He came face-to-face with the deep racial and religious prejudices of the people in Illinois. He saw how strongly people valued property and how far they would go to protect it. He learned how to talk to people about issues that troubled them, and he learned when no talk at all was the best approach. Few occupations could have prepared a man for leadership of people as well as the law did.

Besides learning about people, Lincoln developed a profound respect for the law and an orderly way of doing things. No matter what the situation was — an argument between a husband and wife, a farmer accusing a man of stealing his horse, an angry man trying to get revenge for the murder of his best friend — it was always handled best if the law was fairly applied in a courtroom where proper procedures were observed, allowing each side its say. Lincoln came to believe that at all times the law should be observed, even if it was an obnoxious law. Until a bad law was changed through the legislative process, it was disruptive to allow people to ignore what was written down. The law was the bedrock of civilization.

In a speech before the "Young Men's Lyceum" of Springfield — a political debate club — Lincoln expounded with rhetorical flourishes on his faith in the law and on the violence in different parts of the country he was hearing about. With disgust he told his audience of the gang in St. Louis that lynched a free Negro and of the hanging rampage that occurred in Mississippi. In the latter atrocity the good people of that state hung so many "gamblers" and "Negroes" that the bodies hanging from the trees outnumbered the Spanish moss that droops in gray masses from the trees in the South. Then, referring to the murder of abolitionist Elijah Lovejoy in nearby Alton, Illinois, that year, he said, "Whenever vicious mobs are allowed to throw printing presses into rivers and shoot editors . . . depend on it, this government cannot last." In an atmosphere of chaos and violence, he warned, a dictator would be sure to come forward to restore order.

The answer for their times was strict observance of the law, he concluded. "Let reverence for the laws be breathed by every American mother to the lisping babe that prattles on her lap," he said. "Let it be written in primers, spelling books and almanacs;

let it be preached from the pulpit, proclaimed in legislative halls and enforced in the courts of justice. . . . Although bad laws, if they exist, should be repealed as soon as possible, still, while they continue in force, for the sake of example, they should be religiously observed." (8)

These comments on the disruptions surrounding the abolitionists in the late 1830s, along with his resolution in the legislature denouncing slavery *and* abolitionists, were the only stands Lincoln took on the slavery issue at this point in his career. As a lawyer, a few cases involving runaway slaves came to him. He handled these with sympathy for the African-Americans, but always in accordance with the law — even if the law meant that the "Negro" would have to return to slavery. It was clear that he hated slavery and hoped it would, some day, be legally ended. He believed that people should be allowed their First Amendment right to speak against slavery without being threatened by angry mobs. On the other hand, he believed abolitionists should temper their methods so as not to disrupt the country, and all people should obey the laws concerning slavery as long as they were in effect.

In a practical sense, Lincoln felt moderation would serve the abolitionists' cause better. No one ever won converts to a cause with shouting and obnoxious behavior. In a speech he delivered to the Springfield Washingtonian Temperance Society, a group that promoted temperance (abstinence from alcohol) partly on the basis that George Washington was a teetotaler, he spoke convincingly for the tactic of warming up to those you wished to convert rather than bludgeoning them with your point of view:

> If you would win a man to your cause, first convince him that you are his sincere friend. Therein is a drop of honey that catches his heart, which, say what he will, is the greatest high road to his reason and which, when once gained, you will find but little trouble in convincing his judgment of the justice of your cause, if indeed that cause really be a just one. On the contrary, assume

to dictate to his judgment, or to command his action, or to mark him as one to be shunned or despised and he will retreat within himself, close all avenues to his head and to his heart; and though your cause be naked truth itself, transferred to the heaviest lance, harder than steel, and perhaps sharper than steel can be made, and though you throw it with more than Herculean force and precision, you shall be no more able to pierce him than to penetrate the hard shell of a tortoise with a rye straw. (9)

Although he was advising temperance advocates on how best to win drinkers to their cause, Lincoln would have offered the same advice to abolitionists. He may have heard of William Lloyd Garrison by this time and, if he had, he most certainly deplored Garrison's harsh language and demands for immediate emancipation. William Lloyd Garrison violated Lincoln's sense of the law, of orderly resolution of differences, and of dealing agreeably with people through a willingness to compromise.

5. ROUGH WHIG POLITICS

The slavery issue rarely came up in Illinois, but Lincoln had other problems confronting him as he tried to achieve political success in that state. Although Springfield was more refined than Vandalia, politics were just as bare-knuckled in the new capital as they had been in the old. Lincoln had to be as clever as his opponents and just as ready as the next man to "mix it up' with words or wits, or he would get nowhere. As Carl Sandburg in his great biography of Lincoln put it: "In order to live and stand up and be one of the men among men in that frontier and state in the years around 1840, a man had to know schemers, had to know how to spot a scheme when he saw one coming, and how to meet scheme with scheme." (10)

In the campaign of 1838, Lincoln won re-election to the legislature and helped Stuart win a seat in the United States House of Representatives. In 1840, Lincoln won again and helped the Whig ticket of Harrison and Tyler win the presidency. These contests in Illinois were fought ferociously, sometimes to the point of comedy. Stuart's opponent in the 1838 was Stephen A. Douglas, a short, powerful man with thick, wavy, dark hair. A few years younger than Lincoln, Douglas was gaining a reputation for himself in the Illinois legislature as a leading spokesman for the Democratic Party. Eloquent and vigorous, he could hold his own in any political contest and was earning the nickname "Little Giant."

One afternoon during the campaign Douglas (5'4") and Stuart (6'1") got into an argument in Herndon's store and began wrestling with each other, much to the amusement of the men sitting on barrels and leaning on counters. The two candidates for the United States Congress were soon rolling around on the floor, trying to grab each other in headlocks, and getting soaked with pickle juice. Finally, when both were too tired to strike another blow, Stuart ordered a barrel of whisky for the crowd and the event was turned into a drinking celebration — one of the hundreds that enlivened every frontier political campaign.

Douglas, a man of fiery oratory and fiery temper, added spice to Springfield politics more than once. A few days before the 1838 election he and Stuart had another brawl, this one out on the streets. The altercation ended with Stuart dragging his adversary by the collar through the dust, and Douglas inflicting a blood-drawing bite on Stuart's thumb. After Stuart had gone to Washington, Lincoln wrote to him of yet another Douglas incident: "Yesterday Douglas, having chosen to consider himself insulted by something in the *Journal* (the *Sangamo Journal*, Springfield's major newspaper), undertook to cane Francis (the editor) in the street. Francis caught him by the hair and jammed him back against a market cart, where the matter ended with Francis being pulled away from him. The whole affair was so ludicrous that Francis, and everybody else, Douglas excepted, have been laughing about it ever since." (11)

Lincoln also participated in these types of squabbles in his own races for the legislature. More than once he stopped in the middle of a speech and jumped from the wagon or platform where he was speaking to join in a street brawl — usually to put an end to it. In 1842 he had his most serious altercation. He wrote a series of letters to the *Sangamo Journal* attacking and ridiculing James Shields, the hot-tempered Democratic state auditor. Shields sent a friend (as a "second") to challenge Lincoln to a duel. At first, Lincoln did not take the challenge seriously and suggested, as weapons, "cow dung at five paces." But, when it became clear that Shields was in earnest, Lincoln proposed cavalry swords, with each duelist confined to an area eight feet back from a plank that would be set edge-wise on the ground between them.

The duel was set to occur on a sandbar in the middle of the Mississippi River where the participants would be free from arrest, dueling being illegal in Illinois. On September 22, 1842, Lincoln found himself at the site, whipping a sword around for practice and brooding apprehensively. Shields stood nearby and friends of the two men talked matters over. One witness said it was the longest period of time he had ever seen Lincoln go without cracking a joke. Fortunately, the negotiators were able to arrange some sort of agreement to prevent the antagonists from swinging swords at each other, and Lincoln and Shields returned to shore talking almost amicably — much to the disappointment of a crowd that had gathered hoping to see some blood. For the rest of his life Lincoln regretted this incident because he had lost control of his emotions and put himself into a very dangerous situation. (12)

On a more dignified level, the Whigs and Democrats attacked each other in the years 1837-1842 over a variety of issues. The Democrats accused Lincoln and the Whigs of saddling the state with heavy debts for internal improvements. Bridges, canals, and railroads, the Democrats charged, were not expanding the economy in the state and bringing in great revenues as the Whigs had promised. The Whigs counter-charged that it was the economic policies of the Democratic administration in Washington — particularly Jackson's destruction of the National Bank — that made it impossible for any progressive state to avoid bankruptcy.

To help pay for the internal improvements, the Whigs finally had to pass a bill in the legislature levying a tax of twenty-five cents on every one hundred dollars of assessed property valuation. Some Whigs feared that this would cost the party votes, but Lincoln wrote to one of them telling him not to fear. Such a tax hits not the "many poor," he pointed out, but rather the wealthy few who were not "sufficiently numerous to carry the elections."(13)

Despite this dispassionate statement about rich people, Lincoln seemed to be aligning himself with the party of wealth and privilege. The Whig Party was the choice of Nicolas Biddle, the fat and pompous president of the National Bank, and most other wealthy businessmen. Andrew Jackson's Democrats seemed to be the party of the common people whom Lincoln loved so well. Yet, Lincoln believed that the Whigs had as much claim to the emotional attachment of the average man and the pioneer as the Democrats — and had a program based on more established principles.

The Whig leader was Henry Clay of Kentucky. Affectionately nicknamed "Harry of the West," he was a hard drinking, cigar smoking gambling man, as fully in touch with the people as was plantation owner Andrew Jackson. The Whig presidential candidate in 1840, William Henry Harrison, who was elected in the "log cabin and hard cider" campaign, was also a Westerner who could understand the frontiersmen at least as well as Jackson. Whig principles, while they *were* helpful to banking and business, were also good for the common man. A national bank stabilized the currency so that everyone could make an honest living in an orderly economic system; government support for internal improvements opened avenues of commerce so the farmer could get his crops to market and buy cheaper goods from the East. This economic paradigm would be called "trickle down economics" today.

Proclaiming all these things up and down the state, Lincoln promoted the Whig cause. Although Harrison lost Illinois in 1840, the Whig Party was doing well in the state, particularly in the northern sections where congressional candidates such as Stuart were successful. When Lincoln was re-elected to the legislature for the fourth time in 1840, he began to feel that he had earned a right to a seat in the United States Congress as a representative from Illinois.

Early in 1843, Lincoln began letting it be known among the Whigs of the Seventh Congressional District that he wished to run for Congress. "Now if you should hear anyone say that Lincoln don't want to go to Congress," he wrote Richard Thomas, "I wish as a personal friend of mine you would tell him you have reason to believe he is mistaken." (14) In a campaign circular called "Address to the People of Illinois," he put forth his Whig principles: a tariff to protect domestic industries and to raise money for internal improvements, and a national bank to stabilize the currency. He also urged Whigs to unite as a party, using a biblical quote to warn: "A house divided against itself cannot stand." (Matthew 12:25) (15)

Unfortunately, two other young Whigs were in line for the honor of representing the district. Edward Baker and John Hardin were both in their early thirties as was Lincoln. Furthermore, they were both as successful in politics as he and wanted desperately to go to Washington. Baker was a melodramatic speaker and brilliant young man, consumed with ambition. It was said he actually cried when he learned that his foreign birth (He was born in Great Britain.) made him ineligible for the presidency. He and Lincoln were close friends, and Lincoln would one day name his second son Edward in his honor. Hardin was a tall, distinguished gentleman from Kentucky who had been Lincoln's rival for floor leadership of the Whigs in the legislature. He and Lincoln had a somewhat strained relationship.

When the Whig district convention met at Pekin, Illinois, Hardin had enough votes to assure the nomination. Lincoln then offered a resolution that Baker would be the nominee of the convention in 1844. The resolution passed eighteen to fourteen. Many party men believed that a deal had been hatched whereby Hardin would be succeeded by Baker in 1844 and Baker by Lincoln in 1846. In 1846 Lincoln reminded Hardin of "the proposition made by me to you and Baker that we should take a turn a piece." (16) So it is very likely that a gentlemen's agreement *was* made and that Lincoln, in 1844, was planning to go to Washington two years later.

6. LOVE'S LABOR

In 1839, a wealthy young woman from Kentucky came to Springfield to live in the house of Ninian Edwards, a political friend of Lincoln's in the legislature and a part of the "Long Nine." Mary Todd was the sister of Mrs. Edwards. She was coming to live in Springfield because she could not get along with her stepmother. The Edwards were well-to-do; their brick home was one of the finest in town, so they were able to offer Mary the kind of life she had grown used to in Kentucky. Gala parties and balls at the Edwards' home and outings with the younger social set of Springfield became the important features of Mary's life. Coquettish and pretty, with brown hair and flashing eyes, Miss Todd held forth at social events with the good manners and refined graces she had learned in cultured Lexington, Kentucky, and in a private girls academy.

Mary attracted many of the rising young men in Springfield. Stephen Douglas occasionally escorted her, as did Abraham Lincoln. It was curious that a woman of Mary's breeding should have taken a shine to Lincoln, a man of humble origins who was painfully awkward and unrefined. His pants were always too short and his coat too tight in the shoulders; his hat was usually old and stained. He sat in the plush furniture of the Edwards' home with his bony knees up in the air, and he was known to tell off-color stories in the presence of the ladies. Perhaps Mary sensed something promising in the homely, young politician. It was said that when she was asked whom she would choose as a husband, Lincoln or Douglas, she answered, "Whoever has the best chance of being president." In 1840, she chose Lincoln and they were engaged.

It must have been difficult for Abe to make an engagement with Mary for he had been notably unsuccessful with women prior to her. Back in his New Salem days, he had once been deeply in love with Ann Rutledge, the comely daughter of a storeowner. Their relationship lasted over two years, but during that time Abe was mostly a good listener and a shoulder to cry on because she was waiting for the return of the man she was engaged to. When it finally became evident that her intended groom was never going to reappear, Ann agreed to marry Abe. This match might would have been a good one — Ann and Abe were kindred spirits in many ways — but, tragically, it was not to be. Ann became ill with typhoid fever and never recovered. Her passing plunged Abe into a long period of grief during which some of his friends feared he was suicidal.

Abe's ill-starred romance with Ann explains, to some people, his awkward and sometimes careless treatment of the women who followed Ann into his life. Probably none of them measured up to the gauzy image of Ann he carried in his mind. Mary Owens, a vivacious young lady who arrived in New Salem from Kentucky seemed a likely prospect for the young, would-be lawyer. But Abe thought her too fat, and once, on a horseback ride with other couples, he failed to show her the little attentions she thought a suitor should. As the group of riders approached a stream, the other gentlemen guided their companions' horses across the waters; Lincoln rode on ahead without even looking back to see how Mary was doing. This Abe-Mary relationship did not survive that incident and Abe's subsequent move to Springfield.

When Abe escorted a lady to a social event he often left her on her own while he went off to talk with the other men with whom he felt more comfortable. During extended relationships he would often subject the young lady to lengthy periods of deep brooding and melancholy. He would never explain his problem (if he could have) and would leave her to guess at what was making him so unhappy.

Mary Todd accepted all of this in 1840, but she was to endure even more before Abraham Lincoln became her husband. On New Year's Day, 1841 (which Abe later referred to as "that fatal first of January"), Abe told Mary they would have to break their engagement. He was too confused and too depressed to go through with it. Mary understood and released him from his

Abe Lincoln
in 1840s

Mary Todd Lincoln

promise. Still, Lincoln remained melancholy and spent most of the year bewildered and unhappy, hopelessly unable to decide what to do about his love problems. His depression became so acute that at one point his friends made sure there were no razors or knives in his possession, lest he succumb to his "melancholia" and take his own life. Affairs of the heart did not come as naturally to him as politics did.

When he had first come to Springfield, Lincoln had taken a room above Joshua Speed's store and he and Speed had soon become close friends. For four years Abe and Joshua slept in the same bed in the upstairs room, a fact that has led some recent writers to hypothesize that the two men were homosexual or bisexual. A modern reader might lend a great deal of credence to this since today it is unusual for two men to share accommodations in this way. However, in the 1840's (and probably every other era) this type of sleeping arrangement was common and did not necessarily indicate anything about the sexual preferences of the two men. Furthermore, in long letters to each other, Speed and Lincoln discussed how best to relate to . . . women.

In 1841 Speed moved to Kentucky where he proposed marriage to a young woman named Fanny Henning. Lincoln visited Joshua at his home outside Louisville, met Fanny, and saw in Speed's situation a model that perhaps he could observe. Speed was deeply uncertain that he should go ahead with his wedding, just as Lincoln had been, and he was also wracked with anxiety and depression. When Abe got back to Springfield he wrote, "I tell you, Speed, our forebodings, for which you and I are peculiar, are all the worst sort of nonsense." (17) He urged his old friend to marry Fanny, assuring him that his depression was merely a sign of love and would quickly disappear as soon as the matrimonial bonds were tied.

Speed married as scheduled and wrote to Lincoln that he had never been happier. Serving as Speed's counselor helped Abe rethink his own situation, and then he received some advice from his counselee. Either marry Miss Todd or forget her, Speed advised, because you cannot continue much longer in your present condition. Abe began to feel that he might be able to make a go of marriage after all.

About this time, a matchmaker involved herself in Lincoln's uncertainty. Mrs. Simeon Francis, wife of the *Journal* editor, arranged a party in her home to which she invited Abe and Mary. Surprised and happy at the reunion, Abe and Mary renewed their acquaintance and began to see each other again. They talked again of marriage, but Lincoln needed just a bit more re-assurance from Joshua Speed. "Are you now, in *feeling* as well as *judgment,* glad you are married as you are?" Abe wrote. "Please answer quickly," he continued, "as I feel impatient to know." Speed wrote back within a week assuring Abe that he was still happy in every respect. Lincoln finally believed he had the courage to go through with a wedding. (18)

On November 4, 1842, in the Edwards' parlor, Abe and Mary Todd took their vows and began a marriage that would keep friends and historians guessing for many years. Was Abe Lincoln happy with his wife? Some said an emphatic "no." Mary had a terrible temper, they said, and often turned it on her husband when he showed his lack of breeding or indulged in laziness. She made social enemies with her sharp tongue, frequently causing her husband much embarrassment. She spent money lavishly on clothes and jewelry.

On the other hand, many have contended that Mary was a supportive wife, willing to endure hardships while Abe got ahead. Their first home was a simple room in the Globe Tavern where she gave birth to their first child, Robert. Later, when they moved into a house and had three more boys, she dutifully took care of the home and children while Abe was off riding the circuit or politicking.

We will never know whether Abe was happy with Mary or not since he said very little about his marriage. But, even if he was not happy, he may have heeded one of the few maxims his father ever gave him: "If you make a bad bargain, hug it all the tighter." (19)

7. A MODERATE'S SOUL

In 1841, Lincoln and Stuart dissolved their partnership so that each could concentrate on his own career. Lincoln then teamed up with Stephan Logan, a high-strung meticulous lawyer who taught Abe how to prepare a thorough case. In 1844, however, Lincoln decided he did not like the arrangement whereby Logan got two-thirds of the fees. When Logan asked to end the partnership, Lincoln readily agreed. He turned next to the young man working as a beginning lawyer in the office of Logan and Lincoln and asked him to be a partner in a new office.

William Herndon was a dashing, dark-haired young man whom Lincoln trusted as a lawyer and who, Lincoln felt, would give him contact with the "shrewd wild boys" of Springfield – a politically useful group. Lincoln was already feeling he was old, even though he was only in his mid-thirties! The two men hit it off famously, as Lincoln became a bit of a father figure to "Billy."

However, Billy Herndon quickly became enemies with Mary Todd Lincoln. One evening, when Mary was dressed for a social function, Billy said she looked like a "serpent." Intended as a compliment (meaning she looked graceful and supple), it struck Mary as an extreme insult, and she never forgave her husband's young partner. Herndon soon began to reciprocate the bad feelings. Partly because of their animosity, Herndon was the originator of many stories depicting Lincoln's unhappiness with his "impossible" wife.

The law office of Lincoln and Herndon was an incredible mess. Neither man was tidy, so papers were strewn everywhere. Lincoln was in the habit of sticking important papers in his stovepipe hat or stuffing them into the various pigeonholes of a desk. On a large envelope that the two men might come across as they rummaged through the piles of papers were the words, "When you can't find *it* anywhere else, look in this." (20)

Herndon was interested in a broad range of academic subjects. He would constantly urge Lincoln to read some book or pamphlet, which Abe would set aside as he lay sprawled upon the office couch reading the newspaper. Occasionally Herndon tried to interest Lincoln in the several reform movements he was caught up in, but Abe was usually only amused. Herndon was an abolitionist, and he tried to get Abe to read some of the abolitionist newspapers he received (perhaps *The Liberator* was among them). Lincoln was only mildly interested, and frankly believed that the hotheads who put out those papers were causing so much trouble that the general public would be annoyed and even frightened off.

Lincoln could not fully understand men such as Herndon and other abolitionists who could make simple judgments about good and evil. Thorough study and contemplation of a matter always revealed complexities and shades of meaning that made absolute opinions impossible. He once wrote: "The true rule in determining to reject or embrace anything is not whether it have *any* evil in it, but whether it have more of evil than of good. There are few things *wholly* evil or *wholly* good. Almost everything is an inseparable compound of the two, so that our best judgment of the preponderance between them is continually demanded."(21) Such balance of thought, he believed, served society best, and it had carried him far as a lawyer and a politician. In the years after 1844, he hoped to develop it further and use it as a congressman in Washington and perhaps in other lofty positions as well.

The Radical Agitator

1831-1845

William Lloyd Garrison's childhood and early experiences gave him a moralistic view of the world that led him into a career as a radical reformer. As he established himself as a leader of the anti-slavery movement, he became increasingly more radical until he was ultimately the most extreme abolitionist in the country.

1. PRINTER'S APPRENTICE

William Lloyd Garrison knew that his crusade to free the slaves was going to make him unpopular and a social outcast. He must have also feared that he might never live to see the success of his efforts — that he would remain a social outcast his entire life. He must have pictured days spent working in dingy offices printing newspapers hardly anyone would read and speaking in half-empty halls to hostile crowds; he must have envisioned nights spent in shabby boarding houses talking only with people seeking friendship in a cause. He knew his talents could have secured a more comfortable life for him. Why did he choose to become a radical agitator?

Garrison saw life as a never ending struggle between good and evil, an outlook largely the product of his mother's influence. Fanny Garrison was a strict Baptist who knew the Bible thoroughly and had a clearly defined list of sins. One of the vilest, in her mind, was drunkenness. Her seafaring husband's drinking habits drove him out of their impoverished home in Newburyport, Massachusetts, and off to sea for good. His disappearance left her alone to raise her three children. She severely reprimanded young Lloyd when he did wrong, which he rarely did. She instructed him daily in the Christian virtues of thrift, honesty, hard work, sobriety, and the need to fight evil. When examples presented themselves in the form of drunken men or other unfortunates, Fanny pointed out to her children the punishments awaiting those who break God's rules. She reminded them of their sinful father who was, no doubt, condemned to wander aimlessly on the high seas and go to a watery grave to pay for his intemperance.

By the time he was a teenager, Garrison was a religious zealot who could detect evil as confidently as his mother. Within his family he found new examples of sin's ugly results. His older brother, James, took to the bottle and ran away to sea in a tragic replay of his father's fall from grace. For the rest of his life Garrison's habit of seeing all things as wholly good or wholly evil made it easy — necessary — to take absolute, uncompromising stands for the *right*. Slavery was so clearly a sin that Garrison hardly felt the need to prove it. The "Golden Rule" was all that was necessary. How could one man enslaving another fit the words "do unto others as you would have them do unto you?"

The cause of freeing the slaves had the blessing of his beloved mother. When he was fifteen and serving as an apprentice print-er in Newburyport, she was in Baltimore suffering from yellow fever. She wrote to her son, "Thank God I am well taken care of. . . . I have a colored woman that waits on me, that is so kind no one could tell how kind she is, and although a slave to man, yet a free-born soul, by the grace of God. Her name is Henny, and should I never see you again, and you should ever come where she is, remember her for your poor mother's sake." (1) He fought for the slaves because he saw them as fully equal, righteous people as his mother saw Henny.

From his twelfth to his nineteenth year, Lloyd lived at the home of Ephram Allen and served as Allen's apprentice at the Newburyport *Herald*. During this time he learned the art of set-ting type and publishing a newspaper. This experience became an important element in his makeup as a radical agitator, not only because it gave him the tools of his trade, but also because it taught him how easy it was to denounce people and things from the security of the printing office.

When he was sixteen, Lloyd began sending Allen anonymous letters which he signed "A.O.B." (An Old Bachelor). The first was an opinion piece by an old bachelor (hence the pen name) on the position of women in society. They are too much "idolized and flattered," the bachelor opined. Moreover, "Women generally feel their importance, and they use it without mercy." (2) Other let-ters attacked all sorts of injustices in society. Allen gave them all to Garrison to set into type for the *Herald*. Garrison was flattered that Allen liked the letters, and amused that the man had no idea that his apprentice was the real author.

When his apprenticeship was up in 1825 and he was about to leave the *Herald*, Lloyd wrote one more piece that was appro-priate for "An Old Bachelor." Titled "An Essay on Marriage," his letter concluded: " . . . of all the conceits that ever entered into the brain of a wise man, that of marriage is the most ridiculous." (3) As the next decade was to show, this attitude would change.

What Garrison learned to do as a printer and "An Old Bachelor" was attack things (and people) without coming face-to-face with them. Even after he began signing his own name, he could write and set type in the solitude of his office, sealed away. He would not have to see the people he was attacking or live among them . . . and, perhaps, become more tolerant of the way they were. As time passed, people noticed that Garrison was less a firebrand in person than he was on paper. He could sit for hours at the type case imagining the evil he was writing about and build up anger in order to lash out at it. In person, he had to respond to peoples' looks and feelings and be aware of what they might be thinking. It is possible that without his printing skills, Garrison might not have become a radical agitator at all. With them, and the moralistic approach to life he gleaned from his mother, he was a flaming, uncompromising radical.

A third element in Garrison's make-up came from the social structure of his boyhood home in Newburyport. The town sat at the mouth of the Merrimack River. Along High Street, several blocks up a hill from the water, wealthy families owned magnificent, three story mansions surrounded by beautiful gardens. Young Lloyd was at the other end of the social scale and lived in a small frame house down by the river. His mother could barely keep the family clothed, and Lloyd often had to sell molasses candy on the streets or beg for scraps of food at the mansions. In his adult years, he may have mentally transposed himself into a slave and the Newburyport aristocrats into slave owners. In each case, he wanted to make the high and mighty people take notice of him despite his lowly status.

His experience at the *Herald* proved to him that his best chance for achieving recognition lay in advocating causes. So, when he left the *Herald*, he took on the editorship of another Newburyport paper, the *Free Press*. There, he editorialized on behalf of the Federalist Party — the party favored by the Newburyport aristocrats. But he got almost no attention from the High Street gentry and, when the paper died after only six months, he decided to head for Boston and start getting attention not by pleasing the snobs but by tweaking them. He got a job editing the *National Philanthropist*, a reform paper in which he expounded on the evils of alcoholism, Sabbath violation, and other forms of sin. His goal, rather than to make himself a permanent social outcast, was to find a cause to believe in, work for, and finally ride to fame when he had succeeded in turning society from its evil ways. Shortly after going to Boston in 1827, he wrote in a letter, " . . . if my life be spared, my name shall one day be known so extensively as to render private enquiry unnecessary; and known, too, in a praiseworthy manner." (4) All he needed was the right cause, and this he found a year later when Benjamin Lundy came to Boston.

Slavery, as an issue, fit William Lloyd Garrison's personality well. It was clearly a sin that he could attack with passion and conviction; it was an evil that was perpetrated by people in the South and in the North who enriched themselves from it; and it was a national issue that had yet to be opposed by an effective effort. He intended to make that effort and carry his fame to High Street in Newburyport and beyond.

2. A BEACON OF RIGHTEOUSNESS

During the 1830's Garrison solidified his position on slavery and on other issues that he felt were inextricably bonded to the slavery issue. He also developed a theory of radical *tactics,* a theory he was to put into practice during that decade and after. His ideas and methods were going to isolate him and his followers even from others who opposed slavery, but that isolation was part of the strategy.

Every edition of *The Liberator* fulfilled Garrison's promise to attack slavery without moderation and not retreat a single inch. When some of his friends remarked that they thought his language was too severe, he was pleased. In his farewell to the readers of the *Genius* he had said, "Many have censured me for my severity — but thank God — none have stigmatized me with lukewarmness." (5) To be moderate when attacking a sin as great as slavery was behavior as despicable as committing the sin itself. The cause demanded expressing the truth in plain words, even though they would sound harsh to the slave owners or to people trying to appease the South. Slave owners were "manstealers" and "murderers," and that was what they must be called! There was so much to be done, so many hearts to convert. When Samuel May asked Garrison why he needed to be "all on fire," Garrison answered vehemently, "Brother May, I have need to be *all on fire*, for I have mountains of ice about me to melt!" (6)

In June of 1831, six months after starting *The Liberator*, Garrison went to Philadelphia to speak before a group of "free colored people." He had become popular with these folks when he had solicited money in Philadelphia the previous fall. But, standing in front of those dark faces, he could not help being ashamed of his own whiteness. Some in the audience had only recently thrown off the yoke of slavery by escaping, by purchasing their own freedom, or by being set free by their owners as a special reward for good service. All of them were suffering from northern prejudice. Garrison knew of a school in New Bedford, Massachusetts, where black students were segregated into special corners of the classrooms and, for punishment, white children were forced to sit with them. The black people in Philadelphia were suffering the same kind of treatment, and to them Garrison gave this pledge: "I am determined . . . to give slave holders and their apologists as much uneasiness as possible. They shall hear me, and of me, and from me, in a tone and with a frequency that shall make them tremble. There shall be no neutrals; men shall either like me or dislike me." (7) The African-Americans at this meeting liked him — indeed, adored him. They flocked about him after his speech, pumped his hand and blessed him. No white man had ever taken so strong a stand on behalf of their race. For the rest of his life Garrison was to enjoy the undiluted devotion of the black population of Philadelphia.

Back at *The Liberator* office in Boston, Garrison continued to turn out forceful editorials. In one issue of *The Liberator* he warned slaveholders that they risked tremendous violence and bloodshed if they persisted in carrying on their vile system. He told Southerners that he was advising the slaves to submit to their plight with meekness and to trust in God for their deliverance from bondage, but there was no way to tell how long they would remain passive. He issued his warning in poetry:

> Wo if it come with storm, and blood and fire
> When midnight darkness veils the earth and sky!
> Mother and daughter — friends of kindred tie!
> *Stranger and citizen alike shall die!*
> Red-handed slaughter his revenge shall feed,
> And havoc yell his ominous death cry,
> And wild despair in vain for mercy plead,
> While hell itself shall shrink and sicken at the deed! (8)

Shortly after this poem appeared, Nat Turner gathered his followers about him in Southhampton, Virginia, and began his bloody rebellion. All across the South whites recoiled in shock, revulsion and fear at the news from Virginia. They set up armed patrols to guard the plantation houses and towns at night; they bought new locks for their doors and lay awake at night imagining their slaves, armed with axes, stalking into their bedrooms.

Some Southerners recalled seeing Garrison's *Liberator* with its stern anti-slavery language and its poem about violent uprising. A few began linking *The Liberator* with a pamphlet that had been circulating in the South called *Walker's Appeal*. That pamphlet, written by a free Negro named David Walker, had called on the slaves to rebel, and Garrison had devoted several articles to it in his paper. Southerners reasoned that slaves must be reading these dangerous ideas — it was known that Turner had been taught to read — and therefore Garrison was responsible for the Turner uprising. No one could prove that Turner had ever read *The Liberator*, but few Southerners bothered with that detail. It was enough that Garrison had printed his poem describing the macabre scenario just weeks before Turner acted it out.

Letters began arriving in *The Liberator* office from angry slave owners. Many told Garrison he would be killed if he ever ventured into the South. "Hell is gaping for you," one man wrote. "The devil is feasting in anticipation." In South Carolina a group of "respectable gentlemen" formed a vigilance committee to protect the interests of the slave owners. They offered $1500 for the apprehension, prosecution and conviction of any white person circulating *The Liberator*. The state of Georgia put up a $5000 reward for Garrison himself. (9) Brazenly, Garrison printed the details of all of this in his newspaper.

Garrison's nature would permit nothing other than a radical, uncompromising stand against slavery, and it was becoming obvious to him that such a stand served a tactical purpose. As long as he denounced slavery in the strongest terms possible, Southerners would react. Their reactions — inevitably coarse attempts to silence him — would serve two purposes. They would show the nation that slavery could not exist in a democratic society that allowed free speech, and it would stimulate debate over slavery, forcing people to take sides. At first, people would line up against the abolitionists. He expected that. As the Declaration of Independence makes plain: " . . . all experience hath shown, that mankind are more disposed to suffer, while evils are sufferable, than to right themselves by abolishing the forms to which they have become accustomed." But, eventually, the horrors of slavery would become so self-evident that people would begin to see it as their duty to overthrow it.

As reaction to his ideas intensified and more people began to recognize the existence of the anti-slavery movement, Garrison began plans for an anti-slavery society. Such a group could conduct a coordinated campaign against slavery by printing and distributing literature, sending speakers into the field, and holding well-publicized meetings. In November of 1831, he and others gathered in Sewall's office. Garrison felt that if he could get twelve — the same number as the apostles who began the Christian movement — to agree to his platform, then a society could begin. A fundamental demand of the society, he told the group, must be the *immediate* emancipation of the slaves. Most of the men agreed that immediate abolition of slavery was desirable, but some felt that such a demand, if stated in the platform, would drive away those who felt slavery should be ended gradually. The movement would need all of the followers it could get.

Garrison had heard this reasoning before when people told him that his strong language in *The Liberator* would turn away potential supporters, and he would hear it again. It annoyed him and made him very impatient. If a thing is right, he proclaimed, we must stand with it regardless of how unpopular we may be. Moreover, he continued, a reform group can never stay alive and active if it continues to compromise to suit others. Better to stay small and muscular than to grow large and flabby.

These arguments did not convince everyone at the initial meeting, however, and the vote on the platform was nine for and six against — three short of the "apostolic twelve" Garrison was looking for.

For two months Garrison searched the city for new supporters and tried to "radicalize" some of his old friends. Finally, on the night of January 6, 1832, twelve men who would agree to the principle of immediate emancipation met in a school room of the African Baptist Church in what was called the "Nigger Hill " section of Boston. As a snowstorm raged outside, they solemnly affixed their signatures to the constitution of the "New England Anti-Slavery Society." Nearly all of the men were poor; no one was influential, powerful or well known in Boston. It would have been understandable if some of them had little hope for the success of their tiny society. As they pulled on their coats and prepared to step out into the slushy streets, Garrison lifted their spirits: "We have met tonight in this obscure school house; our numbers are few and our influence limited; but, mark my prediction, Faneuil Hall shall ere long echo with the principles we have set forth. We shall shake the nation by their mighty power." (10)

3. CAUSTIC COLONIZATION

By the time William Lloyd Garrison formed the New England Anti-Slavery Society, he had grown to despise the idea of colonization more than ever. Free African-Americans were repeatedly telling him they did not want to be sent to live in Africa. The whole idea of deporting African-Americans seemed to be based on the idea that they were inferior and therefore unwelcome. The existence of the American Colonization Society inhibited the progress of abolition because by removing free "Negroes" who might cause "trouble," it strengthened the slave system. Garrison was convinced that many slave owners, such as Henry Clay and James Monroe, belonged to the society for that very reason. Furthermore, colonization gave Northerners a false sense that something was being done about slavery.

In 1832 Garrison wrote a long pamphlet entitled *Thoughts on African Colonization* in which he laid before the public his objections to the American Colonization Society's program. Using facts from the society's own reports, he proved that its purpose was not the abolition of slavery, but instead the strengthening of the slave system. Most of the African-Americans sent to Liberia were already free, he pointed out, and one of the leading members of the society, Henry Clay, had specifically said that ending slavery was not a goal of the organization. Even more significant, most of the society's members were slaveholders, and not one had freed a slave and sent him to Liberia. So convinced was Garrison that the Colonization Society was a prop of slavery that he wrote to a friend: "I look upon the overthrow of the Colonization Society as the overthrow of slavery itself — they stand or fall together." (11)

In the spring of 1833, Garrison decided to carry the battle against the society to England. The British were about to pass a bill liberating the slaves in their West Indian colonies — a tremendous victory for the slaves, of course, and for the hearty band of English abolitionists who had struggled for decades to see it happen. The American Colonization Society was going to have its agent, Elliott Cresson, on hand as the representative of the American Emancipation effort. Garrison believed this hoax should not go unchallenged. Therefore, with money raised by the New England Anti-Slavery Society, he set sail from New York in May.

In London, he visited several of the anti-slavery societies and shared the joy of British abolitionists at the pending outlawing of slavery by Parliament. He probably wondered if he would ever have similar reason to celebrate in his own country.

During his first weeks in London an incident occurred he would never forget. Thomas Fowell Buxton, whom many considered the leader of British abolitionism now that the great William Wilberforce was old and dying, sent a letter to Garrison inviting him to a breakfast of British abolitionists. When Garrison came into Mr. Buxton's home, the Englishman stood amazed for a moment, causing Garrison some embarrassment. Finally, Buxton said, "Have I the pleasure of addressing Mr. Garrison of Boston, of the United States?"

"Yes, sir," Garrison answered, "I am he, and I am here in accordance with your invitation."

Buxton threw up his hands in revelation. "Why, my dear sir," he exclaimed, "I thought you were a black man! And I have consequently invited this company of ladies and gentlemen to be present to welcome Mr. Garrison, the black advocate of emancipation from the United States of America!" (12)

For the rest of his life Garrison regarded this as the greatest compliment he ever received. It showed he had argued the cause of the black man so passionately that at least one man assumed he must be black himself!

Pleasurable as it was to become known and appreciated by British abolitionists, Garrison wanted to go beyond social niceties and take on the American Colonization Society's spokesman, Elliott Cresson, who was also befriending anti-slavery people in London. He challenged Cresson to debate, but Cresson repeatedly declined to accept until finally he appeared at a meeting Garrison was holding at the Wesleyan Chapel in Devonshire Square.

Surrounded by a pro-Garrison crowd, Cresson soon began to rue the moment he had walked into the chapel. Garrison lashed out at the Colonization Society, calling it an institution as bad as slavery itself, and the audience shook the room with applause. Voices in the crowd called out for Cresson to respond, but he refused to speak under such unfriendly circumstances. Finally, he stalked out muttering that he was being treated worse than a dog.

Cresson never did debate Garrison even though Lloyd issued challenge after challenge, some of them in the London papers. In lieu of such a confrontation, however, Garrison attacked Cresson in his own anti-colonization meetings. The most successful of these was held at Exeter Hall on July 13th. To a large and friendly British audience, Garrison ridiculed Cresson for claiming that ill health was preventing him from debating. Then, he damned the Colonization Society with his familiar arguments. Finally, working himself into a righteous outrage, he proclaimed that he loved his country but had "solemn accusations to bring against her." She was hypocritical, he pronounced, because she professed belief in the principles of the Declaration of Independence yet practiced slavery; she was "murdering and plundering" the black population by kidnapping slave babies, stealing the labor of black people, and remaining indifferent to their sufferings. When he finished, the crowd roared its approval and Garrison beamed. He had given the Colonization Society and slavery a tongue-lashing the world would long remember. He had also taken a few shots at his own country, and for that he would pay a price. (13)

As he stepped off the ship in New York in October of 1833, William Lloyd Garrison was well pleased with himself. Reduced financially to borrowing money to pay for his return voyage, he had nevertheless won the acclaim of the British abolitionists and had ended forever the Colonization Society's hopes of representing American anti-slavery in Great Britain. For these achievements he was sure he would gain increased notoriety in his native land.

Within days of his return to America he realized he was indeed notorious . . . and hated more than ever. Americans were angry at what they had heard about his speech at Exeter Hall. People fumed that he had criticized his country before a foreign audience. Newspapers in New York City called on citizens to go to Clinton Hall where, it was known, a group of abolitionists were going to meet to form a New York abolition society — a sister group of Garrison's New England Anti-Slavery Society. Perhaps Garrison himself would be there and Americans would show him what they thought of disloyal radicals.

Garrison did go to Clinton Hall, not to participate in the meetings but to watch. Outside he found an angry mob shouting his name and struggling to break into the building. Fortunately, in those days before photography, few people knew what Garrison looked like, so he was able to stand unnoticed among the angry people. He was amused at the thought of what they would do if they knew the identity of the bespectacled, balding young man in their midst. Meanwhile, the abolitionists inside, for safety's sake, adjourned their meeting and went to the Chatham Street Chapel a few blocks away. There they quickly organized their society and departed just before the mob, which had discovered their new meeting place, burst through the doors.

Describing the scene, the New York *Commercial Advertiser* said, "Had Garrison been present, many grave and respectable citizens would have consented to his being tarred and feathered." The paper went on to issue Garrison a warning: "We hope, most sincerely, that not a hair of Mr. Garrison's head will be injured by personal violence, but he will do well to consider that his conduct in England has kindled a spirit of hostility against him at home which cannot be easily allayed. He will act wisely never to attempt to address a public meeting in *this* country again." (14)

The *Evening Post* took a similar position. He is "as mad as the winds on the slavery question," the paper declared. It went on to describe public opinion regarding Garrison's whole movement: "We know of no question of public policy on which public opinion is so unanimous" as that of discountenancing the abolitionists. (15)

When Lloyd returned to Boston, he saw posters all over the city calling on citizens to prevent the escape of the disgraceful American who had slandered his country before a British audience and was threatening to break up the happy union with the South. An angry crowd gathered at *The Liberator* office the evening Garrison returned, but Lloyd managed to avoid them.

Garrison rejoiced in these disruptions and the notoriety he was gaining. The violence and abusive language that were used against him and his fellow abolitionists were stirring the consciences of people who had even mild anti-slavery feelings. Indeed, the time seemed right to call for a national anti-slavery organization to coordinate the efforts of abolitionists everywhere. In *The Liberator* of October 29, 1833, he issued a call for a meeting to be held in Philadelphia for the purpose of establishing an American anti-slavery society.

In November, Lloyd left Boston for "The City of Brotherly Love." Part of the journey involved a steamboat ride from New York to Elizabethtown, New Jersey. It was during this passage that an incident occurred that revealed the difference between Garrison in print and Garrison in person. Samuel May was talking with a stranger about abolition when Lloyd came up to join the conversation. For a long while Lloyd defended the principles of immediate emancipation and Negro equality in the face of the man's skepticism. Finally, the man said, "I have been much interested, sir, in what you have said and in the exceedingly frank and temperate manner in which you have treated the subject.

If all the abolitionists were like you, there would be much less opposition to your enterprise. But, sir, depend on it, that hare brained, reckless, violent fanatic Garrison will damage, if he does not shipwreck, any cause." (16) May and Garrison smiled with amusement as May told the astonished gentleman that he was speaking to none other than William Lloyd Garrison.

In Philadelphia, the police told Lloyd and his group that their meetings could only be held during the day because protection against mob violence would be impossible at night. Undaunted, the small cluster of seventy abolitionists who had come from Boston, New York and Philadelphia, convened each morning and hurried through their business to finish each day before nightfall.

Since most of those present had been converted to abolition by *The Liberator,* and because Garrison had just won the admiration of the British abolitionists, Lloyd was the center of attention. He was asked to write the "declaration of sentiments" and he stayed up all night to complete the task. When Lloyd submitted his document, the group accepted it largely as he had written it, although they deleted a few of his strongest phrases against the American Colonization Society. The paper denounced slavery as a crime in violation of the Declaration of Independence and the will of God; it called for the immediate abolition of slavery without colonization and without compensation to the slave owners; it called for the organization of anti-slavery societies throughout the country and the sending forth of anti-slavery agents to speak on behalf of the slaves and to call the nation to its duty.

The declaration went on to recognize that Congress only had the power to abolish the slave trade, ban slavery from the territories and new states, and free the slaves in the District of Columbia, but it called on Congress to do these things immediately. The final abolition of slavery would come, the statement concluded, when the consciences and hearts of the people were won over.

When the final draft of the document had been transcribed, Lloyd watched proudly as sixty-three men came forward reverently to sign it. He compared the event to the signing of the Declaration of Independence, but felt that this gathering was far more important since the people to be liberated were actually in chains. Several women were present but, in accordance with the custom of the times, they did not sign. Garrison later regretted this sell-out to conformity and vowed it would never happen again.

When the signing was complete, Garrison noted somber expressions on every face. Each member of the American Anti-Slavery Society was hard as iron in his devotion to the cause, but knew that he faced a life-long struggle against formidable and often dangerous opponents.

4. AN ABOLITIONIST WIFE

When William Lloyd Garrison started his career of radical anti-slavery agitation, he might well have assumed he would never marry. What woman would consent to a life of poverty, constant controversy, and social ostracism? "An Old Bachelor" would certainly have agreed that women are too accustomed to pampering to accompany a reformer through life. But despite his old bachelor pretentions, Lloyd had always been a ladies' man. In Newburyport, and particularly in Bennington where he had a "steady" girlfriend (about whom little is known), people commented on his dapper appearance and his interest in a pretty face. Would it be possible to find a woman who would be interested in marrying an abolitionist?

In April, 1833, when he was on his way to New York to begin his trip to Great Britain, Lloyd spoke at the "African Church" in

Providence, Rhode Island. Seated in the audience of mostly free African-Americans was a white man, George Benson, a retired Providence merchant. Benson had organized an anti-slavery society in 1790 and had been speaking out against the Colonization Society before Lloyd had even thought of publishing *The Liberator*. With Benson was his twenty-two-year-old daughter, Helen, who had come to hear the young abolitionist about whom her father had so often talked.

When Lloyd met Helen that evening and again the next day, he was immediately smitten. "If it was not 'love at first sight' on my part," he wrote several years later, "it was something very like it — a magnetic influence being exerted which became irresistible on further acquaintance." (17) Besides her fine features and dark brown hair, Helen's simplicity and modesty attracted Lloyd. She was not the showy, heavily made-up lady "An Old Bachelor" had denounced, but rather a warm, compassionate woman firmly grounded in the Christian virtues, and fully committed to the abolitionist cause. Furthermore, she seemed to admire him, a fact sure to arouse Lloyd's interest in any woman.

It was not until January of 1834 that Lloyd wrote a letter to Helen, and in it he talked endlessly about everything except his feelings for her. When he visited the Bensons in March he went for a carriage ride with Helen, but once again was unable to speak to her of love. That a man could speak so fluently on many matters and yet be so tongue-tied when attempting to speak about love, clearly demonstrates the power of that emotion.

Back in Boston after his March visit, Lloyd wrote more confusing letters, telling Helen how much he admired her whole family — and this from a man who prided himself on always going directly to the point! In one letter he lamented that even though he had many friends in England and America, he had no one to "call his own." "There is none in this wide world whose heart I am authorized to claim, none into whose bosom I can pour the wealth of my affection, " he lamented. (18) Helen must have shrieked in exasperation at her suitor's inability to get on with it! Lloyd's awkwardness was becoming embarrassing. Helen finally made it easy for her stumbling lover by writing that she accepted his proposal of marriage, even though he had never really made one!

In April, Lloyd came to see his new fiancée and was immediately convinced he had made a good choice. Characteristically, for their first meeting as betrothed lovers, Helen wore a simple dress. And, characteristically, Lloyd was pleased with her straightforward simplicity. "Truly," he later exclaimed, "not one young lady out of ten thousand, in a first interview with her lover, but would have endeavored falsely to heighten her charms and allure by outward attractions." (19) In Helen he had found a steady and stalwart companion to accompany him down the rocky road of reform.

On September 4, 1834, Reverend Samuel May performed a marriage ceremony for Lloyd and Helen in the Benson home. He read the simple vows to a small group gathered in the living room at nine in the morning. Lloyd had decreed that there be no music or wedding cake so that the entire affair would be over quickly and the couple, chaperoned by Lloyd's Aunt Charlotte and Miss Eliza Chase, could be on their way to Boston.

Helen knew right from the start that she was marrying a cause as well as a man. Before their wedding day, Garrison had printed in *The Liberator* that those of his enemies who claimed he favored interracial marriage would soon be able to decide if he espoused a white or a black woman. The house Lloyd and Helen rented in Roxbury was going to be shared by other abolitionists, notably Isaac Knapp and his wife, Abigail. And Lloyd, within a week of the wedding, was inviting all his "abolition friends" to visit at his house. But, Helen adjusted well to all of this. She would be Lloyd's devoted and supportive wife. In the trials to come, he would need all of the help she could give him.

5. WILLING MARTYR

The anti-abolitionist violence Garrison and his supporters had been experiencing from the beginning increased dramatically in 1834 and the years immediately after. In May of 1834, the City of New York witnessed another scene similar to the one that occurred when Garrison returned from Great Britain. An angry crowd burst into the Chatham Street Chapel to disrupt the first annual meeting of the American Anti-Slavery Society. The New York papers reported that "some of the ruffians bawled out for Garrison, but he was out of their murderous reach." The *Courier and Enquirer* warned the abolitionists never to meet in New York again. (20)

Unruffled, the abolitionists met at the Chatham Street Chapel on the fourth of July, only to have their speakers drowned out by rowdy young men who sat in the doorways and made loud, derisive comments. (Lloyd and other movement leaders had decided to hold major abolitionist events annually on the Fourth to highlight the anomaly between the Declaration of Independence and slavery.) On July 9th, Lewis Tappan, brother of Arthur Tappan (the man who had paid Garrison's bail), lost his home to a fire set by anti-abolitionist mobs. During the same months, pro-slavery riots shook towns in Pennsylvania, Ohio and Connecticut. Free African-Americans were attacked and beaten and their homes set on fire. In Boston, the *Commercial Gazette* proposed that Garrison be indicted as a public nuisance or, perhaps, tarred and feathered at public expense.

Some of the violence was inspired by the usual southern demands that the abolitionists must be silenced. Northerners —

businessmen in particular — were anxious to keep the profitable union with the South in tact, and wished to prove to the South that the abolitionists were not welcome in the North any more than they were in the South. Furthermore, Garrison had whipped up new controversy by inviting the British abolitionist, George Thompson, to speak in the United States. Newspapers and public officials up and down the land deplored the meddling in American affairs of a "foreign fanatic." Men in several northern cities proclaimed that if Thompson spoke within their grasp he would not return to England alive.

Unmindful of these threats, the dynamic Thompson spent much of 1835 delivering anti-slavery lectures throughout the Northeast. In Lowell, Massachusetts, Concord, New Hampshire, and several other towns he was pelted with rotten eggs and stones. In almost every place, small groups of abolitionists tried to hear him speak while pro-slavery mobs shouted him down, threw things at him and threatened his life.

With Thompson in the country, the smoldering outrage against the abolitionists became a raging fire. Southerners and their northern supporters were determined to silence the troublemakers once and for all. Nearly every southern postmaster searched the mails for abolitionist literature and burned any he found. The Postmaster General, Amos Kendall, condoned this and President Andrew Jackson, a slave owner, supported it as well. Garrison, Thompson and Arthur Tappan were all marked for assassination; three thousand dollars was offered for Thompson's ears; twenty-thousand dollars was offered for Garrison, dead or alive; and southern businessmen were threatening to cut off trade with Northerners known to be friendly with the abolitionists.

William Lloyd
Garrison

Helen Benson
Garrison

In this inflamed atmosphere, prominent businessmen in Boston felt the time had come to prove their good will toward the South. Benjamin Curtis, a lawyer and future Supreme Court justice, wrote to a friend: " . . . so great have been the commotions excited in many parts of the South, and so excited is the public mind there, that there are strong fears felt here by friends of the Union that, unless something is done here to check the abolitionists and convince the South that the great body of the people of the northern states are unfavorable to the (Anti-Slavery) Society, the Union will not continue for a single year." (21)

A meeting at Faneuil Hall was called for August 21, 1835, for the purpose of passing resolutions against the abolitionists and soothing the tempers of the Southern slaveholders. Mayor Theodore Lyman presided as one prominent man after another expressed his abhorrence of abolitionism and his good will toward the South. Speakers accused the abolitionists of inciting slave rebellion and threatening the Union with their incendiary ideas. Many of the orators emphasized that the abolitionists were merely a small and fanatical group that would quickly be destroyed by the "sensible" people in the North.

Garrison was outraged by this meeting. In *The Liberator* he proclaimed that Faneuil Hall could no longer be called the "cradle of liberty;" instead it was the "refuge of slavery!" In a letter to one of the participants, he took issue with the often-repeated claim that the abolitionists were few in number and therefore insignificant. " . . . the success of any great moral enterprise does not depend upon numbers," he wrote. "Slavery will be overthrown before a majority of the people shall have called voluntarily, and on the score of principle, for its abolition." (22) His words would prove to be prophetic.

The fact that the meeting had taken place, however, indicated that the danger to abolitionists was increasing. But Garrison did not fear violence. He knew that injuries to his person or his death would win more converts to the cause. "I presume that our principal cities will be visited by assassins," he wrote to Henry Benson, his brother-in-law. "It matters not. If we perish, our loss will but hasten the destruction of slavery more certainly." (23) George Thompson, writing to Lloyd from Marblehead, expressed a similar opinion. "(Samuel) May, who was with me today, informed me that a recent Southern paper has stated that if the prominent fanatics were not put down by the strong arm of the law in the North, ASSASSINATION *would cease to be reprehensible or dishonorable.* Such writing must do good. Let the South go the whole length of the rope, and let there henceforth be no mistake about the meaning of the words "Southern chivalry." (24)

In October, Thompson was scheduled to speak before the Boston Female Anti-Slavery Society, a small group of women who, in an open challenge to the accepted role for women in 19th century society, had organized themselves to speak out for the slaves. Hostile notices went up in hotel lobbies and taverns all over town informing the public that Thompson was going to be at the anti-slavery offices on Washington Street on October 21st and that this was the opportunity for friends of the Union to "snake Thompson out." One hundred dollars was offered to the first man who could lay violent hands on the Englishman and bring him to the tar kettle.

When the day of the meeting came, the abolitionists had deemed it advisable for Thompson to be out of town, so the ladies convened with Lloyd to replace Thompson as the speaker of the day. Nevertheless, a large crowd of men, many of them respectable businessmen and men of influence in Boston, gathered on Washington Street in front of the anti-slavery offices. The well-tailored suits some of the men wore led Lloyd later to refer to the group derisively as "The Broadcloth Mob." Garrison arrived and went up to the meeting hall on the second floor where he found fifteen ladies trying to conduct their meeting in the midst of several jeering and taunting young men. Putting on his most deferential airs, Lloyd told the men that this was the Boston *Female* Anti-Slavery Society and invited them to leave — unless any of them were ladies in disguise, in which case he would introduce them to the rest of their sex and allow them to take their seats. Startled, the men whispered to each other that they were looking at none other than Garrison himself.

Miss Mary Parker, president of the society, suggested that the situation might become less tense if Garrison would leave the room. Sensing that she was right and that the men might vent their anger at him now that Thompson was clearly unavailable, Lloyd went into the office next to the meeting room and closed the door. Mayor Lyman, accompanied by three policemen, came into the room and begged the women to leave for their own safety. Refusing to be rushed by a man they felt was an enemy to their cause and a friend to many in the mob, the ladies calmly voted on a motion to adjourn. Then, they marched down the stairs to the street, white women paired with black, "thus giving," as society member Maria Chapman later put it, "what protection a white skin could ensure a dark one." (25)

By this time Lloyd was leaving the building through a rear window. As he jumped onto the roof of a shed and ran to hide in a carpenter's shop, he could hear the crowd and knew that some of the men were coming to find him. Though he hid behind a pile of lumber on the second floor of the shop, a few of the rowdies soon clambered up the stairs and grabbed him. With shouts of blood-thirsty glee they began tying a rope around his waist. Some of the meaner ones wanted to throw him out the window, but cooler heads prevailed and they finally allowed him to climb down a ladder to the furious crowd below. When he was in their midst, the men ripped his clothes and dragged and pushed him down the street. Only the strong arms of two or three large men, who for some reason felt protective, kept him from being clubbed, or perhaps killed.

Lloyd's protectors brought him into City Hall and the door was locked against the crowd. With angry shouts blaring through the windows, Mayor Lyman and the police debated what to do. Someone gave Lloyd an old coat, baggy pants and a cap to wear. Finally, Lyman concluded that this hated man could only be safe in jail. He ordered him arrested for "disturbing the peace," and summoned a carriage to be drawn up at the door to take Garrison to the Leverett Street Jail.

When Garrison emerged from City Hall with Lyman and several guards, the crowd must have been deceived by the borrowed clothing for it did not act until he was in the vehicle. Then, realizing their mistake, the men surged forward, surrounding the carriage and the horses. They pounded on its sides, kicked the doors, and, at one point, almost tipped it over. The driver frantically whipped the horses and at last the carriage leaped ahead and began careening down the street with the mob in hot pursuit.

When the almost comical procession of frightened horses, carriage and enraged citizens reached the Leverett Street Jail, Garrison was once again in danger. The police had to rush him into the building past frustrated and angry men. Then, the editor of *The Liberator* was locked into a cell for the night. For the second time in his life William Lloyd Garrison was in jail for his abolitionist beliefs.

All who saw Garrison during this episode reported that his face was calm and serene during all the indignities he suffered. As he had said, he was fully prepared to die for immediate emancipation, and he was happy in the thought that such gross treatment only served to draw attention to his cause and elicit sympathy for it.

Just as he had done in Baltimore, he used his overnight stay to promote his martyr image. On the walls of his cell he wrote, "(William Lloyd Garrison was confined here) to save him from the violence of a 'respectable and influential' mob, who sought to destroy him for preaching the abominable and dangerous doctrine that all men are created equal and that all oppression is odious in the sight of God." (26)

For Helen, waiting at home, the fragments of news she received about the incident heightened her anxiety until she prepared herself to hear that her husband had become a martyr to the abolitionist cause. She was six months pregnant with their first child and she prepared to raise the baby, due in February, as a widowed mother who would tell the little boy or girl of the father's great moral crusade and his bravery in the face of martyrdom.

Though his friends and Helen feared for his safety, Lloyd was pleased as he left jail the next day. In the weeks following his encounter with violence, events seemed to prove that such incidents served to further the cause of abolitionism. In a letter to Helen he wrote, "New subscribers to *The Liberator* still continue to come in — not less than a dozen today. Am much obliged to the mob." (27)

In his paper Garrison repeatedly reminded the North that Southerners were attempting to squelch freedom of speech by inciting people to do violence against abolitionists. This type of appeal to conscience, unlike pure abolitionist appeals, had an effect. Even some Northerners who did not favor emancipation of the slaves began to sympathize with the abolitionists because of the injustices being done to them. The issue of "southern control over northern liberties" was to become a major weapon in Garrison's struggle to overcome northern hostility and apathy.

In February, 1836, Helen gave birth to the Garrisons' first son. They named him George Thompson Garrison in honor of their good friend — the steadfast abolitionist whom the Boston mob had set out to kill.

Surprisingly, during the three years following the attack on Garrison, a gradual change in public attitude became evident in Boston. Three events converged to bring this about: President Jackson, in his 1835 annual message to Congress, virtually condoned violence against abolitionists, thus making it clear to New Englanders that even the president, when it came to slavery, was willing to deny freedom of speech. Also in Washington, the House of Representatives, at the insistence of the southern delegates, passed a "Gag Rule" outlawing the reading of anti-slavery petitions on the floor of the House, thus adding Congress to the list of enemies of free speech. Finally, and worst of all, an abolitionist editor was actually killed. Elijah P. Lovejoy, editor of an anti-slavery paper in Alton, Illinois, was shot dead while attempting to protect his press from being thrown into the Mississippi River by an irate mob. Each of these atrocities — Jackson's speech, the "Gag Rule," and Lovejoy's murder — caused Bostonians of conscience to pause and think.

At Faneuil Hall a meeting to protest the Lovejoy murder took place. Some of the "respectable" men of the city attended and applauded speeches denouncing that gross overreaction to an unpopular idea. Although the gathering did not represent a majority of the city's population by any means, the fact that over one hundred people gathered on behalf of a murdered abolitionist, less than three years after a similar incident in their own city, revealed a significant sea change in public opinion.

Most significant of the new converts to the anti-slavery cause was the man who gave the most eloquent speech on behalf of Lovejoy. Wendell Phillips had witnessed Garrison's ordeal with the mob from the windows of his law office and had decided, on the spot, to join the crusade of the man being so greatly abused. Phillips was wealthy and a member of Boston's "blue blood" aristocracy, yet he jeopardized his law practice and his social standing by becoming a despised abolitionist. He was sacrificing for the cause, just as Garrison was. Such was the effect that the persecution of abolitionists had on many thoughtful Northerners. Phillips, along with several other wealthy men, became financial supporters of *The Liberator* and the Garrison family, keeping them afloat in hard times. Lloyd and Helen needed all the help they could get as their family added six additional children after the birth of George Thompson: William Lloyd, Jr. 1838; Wendell Phillips, 1840; Charles Follen, 1842; Helen Frances, 1844; Elizabeth Pease, 1846; and Francis Jackson, 1848.

6. PURGE

Despite the sympathy they were winning from some Northerners and the conversion of men such as Phillips, not all abolitionists agreed that their cause was well served by extreme radicalism and its resulting violence. Indeed, many people felt that softer language and greater willingness to work with people who favored gradual emancipation — or even colonization — would allow the movement to grow in numbers and influence and would hasten its eventual success. In the years after 1835 these more conservative abolitionists feuded with Garrison to such an extent that the movement ultimately split, leaving Garrison and his small group of followers standing alone on the most radical anti-slavery ground.

It was partially the growth of the movement after 1835 that caused the split. Prior to that year, when the abolitionists were just a handful of "fanatics" and "troublemakers," they could have their differences over immediate versus gradual emancipation and other issues and still stick together, if only for their own protection. After 1835, as more people joined the movement, the various members could feel more inclined to give vent to their differences of opinion. The New England clergymen were the first to resent Garrison's anti-moderate wrath and the first to speak out against him.

From the early days of *The Liberator*, Garrison frequently devoted space in the paper to denunciations of New England ministers. He argued that since they were the spiritual leaders of their communities, they should be in the vanguard of abolitionism, and he was outraged that they were not. When ministers refused to allow anti-slavery notices to be read from their pulpits or to open their churches to abolitionist gatherings, he berated them in print. When the Massachusetts Anti-Slavery Society could find only a stable in which to hold its 1837 meeting, he remarked sarcastically that there was not a pulpit in the city "to which a slave-holding preacher could not find ready access, even for the avowed purpose of vindicating the soul-destroying system of slavery as a divine institution." (28) When ministers, in their convocations, failed even to express sympathy for the abolitionist cause, Garrison showered them with verbal abuse, once calling the Methodist ministry a "cage of unclean birds." (29)

By 1837 Garrison had evolved a unified philosophy that he summed up in the word "Perfectionism" which meant that there was a perfect, Christ-like life to which all people should aspire. The perfect life included abstinence from all impure substances such as alcohol, respect for the dignity, worth and liberty of all human beings, and total non-violence. Denunciation of slavery was, of course, a duty of every "Perfectionist" since the slave system destroyed the dignity, worth and liberty of all black human beings, and it depended on violence and force for its existence.

But a "Perfectionist" had other duties. He or she had to support fully the right of women to be the complete equals of men in all things — an outlandish idea in 1837. He had to refuse to fight, even when attacked. Lloyd demonstrated his pacifism when he was attacked by the mob and when he advised abolitionists and slaves to take their abuse with meekness, for the meek would inherit the earth. Those who thought Garrison condoned violence at the time of the Turner rebellion were blind to the fact that he only *predicted* violence, basing his prediction on the fact that most slaves were not pacifists.

Finally, a Perfectionist had to disassociate himself from all governments since governments depended on force to sustain themselves. It was especially necessary, Garrison was convinced, to divorce oneself from the United States Government since it upheld slavery with its army and its constitutional guarantees of property.

By 1837 the clergymen in Massachusetts who considered themselves abolitionists were ready to move against Garrison and his perfectionist ideas. They authored the "Clerical Appeal," a protest against Garrison's anti-clerical statements. Garrison answered the "Appeal" with scathing editorials in *The Liberator* calling the clergy "dumb dogs" and "hindrances to the march of human freedom." (30) The ministers began talking among themselves about starting their own anti-slavery organization, separate from Garrison's and away from his influence.

A feud was evolving and Garrison hoped to be supported in it by the American Anti-Slavery Society. But Lewis Tappan, brother of Arthur Tappan who had freed Lloyd from the Baltimore jail seven years earlier, agreed with the ministers' attacks on the fiery editor. In a letter to Garrison, Tappan asked him to discontinue his quarrel with the ministers. They speak for most of the members of anti-slavery societies, Tappan said, and he warned Lloyd that abolitionism could not afford to "drive away" or "knock on the head" friends who were substantially right. In a heart-felt plea he asked, " . . . would it not be magnanimous to overlook it all for the sake of the cause — THE CAUSE?" (31)

But Garrison, headstrong as usual, had no intention of moderating his tone or backing away from Perfectionism. Thus, in an editorial on December 15, 1837, he announced a new policy for *The Liberator*: "In entering upon our eighth volume, the abolition of slavery will still be the grand object of our labors, though not, perhaps, so exclusively as heretofore. There are other topics which, in our opinion, are intimately connected with the great doctrine of inalienable human rights. . . . These we shall discuss as time and opportunity may permit. Our motto "Universal Emancipation," he went on, "will now mean freedom from slavery, freedom from government of brute force," and freedom from sin. "The cause of peace will command our attention, and so, too, will the rights of women." (32)

Garrison's support for equal rights for women, his refusal to vote, and his bout with the clergy drove a wedge between himself and most of his fellow abolitionists. The majority of anti-slavery men wanted to cooperate with influential ministers, even if those ministers were not fully committed to *immediate* abolition of slavery. Most did not want to lose potential supporters who objected to seeing women speaking in public. And most were firmly of the opinion that abolitionists should not only participate in government but, indeed, form a political party and run a candidate for president in 1840.

Garrison was appalled at the very idea of a political party. Such a move would dilute the abolitionist cause. How could anti-slavery continue as a moral force — a force for the right no matter how unpopular the right might be — when its supporters were bargaining for power and making compromises, as they would inevitably do if they were trying to win elections? As 1840 and the presidential election approached, Garrison knew a showdown would have to come.

It came at the 1840 meeting of the American Anti-Slavery Society in New York. Weeks before the meeting was called to order, Garrison learned that his opponents within the movement would be in New York in great numbers to expel him from the society by denouncing his harsh language, his attacks on the clergy, and his non-resistant principles. After that, they would organize a political party and pass resolutions calling on abolitionists to vote. Desperate to maintain control of the society he had begun, Garrison marshaled his forces for the impending showdown. He wrote letters to all his anti-slavery friends begging them to be in New York. He even chartered a boat to provide transportation for all "true Garrisonians." Trains and stagecoaches carrying Garrison's friends, many of them women, arrived in Providence, Rhode Island, the embarkation point. On a moonlit night, the boat glided softly through the Atlantic and the inspired passengers sang hymns as if they were on a crusade.

When the meeting opened in New York's Fourth Free Church, Francis Jackson, a Garrisonian, presided. His first duty was to appoint a business committee, and to this he named a woman, the fiery and outspoken Abby Kelley. The committee list was approved by a vote of 571 to 451 and, with that, Lewis Tappan and two other men who had been appointed to the committee resigned. Tappan told the gathering, " . . . to put a woman on a committee with men is contrary to the constitution of the society; it is throwing a firebrand into the anti-slavery ranks; it is contrary to the usages of civilized society." (33) He and several hundred others walked out of the room and went to the basement of the church to form their own anti-slavery society — "The American and Foreign Anti-Slavery Society" — based on political activity and an inactive role for women. Garrison and his supporters were left upstairs to run the American Anti-Slavery Society as they pleased.

"It was our anti-slavery boatload that saved our society from falling into the hands of the new organizers . . . . ,"Lloyd wrote to Helen. "We have made clean work of everything — adopted the most thoroughgoing resolutions, and taken the strongest ground with *crashing* unanimity." (34) Those resolutions deplored political activity and denounced the clergy for lack of anti-slavery zeal.

But the "crashing unanimity" was confined mostly to those people Garrison had brought with him. Around the country, the majority of anti-slavery people opposed Garrison's extreme stand and endorsed the idea of a political party. Later in 1840 the Liberty Party was formed and many abolitionists took the opportunity to vote for its candidate. James Birney received only 7,000 popular votes and no electoral votes for president.

Garrison was unconcerned that most abolitionists favored the Liberty Party. He had never believed that the power of a moral reform movement depended on the number of its members. It depended only on the righteousness of its ideas. His tiny group, he believed, was the only abolitionist group that maintained the purity of its position. The Liberty Party abolitionists, he warned, would "lose the reputation of honest enthusiasts, and come to be considered as hypocritical seekers after place and power." Furthermore, they could not meet the slaveholders on moral grounds, but only at the polls where they would lose overwhelmingly, as Birney's defeat showed. As for himself, he believed his voice would be heard more than ever. "The many base attempts that have been made to cripple my influence, and to render me odious in the eyes of the people," he wrote to a friend, "have only served to awaken sympathy, excite curiosity, and to open a wide door for usefulness." (35)

Lloyd had once told a Philadelphia abolitionist whom he considered to be too moderate: "Your cause will not prosper . . . until it excites popular tumult, and brings down upon it a shower of brickbats and rotten eggs, and is threatened with a coat of tar and feathers." (36) Most abolitionists had grown morally soft, he believed, and were lowering their standards to participate in normal public life. In doing this they were diminishing their own influence and forsaking the slaves. In contrast, by maintaining the purity of his principles, he was disturbing the consciences of people and remaining a force to be reckoned with.

His purist platform, he believed, needed only one more plank, and this he added in the early 1840's. He had long believed that slavery depended on the American Union: the United States Army was essential to protect Southerners from slave revolt, and northern markets were necessary to maintain southern cotton plantations. Moreover, he had long held that Northerners were as guilty for the crime of slavery as Southerners as long as Northerners were part of the same union.

In 1843 the Massachusetts Anti-Slavery Society passed a very radical resolution:

" . . . the compact that exists between the North and the South (the U.S. Constitution) is a covenant with death and an agreement with hell — involving both parties in atrocious criminality — and should be immediately annulled." (37) A year later Garrison's American Anti-Slavery Society Resolved: " . . . until slavery be abolished, the watchword, the rallying cry, the motto on the banner of the American Anti-Slavery Society shall be 'NO UNION WITH SLAVEHOLDERS!'" (38) The intent was that the North should leave the Union and wash its hands of slavery. The

South, left on its own with no help from the North in returning fugitive slaves or putting down slave rebellions, would eventually give up the vile system as a lost cause.

In thirteen years (1831-1844) William Lloyd Garrison had radicalized his position to the point where, more than all other abolitionists, he was completely outside the mainstream of American life. He had moved quickly from gradual to immediate emancipation, and then into a host of "perfectionist" ideas, and finally, to a complete withdrawal from the American political process. Every step had followed logically from the one before it, driven forward by righteous thinking.

Moralistically, Garrison felt he could take no other position; practically, he felt his position was good strategy. It was, in his mind, the only strategy that could ever bring American society to the point where it could free the slaves. Only extremism could keep the political cauldron bubbling and give people the moral fortitude they would need for so unsettling a change as the emancipation of three million African-Americans. As Garrison knew all too well, men who ran the country and had the power to make changes — the politicians — needed to see a strong moral feeling sweeping the populace before they would make a decision based on moral rather than practical concepts. William Lloyd Garrison felt nothing but disdain for the morality of all politicians; they had to be harshly goaded to do the right thing.

CHAPTER FOUR

Garrison and Lincoln in 1845

By 1844 William Lloyd Garrison and Abraham Lincoln had each established his career and values. Their careers grew from their abilities and their views of American society. Their values, closely tied to their careers, were the products of their upbringing and the cultures that surrounded them as they matured. In some ways the two men thought alike; they were both very ambitious. But, in many ways, they were exact opposites. In the 1840's, as they reacted in their different ways to the momentous events that unfolded, they would never have guessed that they were moving toward a rendezvous with emancipation.

From his earliest days in Newburyport, Garrison associated mostly with people who "had the answers" and who looked down on those who did not. His mother was morally self-righteous. The newspapers Lloyd worked for or edited were, like most papers at the time, dedicated solely to one point of view. Finally, the men and women who clustered around him in the anti-slavery movement were moralists who condemned even neutral people as sinners. In this environment, Garrison thought in absolute terms and, since he was ambitious and wished to lead, he had to be the most absolute of all. His values came under the heading, "Those who are not for us are against us." He permitted no compromise with evil, particularly the evil of slavery. He would tolerate no talk of delay in purging the nation of its towering sin.

Garrison had the ability to denounce evil very effectively and to use language that would stir people and arouse their passions. He believed that kindling anti-slavery flames and fanning them was the only way to force American society to begin to think about slavery. People were prospering too much because of slavery or were too apathetic to be moved by mild arguments. He was convinced that even if he were despised at first, he would be vindicated when the pro-slavery people took extreme measures to silence him. The people would then see the evils of the slave system. Thus, the government's refusal to allow *The Liberator* to be delivered in the South was a victory; so, too, was the Boston mob in 1835. These exposed the anti-democratic nature of slavery and won converts to abolitionism.

Garrison also believed that, for righteousness sake and for practical reasons, abolitionism needed to maintain its purity. An abolitionist must disassociate himself from all types of behavior and all institutions that were part of slavery. Thus, abolitionists should be pacifists because force was the tool of slaveholders. Abolitionists should divorce themselves from the American government by refusing to vote, because the government supported slavery. Finally, abolitionists should demand separation of the North from the South so that free men would no longer have to participate in slavery. By placing themselves in these advanced positions, the abolitionists would be shining examples of moral purity — people who had no link whatever with sin — and people to whom the Americans could look for moral guidance. Political participation, such as that engaged in by the Liberty Party abolitionists, was a great betrayal of principle and bad policy, for it involved abolitionists in political deals and compromises that tarnished their image and destroyed their moral leadership.

On the slavery issue, Lincoln was like Garrison in some ways. He sympathized with the African-Americans and thought slavery was wrong. But Lincoln was a product of the frontier, the great leveling ground of young America. Moving from Kentucky to Indiana to Illinois, he followed the edge of the frontier and associated not with moralistic church people, partisan editors and self-righteous reformers, but rather with the broad parade of the human race. He lived not with the scent of elitism but with the earthy smell of equality. In his environment, a man did not make high-minded pronouncements or heavy moral judgments. Instead, he worked shoulder to shoulder with his neighbors and respected their opinions.

Lincoln lived on the land, and the land yielded slowly to the advance of man. He worked with people who knew the stubbornness of the soil and the difficulties of "making a go of it" when success or failure sometimes hinged on a single rainstorm. People on the frontier expected to keep things that took hard work and sweat to acquire. What had brought them even small success they were reluctant to change. Lincoln understood the gradual process of change — the need to move in rhythm with nature and with nature's servant, man.

Lincoln's career was politics and law. He believed in American institutions and procedures and wanted to work and achieve success within them. His physical abilities and his understanding of human nature helped him deal with the people and win their votes. In the Illinois State House, in the courts, and on the campaign trail, Lincoln learned that victories were usually won by those people who were willing to see the other side of issues and to compromise when necessary. Successful men maneuvered, struck bargains, carefully timed their moves, and often settled for some, not all, of what they wanted. In the final analysis, it usually did not matter whether you were right or wrong. What counted were votes.

Avid newspaper reader that he was, Lincoln had probably heard of William Lloyd Garrison by 1845. "Oh yeah," he would have said, "he's that Boston abolitionist, the most radical of them all, the one who was mobbed and almost hanged. He'll do his cause more harm than good with his overheated words, and, in the process, he'll cause a lot of trouble!"

Lincoln was baffled by the abolitionists' demands. What disruption it would cause to set three million African-Americans free at once! How intolerant the mass of people would be of such a change! Those fanatics were wrong. They should believe that most people's hearts are good, that they will listen to reason, and that some orderly resolution of the slavery question will come about if thoughtful people would just be patient.

In 1845 Garrison had probably never heard of Abraham Lincoln, an Illinois state legislator who had never been east of Kentucky and was unknown nationally. If he had, he would have categorized Lincoln with all other politicians — a group incapable, by the very nature of its profession, of taking a moral position. If Lincoln was baffled by the abolitionists, Garrison was even more baffled by any man who could permit an evil institution to exist even a single day.

Yet, William Lloyd Garrison knew, even though he rarely, if ever, said it, that if he really would ever "be heard," the politicians would have to be the most important group to do the listening. If slavery were to be abolished in Washington, D.C., if the North really were to withdraw from the Union leaving the South to hold its slaves alone, and if slavery were ever to be outright abolished, the politicians were the ones who were going to have to do it. The reason he did not say this is because it was too early. The moral purity of his movement had to be maintained; there was much work still to be done and many more hearts to convert before any politician would dare make a move against slavery.

Fortunately for Garrison, after 1845 his major ally — the South — began doing its work more effectively than ever. The South had manufactured many abolitionists in the North by trying to restrict Garrison's freedom of speech. It was about to make even more abolitionists — and jolt the sensibilities of moderates such as Abraham Lincoln — by pushing westward and proving that Garrison was right when he claimed the nation was dominated by the "slave power" – the grotesque alliance between the slave owners and their allies.

CHAPTER FIVE

"By the Fruit the Tree is Known"

1845-1850

During the great period of westward expansion, Americans hotly debated the question of whether or not slavery would be allowed in the new lands acquired by the United States. William Lloyd Garrison took uncompromising positions on slavery's growth, but mostly refused to discuss the issue because the real problem was slavery itself. Lincoln, ever a loyal party politician, worked hard for the election of Whig candidates and tried to persuade those who opposed slavery's extension, as he did, that the Whig candidates offered the best chance of keeping slavery from spreading. When the Compromise of 1850 settled the issue of slavery's expansion, seemingly for good, each man viewed the deal through his own very different lens.

1. WESTWARD EXPANSION AND SLAVERY

In the year 1844, a traveler coming to the door of a log cabin in Kentucky sees a sign scrawled on the planks: "Gone to Texas." A mill owner in Lowell, Massachusetts, has to hire several new workers to replace those who have gone to Oregon. A plantation in Alabama is decaying, with weeds growing in the cotton fields and the wooden doors of the slave cabins creaking in the breeze; the planter has moved his family and his "bondsmen" to new land in Texas. The country is in the midst of a great migration. Western fever has struck. The flow of wagons Lincoln saw in St. Louis in 1831 is reaching flood proportions as thousands of people pack their belongings and set out for the frontier.

One destination is Oregon Territory, a huge expanse of wooded land in the far Northwest that comprises what is now Oregon, Washington, British Columbia, and parts of Idaho and Montana. Reports have spread throughout the country of the lush soil in the Willamette River Valley in Oregon, and thousands are willing to make the arduous trip to start a farm there. In the spring of each year, wagon trains form in Independence, Missouri, and head out across the green prairie grass. After covering hundreds of miles of flatlands inhabited by "hostile Indians," the wagons proceed through the passes of the Rocky Mountains to begin the most difficult part of the journey. If they are lucky, they reach the Willamette by October before snow blocks all hope of getting through. The trail from Independence is dotted with chests of drawers and tables left by those who needed to lighten their loads. Along the way simple crosses mark the graves of those who succumbed to disease, starvation or Indian arrows.

Oregon was not officially United States territory in 1844. It was claimed also by Great Britain; indeed, north of the Columbia River most of the settlers were British subjects from Canada. To solidify the United States' claim to Oregon, the Americans in the Willamette Valley organized their own territorial legislature with a document called the Champoeg Compact. Besides creating a government, this compact outlawed slavery and banned all free African-Americans from the territory. The Oregon settlers did not want to compete with the slave system, nor did they want to live side-by-side with "Negroes." Thus, Oregon was following the pattern of the northern free states that outlawed slavery but also discriminated severely against black people.

Another destination for those moving west, particularly plantation owners, was Texas. In 1820, the Mexican government had given a land grant in its northern provinces to Moses Austin, an American businessman and banker. Under Moses' son, Stephen, an American colony in Texas prospered. Southern planters were attracted by Austin's offer of 177 acres of farmland and 13,000 acres of pastureland to each family. By 1834, there were twenty thousand white colonists and two thousand slaves in Texas.

The Mexican government made several attempts to outlaw slavery in Texas before 1834, but the Texans always successfully ignored edicts from Mexico City. In 1835, however, President Santa Anna proclaimed a unified constitution for Mexico that denied the Texans their right to self-government and banned slavery. Angered at this attempt to rule them and steal their "property," the Texans set up their own government in San Antonio and expelled the Mexican soldiers stationed in the town. Calling their state the "Lone Star Republic," the Texans prepared to fight Santa Anna and his army, which was advancing northward to put down the rebellion.

One hundred and seventy-nine Texans defending a Spanish Mission called the Alamo outside San Antonio were wiped out by Santa Anna's force of three thousand men. Several weeks later, however, a Texan force under Sam Houston caught the Mexicans off guard near the San Jacinto River and, with the rallying cry "Remember the Alamo!" won an overwhelming victory, capturing General Santa Anna himself in the process. The Mexican president, in the presence of towering (6'6") Sam Houston — and Sam's Bowie knife — agreed to full Texan independence.

As an independent slave republic, Texas was more attractive to Southerners than ever. By 1844 wagons were rolling across

Louisiana toward Texas every day. The grasslands of eastern Texas were becoming dotted with cotton plantations.

Sam Houston and the Texan leadership appealed to the American government for admission to the Union as a state. Southerners pushed the appeal claiming they needed new slave territory if they were to maintain their equality with the North in Congress. The number of slave states to free was even at thirteen, but only Florida was left to join the Union for the South, while Wisconsin, Iowa, and Minnesota would soon be coming in for the North. Moreover, Southerners were terrified that Texas might become a protectorate of Great Britain who was making overtures to the Texas government. Britain would almost certainly demand an end to slavery in Texas; then Texas would become a haven for runaway slaves right at the South's doorstep. Before Britain made any kind of deal with the Lone Star Republic, Texas must become a slave state.

Abolitionists were appalled at the idea of taking more slave territory into the Union. Garrison's mentor, Benjamin Lundy, wrote a pamphlet in 1836 called "The War in Texas," which claimed the Texan revolution had been promoted by the South to gain new slave markets and more slave territory. Garrison agreed, but for a while he did not focus on Texas since he felt it was just another example — by no means the only one — of the stranglehold the slave owners had on the Union.

Most Northerners, although they supported southern arguments for slavery and persecuted abolitionists, opposed annexing Texas to the Union. Congenial as most Northerners felt toward the South and slavery, they felt uneasy about extensive additions of southern territory and the corresponding increase in southern voting power that would result. If it controlled the national government, the South would lower the tariff, which most Northerners deemed essential to the development of industry, and which Whigs considered necessary for internal improvements.

Southerners, by contrast, were almost apoplectic at the prospect of seeing Oregon enter the Union while Texas remained outside: " . . . the whole of the non-slaveholding states have manifested a great disposition to trample upon and disregard the rights of the southern, as slaveholding states!" screeched the Jacksonville (Alabama) *Republican*, "Under these circumstances, the addition of Texas with its slaves is the only possible means of saving the South." (1)

The dissension over Texas made its admission a hot issue that most political leaders prior to 1844 refused to handle. But the organization of territorial government in Oregon, the increasingly strong demands for Texas's annexation, and the fact that the settlement of both of these territories was proceeding rapidly, indicated that the presidential election of 1844 might center on westward expansion.

Henry Clay, the perennial leader of the Whigs, was certain he would be the candidate of his party. Although he had lost to John Quincy Adams in 1824 and Andrew Jackson in 1832, there was no Whig available to deny him a third try. On the Democratic side, Martin Van Buren, the New Yorker with bushy side-whiskers who had succeeded Jackson in 1836 but had lost to William Henry Harrison in 1840, was sure he would again receive his party's nod. Two years before the election, Van Buren and Clay got together and agreed that rather than put the country, and themselves, through a wrenching debate over Texas, they would each renounce any intention of annexing the Lone Star Republic. Van Buren issued a statement saying that rushing the admission of Texas into the Union would mean war with Mexico since Mexico had not resigned herself to losing it. Clay said he would welcome

Texas to the Union only if all sections of the country approved and war with Mexico could be averted. The two men prepared to face each other in a Texas-free campaign.

However, plans often go awry in presidential politics. In 1844, Clay and Van Buren's scheme was blown to pieces when Van Buren lost the Democratic nomination to James K. Polk. Polk, a nervous, sickly Tennessean, was a protégé of Andrew Jackson. He won the nomination by coming out strongly for the annexation of Texas and Oregon (the Mexicans and the British be damned!), and promising the acquisition of more land in the west, particularly California. Polk was an apostle of the idea, later called "Manifest Destiny," that it was God's will for the United States to extend its border all the way to the Pacific Ocean. The Democratic Party was going to go all out for expansion. The people wanted it, the country would grow because of it, and abolitionists and tariff-minded Whigs had better step out of the way!

Polk had support in the South where desire for Texas grew into out-right lust after his nomination, and in the North among folks who dreamed of Oregon and favored American power and growth even if it did mean more southern votes in Congress. Clay had the votes of most Whigs who hoped, at last, to see enacted his program of internal improvements and a restored United States Bank. This would only happen if Texas stayed out of the Union and its anti-tariff votes never materialized.

William Lloyd Garrison, fresh into his "NO UNION WITH SLAVEHOLDERS!" position, condemned both candidates as slaveholders. He proclaimed that, like all politicians, they were tools of the slave interests. Garrison heaped special scorn on the Liberty Party that was trying once again to elect James Birney on an anti-slavery platform. The party would be humiliated as it had been in 1840, Garrison predicted, proving once again that abolitionists who tried to win votes were deluded. In fact, he added, they were harmful to the cause because they allowed some anti-slavery people to believe they were doing their duty to the slaves when they voted for the Liberty party candidate every four years. The whole election was immoral lunacy, and Garrison had little interest in it except insofar as it proved him correct.

Abraham Lincoln spoke up and down Illinois for Clay. Abe knew that Clay, at age 67, was making his last bid for the presidency, and so he was putting in extra effort to elect his hero, the founder of the Whig Party. Campaigning for Clay improved Lincoln's own standing in the party and his recognition in the state in preparation for his race for a seat in Congress in 1846. In town halls, court houses, and village squares, he urged his home-spun western audiences to support the Whig program of sound money and industrial progress by voting for the man who had proved his love for his country, Henry Clay.

Abe's efforts were in vain. Polk carried Illinois and the nation, winning 1,337,000 votes to Clay's 1,299,000. It was a bitter defeat for Clay. If just a few thousand anti-slavery Whigs in New York State had voted for him instead of Birney, the Liberty Party candidate, New York's electoral votes –- and the presidency – would have been his.

It was also a sad and puzzling election for Abe Lincoln. Sad because Henry Clay would never be president. Puzzling because it seemed as though anti-slavery Whigs in New York had thrown away their votes on Birney and had, at the same time, brought about the result they did not want – the election of James K. Polk, the man who wanted to annex slave-holding Texas. A year later Lincoln wrote to Williamson Durley, an abolitionist: "If by your votes you could have prevented the extension . . . of slavery, would it not have been good, and not evil, so to have cast your votes, even though it involved casting them for a slaveholder (Clay)? By the *fruit* the tree is to be known. An evil tree cannot bring forth *good* fruit. If the fruit of electing Mr. Clay would have been to prevent the extension of slavery, could the act of electing him have been evil?" (2)

Lincoln's political mind could not conceive of a man's voting for principle if it meant losing a practical, and more significant, issue connected with that principle. In his thinking, the moral bullheadedness of the anti-slavery Whigs had given Polk the election. Now the slave republic, Texas, was straightening her gown and waiting to be led down the aisle into the Union.

2. A WAR TO EXPAND SLAVERY

With the country clearly in favor of expansion, Congress acted to annex Texas even before Polk took office. On February 28th, 1845, it passed a joint resolution making Texas a state.

In Boston, people were outraged over the Texas annexation. Before Congress acted, a convention was held in Faneuil Hall to protest the imminent annexation. Garrison attended and spoke to a respectful audience, one far different from the one that met at the same hall ten years earlier to discuss ways to shut up the "dangerous fanatic." For two years he had been warning that Texas's annexation was inevitable, and he had been advising the North to secede from the Union before it had to participate in that immoral act. Now annexation was upon the country; now the North was an equal partner with the South in the extension of the slave dominion.

In March, after the deed was complete, Garrison called it "a crime unsurpassed in the annals of human depravity!" What further proof did the North need that the South now held mastery over the nation? Massachusetts should "treat the general government as a nullity .... NO UNION WITH SLAVEHOLDERS!" (3)

Candidly, Lloyd had to admit he was pleased with the annexation of Texas. It proved to the North that the slave power was strong, greedy, and reckless. Also, it was turning the tide of northern public opinion against the South. He wrote that even though the slave power seemed invincible after its Texas victory, "Never has it been so near its downfall as at this moment." (4) He was confident that the South's increasingly extreme demands would drive more Northerners toward abolitionism.

Garrison believed that under Polk, a Tennessee slaveholder and rabid expansionist, the South would make more attempts to seize territory for slavery. At a rally to "consider the encroachments of the slave power" held in Concord, Massachusetts, on September 22, 1845, he warned that if the North continued to stand with the South in her aggressions upon Mexico, then the North was as vile as the South. We must get out of the Union now, he cried, and cleanse ourselves of this awful complicity.

In Illinois, Lincoln was only mildly concerned about the annexation of Texas. He did not think it would "augment the evil of slavery" since slavery was already in Texas. He did have a concern similar to Garrison's, however, that the South would take slavery into other lands that might be acquired by the aggressive Polk. To such an extension of the slave system he was unalterably opposed. As he told his abolitionist friend, Williamson Durley, he felt it was the constitutional duty of the North to let slavery alone where it already existed, but he believed the North should never "prevent slavery from dying a natural death" by finding "new places for it to live in, when it can no longer exist in the old." (5) This was one of Lincoln's first expressions of his belief that slavery should be contained, a belief that inched him a tiny bit closer to William Lloyd Garrison.

Lincoln and Garrison were right in predicting that the Polk administration would, as it had promised in the election, add new territory to the United States. During 1845, Polk negotiated the Oregon question with the British and finally, in 1846, signed a treaty dividing the territory along the 49th parallel, the same line that formed the American-Canadian border west of the Great Lakes. Oregon became a United States Territory free of slavery.

Polk, of course, was interested in much more than Oregon. In 1843, John C. Fremont had led an expedition through the Sierra Nevada Mountains into California, the northern Pacific coast province of Mexico. The journals of his expedition told of the lush valleys and magnificent harbors at San Francisco, Monterey, and San Diego. They also revealed how poorly Mexico administered and defended its beautiful possession. Polk's eyes lit up at the thought of grabbing this jewel for the United States. Time was of the essence, however, because reports were coming to Washington that Great Britain and Russia were contemplating the jewel as part of *their* empires.

In late 1845, Polk sent John Slidell as ambassador to Mexico City to offer five million dollars for New Mexico (the area between Texas and California) and any amount the Mexicans asked for California itself. The Mexicans, still burning with indignation over American annexation of Texas, refused to see Slidell. Based on this snub, Polk was prepared to ask Congress for a declaration of war, but he managed to maneuver the Mexicans into a more outrageous provocation.

An American army under General Zachary Taylor was in Texas. Polk ordered it to advance to the Rio Grande River across from the Mexican town of Matamoros. Mexico was claiming that the southern boundary of Texas was the Nueces River, a hundred miles north of Matamoros. The Mexicans saw Taylor's advance as an aggression into their territory. On April 26, 1846, a small unit of Mexican cavalry crossed the Rio Grande, killed several American troopers in a brief skirmish, and withdrew. News of this incident reached Polk on May 9, 1846, just as he was about to ask Congress for a declaration of war based on Slidell's snub. Now his war message would say that American blood had been shed "upon American soil," since he chose to believe the Rio Grande was the southern border of Texas. On May 13th Congress declared that "by act of the Republic of Mexico, a state of war exists between that government and the United States." (6) Polk had his war, and he hoped it would net California as a conquest.

The war was immediately popular in the South and up the Mississippi Valley into the Northwest. Dreaming of joining Zachary Taylor's army and marching victoriously into Mexico City, men rushed to enlist. In Springfield, Lincoln felt uneasy about the way Polk had engineered the Mexican attack. Yet he attended a great mass meeting in the Springfield square and joined Governor Ford, and others in speaking for swift and united action against the enemy. The crowd gave loud "hurrahs!" to every hawkish statement, and seventy men stepped forward to volunteer. Any misgivings Lincoln had about the causes of the war he kept to himself. After all, once war was declared, a man could only retard victory by casting doubt on the righteousness of the war effort. Besides, it was an election year, and he would be running for Congress. It would not be wise to alienate voters by throwing icy water on their inflamed spirits.

Amidst the excited atmosphere of men going off to war, Lincoln's campaign for Congress drew little attention. His deal with Hardin and Baker almost came apart when Hardin considered running for the seat again. But, with some prodding from Lincoln, he withdrew from the race and went off to fight in Mexico. He hoped he would come home a war hero and a strong candidate for high office. Instead, a year later, he came home in a pine box.

Lincoln's Democratic opponent for the congressional seat was Peter Cartwright, a Methodist minister who traveled the countryside preaching the gospel to evangelistic gatherings. On the revival stump, Cartwright could convert gruff frontiersmen to religion and bring sinners to their knees in repentance, but on the campaign trail he was a flop. Lincoln spoke in his usual folksy style and endeared himself to voters far more than the bombastic Cartwright could. When Abe extolled the virtues of Whig principles, folks listened. At the polls, he whipped Cartwright handily.

In Boston, William Lloyd Garrison, as would be expected, was outraged at the declaration of war and the call for volunteers. No need to be patriotic or to appeal to voters stymied *him*. He scoffed at the volunteers who drilled on the common and compared them to Falstaff's ragged band. He hoped that Mexico – *slave-free* Mexico – would be "victorious in every conflict, until not an invading foot (trod) upon her soil." (7) Clearly, he wrote, this was a war contrived by the slave power to enlarge Texas, seize Mexican land, and extend the slave empire.

For the most part, however, Garrison paid little attention to the Mexican War in his editorials and speeches. At its outbreak, he was planning another trip to England where he hoped to persuade the Scottish Presbyterian Church to return the money it had raised in the American South from slaveholders (tainted money!). He also hoped to renew contacts with the British abolitionists. When he returned from England in the fall of 1846, he began planning a speaking tour of Ohio, a tour on which he was going to concentrate on "NO UNION WITH SLAVEHOLDERS!" using the war with Mexico as just another example of the slaveholders' control of the Union.

Other New Englanders, even some who had never before opposed slavery, took up the anti-war slack created by Garrison's journeys. Henry David Thoreau, the nature-loving pacifist of

Concord, refused to pay his state poll tax in protest against the war. He spent a night in the Concord jail and would have spent more had friends not paid the tax for him. The Massachusetts Legislature made official protests against the war, calling it an "unconstitutional" war with a "triple object of extending slavery, of strengthening the slave power, and of obtaining control of the free states." (8)

Because of the success of American armies, the war ended quickly. In California, American settlers rose in rebellion against Mexico, easily conquered the scant Mexican forces there, and declared California part of the United States — all within four months of the declaration of war. In northern Mexico, General Taylor won quick victories, culminating in the Battle of Buena Vista. In this bloody affair, fought on a scorching plain, the Mexicans were routed, bringing glory to "Old Rough and Ready" Taylor and Colonel Jefferson Davis, whose regiment stopped a fierce charge by Mexican cavalry.

Meanwhile, General Winfield Scott advanced on the Mexican capital. "Old Fuss and Feathers," as his men called him, won several brilliant victories and, on September 17, 1847, rode triumphantly into Mexico City as bugles blared, and Mexican civilians watched from windows and rooftops. The war had been won. Soon Mexico would be compelled to turn over California and New Mexico to the United States and to recognize the Rio Grande as the southern boundary of the United States.

Lincoln did not take his seat in the House of Representatives until the fighting was largely over. Still, the Congress that assembled in December, 1847, was going to have to approve the final treaty with Mexico and the spoils of war it would contain, and so the justification for the war was still an issue. A major question was what would be the status of the new land the U.S. would take from Mexico – would it be open or closed to slavery? On these concerns, Lincoln was to get his first taste of standing on principle in the face of strong opposition.

Whigs had questioned the justification of Democrat Polk's war from the beginning, and their criticism did not abate as the war drew to a close. Henry Clay called the war one of "offensive aggression," and told the man who had defeated him for president that it was Mexico, not the United States, who was fighting to defend itself.

Lincoln's early doubts about the war solidified as he listened to Clay and other Whigs. Finally, he rose on the floor of the House to make his own position clear. Speaking in his high-pitched, western drawl, he asked President Polk to prove that the spot on which American blood was first shed was truly American soil. He introduced a resolution asking for Polk's proof (which Polk never gave), a resolution that became known as the "Spot Resolution."

Thereafter, Lincoln voted with the Whigs on all motions designed to put the president in the wrong. Even a resolution of thanks to General Taylor was amended to praise Taylor's efforts "in a war unnecessarily and unconstitutionally begun by the President of the United States." (9) However, when an extreme group proposed that the United States disavow all claims to Mexican land and withdraw United States forces to north of the Rio Grande, Lincoln voted "nay," standing with the majority who favored annexation of territory.

Back in Illinois, as word spread around Sangamon County of Lincoln's opposition to the war, people began calling him a new Benedict Arnold, a traitor to his country. The *State Register*, an important Illinois newspaper, ridiculed Lincoln as a man afflicted with "spotted fever," a "spotty gentleman" who, fortunately, was the only man in Washington afflicted with the disease since it would most likely "carry him off." The word in the seventh district was that Lincoln could not win another term if he ran.

Lincoln's feelings about this were expressed in a letter to Billy Herndon. He said, in essence, that he had to choose between standing by his convictions and telling a lie, and faced with that choice, the only honorable thing he could do was condemn Polk's war. (10)

The question of whether the new lands acquired from Mexico would be open to slavery had been raised the year before Lincoln came to Washington by David Wilmot, a representative from Pennsylvania. Wilmot proposed an amendment that stated that in any lands annexed as a result of the war, "neither slavery nor involuntary servitude shall ever exist." This "Wilmot Proviso" aroused consternation among Southerners. An attempt by Congress to keep slavery out of the new territories was, in their eyes, akin to an attempt to strangle the slave system. Southerners, their argument went, had as much right to bring their property into the new territories as Northerners did. The South would not tolerate this invasion of its constitutional rights. Unable to defeat the proviso in the House, where the North held a majority, the South stopped it in the Senate and Southerners hoped it would never raise its ugly head again.

After Lincoln took his seat, he supported the concept of outlawing slavery in California and New Mexico. As he had written to Durley in 1845, he thought the constitution protected slavery under the right of property, but did not guarantee its extension into new territory. Because it had the power to govern territories, Congress could ban slavery from them. Thus, it was the duty of all those who thought slavery was wrong to vote slavery out of the west. Lincoln later claimed he voted for one or another version of the Wilmot Proviso forty different times. The proposal never passed, however, and the question of whether slavery could go into New Mexico or California was unresolved as the elections of 1848 approached.

William Lloyd Garrison was unconcerned about the fate of the Wilmot Proviso. In his mind, those who were attempting to attack slavery by preventing its extension into the West were engaged in a futile effort totally devoid of moral strength. "We regard it as a matter of comparative indifference whether the proviso receives the sanction of Congress or not," he wrote, "feeling that the attempt to restrain slavery by laws and constitutions is precisely equivalent to damming up the Mississippi with bulrushes, and that any man who expects anything but failure from such a plan has still the a b c of his country's history to learn." (11) The South had always gotten its way in the Union in regard to slavery, he argued, so the only answer was to desert the South.

Curiously, in 1848, Garrison was gratified to see the beginning of a new political party dedicated to keeping slavery out of the territories. The "Free Soil Party" was made up of anti-slavery Whigs, anti-slavery Democrats, and abolitionists who had been part of the Liberty Party. (As Garrison had predicted, the Liberty Party died in 1848 from lack of success at the polls and arguments among its members over political strategy.) Although Garrison believed that the issue of "free soil" was "weaker than a spider's web," and that "a single breath of the slave power" would blow it away, (12) he was pleased that the movement showed that at least a moderate anti-slavery feeling was beginning to work its way into the hearts of average Northerners.

There would come a time, Lloyd was sure, when this moderate feeling would turn into a passion — the slave owners' insistence on spreading slavery would ensure that — and then the debate with the South would reach its climax. The North would leave the Union and cut off slavery from its source of nourishment, leaving it like a fish washed up on the beach. In July, 1848, he wrote to Helen: "I long to see the day when the great issue with the slave power, of the immediate dissolution of the Union, will be made by all the free states, for then the conflict will be a short and decisive one, and liberty will triumph. The Free Soil Movement inevitably leads to it, and hence I hail it as the beginning of the end." (13) Although he was wrong in predicting that the North would leave the Union — and that the conflict would be short — his belief that the issue of slavery in the territories would lead the North into a Union-rending crisis with the South and result in freedom for the slaves was quite correct.

Lincoln was not disposed to join the Free Soil Party. Although he was a Wilmot Proviso man, he believed in working within the two party system. Only the major parties had a chance of winning elections, he reasoned, so a wise and practical man tried to bring success to the party that most closely fit his convictions on all issues. In 1848, Lincoln was still a Whig politician.

3. THE QUINTESSENTIAL WHIG

During his first year in Washington, Lincoln, like most freshman congressmen, had to adjust to life in the nation's capital. The city was quite different from Springfield. He, Mary, and their sons Robert and Eddie took rooms in a boarding house across from the Capitol building. There they shared a dining table with other congressmen and tried to make a go of it as a family. But Mary soon became bored with life in a place where the men were constantly talking politics, and the women — the few who had accompanied their husbands — were snobbish and unfriendly. After three months, she took the boys to Lexington, Kentucky, to live in more comfortable surroundings with her family while she waited for Abe to finish the session. Lincoln was left on his own to fraternize with the boarding house crowd, attend committee meetings and legislative sessions, and learn the ways of Washington.

In 1847, Washington was a city of contradictions. The main thoroughfare, Pennsylvania Avenue, was a straight ribbon of crushed stone "pavement" stretched between the Executive Mansion and the Capitol. Along its sidewalks on a Sunday afternoon, one could see senators and congressmen, some of the most famous men in the country: Henry Clay, Thomas Hart Benton, John C. Calhoun and Daniel Webster, to name a few. Off Pennsylvania Avenue, however, the city was a mire of muddy, unpaved streets, mosquito infested marshes, and run-down wooden buildings. Eight thousand free African-Americans made up a third of the population of the city, and many of them lived in squalor within sight of the nation's centers of power.

More cruel and ironic, Lincoln thought, was the presence of two thousand slaves and liveries for the slave trade in the shadow of the Capitol. In these liveries, he observed, "droves of Negroes were collected, temporarily kept, and finally taken to southern markets, precisely like droves of horses." (14) The same disgust that had engulfed him at the sight of the slave auctions in New Orleans crept into Abe's heart in Washington. Surely, he thought, Congress should not tolerate this gross display of human cruelty in its own back yard!

In the House of Representatives chamber, where he held one of the back-row seats customarily assigned to newcomers, Lincoln followed tradition and allowed Whig Party leaders to carry the debates. Until he got "the hang of the House," he spoke only to introduce and argue for his "Spot Resolution." On nearly every issue he voted straight party line, following the Whig leadership loyally. He was a conscientious, hard-working congressman who rarely missed a vote and served his party and his constituents well. After his "Spot Resolution," however, his constituents were too angry to notice much that he did.

In 1848, the Whig leaders tried to line up a winning presidential ticket for the fall campaign. There was always Henry Clay, but his defeats in 1824, 1832 and 1844, and his seventy-one years, soured many Whigs who wanted a sure-fire winner. The man on everyone's mind was the hero of the Mexican War, "Old Rough and Ready" Zachary Taylor. Heroic generals had proven to be highly successful vote getters (witness Andrew Jackson and William Henry Harrison), and Taylor had the virtues of being a well-known hero who was obscure on the issues. He could be "sold" to Southerners as a slaveholder (which he was), to Northerners as an opponent of slavery's extension (Who was to say he wasn't? He had never voted or made a speech), and to everyone as the "man of the hour."

Lincoln was an early proponent of the Taylor candidacy, and his reasons were purely practical. "In answer to your inquiries," he wrote fellow representative Thomas Flourney in February, "I have to say I am in favor of General Taylor as the Whig candidate for the presidency because I am satisfied we can elect him, that he would give us a Whig administration and that we cannot elect any other Whig." (15) Better to have a Whig administration under a man who might not be qualified to be president, Lincoln reasoned, than to have any sort of Democratic administration. In numerous letters back home he urged Illinois Whigs to support Taylor. Finally, at the June convention of the Whig Party in Philadelphia, he watched with gratification as the general was nominated with the help of Illinois votes.

The Democrats chose Lewis Cass of Michigan to oppose Taylor. Incredibly ugly (which mattered little in pre-television elections), Cass was an ardent supporter of expansion. As far as the already-acquired territories were concerned, he felt Congress should not pass the Wilmot Proviso or any other law outlawing — or guaranteeing — slavery in New Mexico or California. Whether slaves could be brought into those places or not, he believed, should be left entirely to the people who lived there. Letting the people decide — "popular sovereignty" — was a way of taking the debates on slavery out of Congress, thus reducing the tensions in the country. Or, so he thought.

Although Taylor was not an avowed supporter of the Wilmot Proviso, Lincoln had a way of coordinating his own Wilmot Proviso sympathies with his support of Taylor. On July 27, 1848, as he spoke in the House of Representatives for Taylor, he said, "I am a northern man, or, rather, a western free state man, and with a constituency I believe to be, and with personal feelings I *know* to be, against the extension of slavery. As such, and with the information I have, I hope and *believe* General Taylor, if elected, would not veto the Proviso. *But* I do not *know* it. Yet, if I knew he would, I would still vote for him. I would do so because, in my judgment, his election alone can defeat General Cass, and because, *should* slavery thereby go to the territories we now have, just as much will certainly happen by the election of Cass, and in addition, a course of policy, leading to new wars and new acquisition of territory, and still further extension of slavery." (16) As usual, Lincoln was thinking of the practical consequences of political action. What good would it do to reject Taylor only because he was not strictly in line with your opinions on slavery and was a slaveholder himself? If you rejected him, you helped Cass, who was surely a slavery expansionist!

In the late summer of 1848, Lincoln took his arguments for Taylor on a speaking tour of Massachusetts. He hoped to convince anti-slavery Whigs who might be tempted to vote for the Free Soil candidate, Martin Van Buren, to stick with the party. At Worcester, New Bedford, Chelsea, Cambridge, and other towns, he spoke to small crowds who had come to hear their local politicians and also to see a tall, funny looking congressman from the west who told a lot of stories. Humorous though he was, Lincoln, as always, had a serious message. Whig principles on slavery are, in general terms, the same as Free Soil principles, he pleaded. If you vote for Taylor you will be getting about the same thing you would if you could, by some miracle, elect Van Buren. But you can *never* elect Van Buren. So, if you vote for him, you will deprive Taylor of your vote and you will help elect Cass, whom *none* of us wants! It was the classic argument against voting for a third party candidate.

At Tremont Temple in Boston, Lincoln followed the Governor of New York, William Seward, to the platform. This dignified little man with a beak nose impressed Lincoln when he delivered a polished speech opposing the extension of slavery into the territories. Lincoln, a homespun orator speaking before cosmopolitan city people, followed with his usual plea to support Taylor as the best way to stop the spread of slavery. Afterwards, when he talked with Seward at their hotel, he complimented the governor (soon to be elected senator from New York) and told him: "I reckon you are right. We have got to deal with the slavery question, and got to give much more attention to it hereafter." (17) Little could Seward have imagined that he would one day serve in the cabinet of this tall, rustic man who would be the president, and they would "deal" with the slavery question together.

From Boston, Lincoln went west to Albany, New York, where he met Millard Fillmore, the Whig vice-presidential candidate. From there, he took the train to Buffalo. After visiting Niagara Falls, a sight that impressed him deeply, he boarded a steamboat that took him across Lake Erie to Detroit. From there, he traveled overland to Chicago, a town that had only been a bit larger than New Salem when Lincoln first arrived in Illinois, but was now the fastest growing city on the Great Lakes. In his stump speech, now finely tuned, he spoke for Taylor for two hours in the public square. Finally, during the last two weeks before the election, he traveled about his home district, scaring up last minute votes for the Whig ticket.

On election day, Taylor defeated Cass 1,360,752 to 1,219, 962, with 291,342 votes going to Van Buren. Taylor lost Illinois, but carried Lincoln's district by fifteen hundred votes, and so, on the whole, Lincoln was pleased by the results. He believed he had contributed no small share to the Whig triumph and that his efforts would be rewarded in some way. Because of the Whig practice of "taking turns," in Congress, Abe had not run for re-election to his congressional seat, and might have lost anyway because of his "Spot Resolutions." But, there were jobs to be handed out to deserving Whigs by the new administration and perhaps he could land a choice position.

Back in Washington for his last congressional session in December, 1848, Lincoln resumed his role as a conscientious Whig stalwart. The question of slavery in the new lands was still unresolved, and Abe watched with disapproval as Northerners and Southerners began to harden their positions. He was particularly dismayed by the attitudes of a few southern spokesmen who were saying that slavery would have to be guaranteed in the new territories or the South would leave the Union. He continued to vote for Wilmot Proviso type proposals (none of which succeeded), but spoke little on the subject, believing it was best left untouched until passions cooled.

He was, however, moved to make one stand against slavery. Joshua Giddings, the anti-slavery Whig from Ohio whom Lincoln admired, spoke eloquently one day on the crime of slavery, and proposed that it be abolished in the District of Columbia. Mindful of the terrible slave liveries he saw every day, Lincoln approved of Gideon's idea and believed he could draw up a moderate bill that would get enough votes for passage. And so, he prepared a bill that would free all children born of slave mothers in the district after January 1, 1850, and paid federal money to any slave-owners in the district who wished to free their adult slaves after that date. The plan would have to be approved by the people in the district, and there would be provision for the prompt return of runaway slaves from elsewhere in the South who might enter the district. Since the bill paid Southerners for their property, since it *gradually* freed slaves, thus allowing racial adjustments to proceed comfortably, and since it prevented Washington from becoming a haven for runaways from Maryland and Virginia, Lincoln believed it would get the support of all but the most fanatically pro-slavery or anti-slavery congressmen.

A few days before he was to propose his bill, however, Lincoln realized it would surely fail because he was "abandoned by his former backers," men who had lost their stomach for the fight that would surely be stirred up by the proposal. Not one to put forth an idea just for principle's sake, he never introduced his District of Columbia Emancipation Bill. Paradoxically, because the bill provided for the return of runaway slaves, the incident left Lincoln in the position of being regarded by the abolitionists as a man who would track down runaways and return them to bondage. Wendell Phillips later branded him that "slave hound from Illinois," (18). At the same time, because the bill would have freed some slaves in the District of Columbia, Southerners saw him as a radical abolitionist.

At the end of the session, Abe stayed on in Washington hoping to have some influence on the political appointments being made by President Taylor and to secure a job for himself. He wrote letters to members of the cabinet and waited to be consulted about appointments that might be made in Illinois. When nothing came of his efforts, he returned reluctantly to Springfield, still hoping something would come his way. As a loyal Whig for many years, he felt he was entitled to at least some of the spoils of victory.

His attention focused on the job of Commissioner of the General Land Office in Washington that had been promised to someone from Illinois. When it became clear that the choice would be between Justin Butterfield of Chicago and himself, he went after the job with vigor. Butterfield did not deserve it, Lincoln believed, because he had not supported Taylor for the Whig nomination and had not campaigned for Taylor in the general election. Political rewards should go to those who had earned them. He asked everyone who might have influence in the administration to speak up for him and finally, in desperation, he went back to Washington to plead his own case. However, for reasons never explained, the job went to Butterfield.

Returning once more to Springfield, Lincoln felt he was out of politics. At the age of forty, he considered himself an old man who had had his fling in Washington and was now out to pasture. There was nothing to do but resume his law practice with Billy Herndon and perhaps be more of a family man again. He would once more argue suits and libels before local juries and spend long weeks on the circuit. He would chop wood behind the house and do the marketing with a basket over his arm. He would romp in the yard with his sons and take Mary to Springfield social events. The political forces that were organizing around the slavery question would fight their battles without him.

4. THE ABOLITIONIST LIFE

By the late 1840's, William Lloyd Garrison had settled comfortably into his role as a radical reformer. More "respectable" to others than he had been a decade earlier — a fact, he said, that concerned him very little — he was convinced he was doing the right thing (which was paramount) and that his cause was gradually gaining ground. What he needed to do now was maintain his position firmly, spread the truth about slavery and the "slave power" as widely and effectively as he could, and watch for signs that events and peoples' hearts were turning his way.

In 1847, Lloyd felt the time had come to bring his brand of uncompromising abolitionism to the West. Before this, he had gone east — to England — in his abolitionist travels, but had ventured little further west than Worcester, Massachusetts. The focus of the country was moving westward, and there was strong anti-slavery sentiment in Ohio to be stimulated. In the last ten years, religious revivalism had swept the state, and the revivalist speaker, Theodore Dwight Weld, had spread the anti-slavery message. After the split in the American Anti-Slavery Society in 1840, most Ohio abolitionists had gone political, giving their support to the Liberty Party. Now, with Weld in semi-retirement, and the Liberty Party dying, Ohio was ripe for an alliance with the Garrisonian East.

Lloyd took with him a traveling partner, a former slave named Frederick Douglass. A huge man with thick, bushy hair and piercing eyes, the thirty-year-old Douglass had developed into a superb public speaker since his escape from slavery in 1838. Garrison discovered him at the Massachusetts Anti-Slavery Society meeting on Nantucket in 1841. At that meeting, Douglass spoke simply but eloquently — and, with first-hand knowledge — about the horrors of slavery. Lloyd followed with a crowd-stirring appeal:

"Have we been listening to a thing, a piece of property, or a man?" he cried.

"A man! A man!" the five hundred men and women shouted.

"And should such a man be held a slave in a republican and Christian land?" Garrison continued.

"No! No! Never!" responded the crowd.

"Shall such a man ever be sent back to slavery from the soil of Massachusetts?" Garrison asked.

"No!" roared the people again.

"No!" Lloyd echoed, "a thousand times no! Sooner (let) the lightning of heaven blast Bunker Hill Monument till not one stone be left standing on another!" (19)

And the crowd cheered.

From that day on, Frederick Douglass was one of the American Anti-Slavery Society's most effective and sought-after speakers. He had, as one abolitionist put it, his diploma as a graduate of the "peculiar institution" written in scars on his back. With such a "degree," he could command the attention of any open-minded Northerners.

Garrison and Douglass met in Philadelphia to begin their trip and went from there by train to Harrisburg, Pennsylvania. As Douglass sat quietly in a seat near the rear of the railroad car, a drunken young man approached and yelled, "Get out of that seat!" Douglass looked up calmly and replied that he would do so if the man would make the request in a gentlemanly fashion. With that, the man grabbed Douglass by the coat and dragged him from the car. As a non-resistant like Garrison, Douglass submitted to this without a struggle. Lloyd followed and the two men quietly took seats in the rear of another car. The incident was a harbinger of the non-violent protests for civil rights that would occur over one hundred years later.

At Harrisburg, Garrison and Douglass stayed with local abolitionists and spoke in the evening to a crowd of citizens packed into the courthouse. Garrison spoke in his usual calm yet forceful style, emphasizing the horrors of slavery and the need for disunion, and the crowd listened with respect if not agreement. When Douglass rose to speak, however, a group outside the building began shouting, smashing windows and throwing rotten eggs. One egg spattered on Lloyd's coat and discharged its terrible odor about the platform; a rock thumped against Frederick's back; shouts of "Out with the damn nigger!" filled the air. When he could finally be heard, Lloyd told the audience that if this were an example of Harrisburg's "love of liberty," he and Douglass would leave the city and spare themselves any further breath. They did, however, speak the next evening before a "colored audience" that was a model of politeness.

When the two abolitionists rode the stagecoaches from Chambersburg, Pennsylvania, to Pittsburgh, Frederick was refused permission to eat at the same tables as the white travelers whenever they stopped at wayside inns. Lloyd would join him at a separate table. Such was the hospitality shown to free people of color in the North in 1847.

Pittsburgh reminded Garrison of Manchester and other manufacturing towns in England. For several days he and Douglass spoke to gatherings in the city and in the towns and villages in the surrounding countryside. " . . . meetings continually from day-to-day – little or no sleep. . . . ," Lloyd wrote Helen. Still, he was happy with the uplifting response of the people. It appeared to him, overoptimistically, that the whole area was becoming "abolitionized." (20)

At New Brighton, Garrison and Douglass had to hold their meeting in a large room above a store. As they spoke to about a hundred people gathered before them, mice were at work in the barrels of flour that rested on the rafters overhead. The speakers were soon sprinkled white — a sign, Lloyd said, that the mice wanted the speeches to be more *"floury."* (21) (Humor was a bit feeble at abolitionist meetings.)

As they moved from town to town through Ohio, Lloyd felt extreme fatigue. Speaking energetically several times a day in the hot sun was causing him to sweat profusely and lose weight. "I have never perspired so much in my life," he wrote to Helen. "The quantity of water thus exuded through the pores of the skin has astonished me, and I marvel that anything is left of me in the shape of solid matter." Still, he assured her, he was holding up "better than he anticipated." (22) Better, it seems, than Frederick who was rapidly losing his voice. Several times Douglass had to sit down, too hoarse to continue, leaving Garrison to tell the former slave's story for him. In the end, Douglass could move the audience to tears without saying a word by simply displaying the welts across his back.

At New Lyme, Ohio, four thousand people crowded into a great tent. Despite a chilling rain that capsized the tent the afternoon before the meeting, people came from all over the region to hear the famous — or infamous — William Lloyd Garrison and the magnificent Frederick Douglass. One black man, Lloyd noted, "rode three hundred miles on horseback to be at the meeting!" (23) The people stayed for three days, braving the cold dampness, to hear special hymns written for the occasion and to listen to Garrison and Douglass, who had partially regained his voice. A few politicians came, including Joshua Giddings, an anti-slavery congressman whom Garrison respected. When it was over, the people returned to their homes renewed in abolitionist spirit.

The word was reaching Ohio. At most stops, Garrison signed up new subscribers to *The Liberator.* Everywhere abolitionists were thrilled to meet the famous William Lloyd Garrison in the flesh. Lloyd did write home to Helen, however, that the Ohioans were a little less liberal with their contributions to the cause than New Englanders.

When his tour reached Oberlin, Lloyd's interest in Oberlin College temporarily drove away his exhaustion. Oberlin was a haven for reform in Ohio. It had been the first college to admit women and African-Americans; it was a refuge for fugitive slaves; and it refused to associate its church with the pro-slavery churches in the South. Such a place Garrison wanted to see.

He was just in time to attend the graduation ceremony for theological students. This group of young men interested him deeply for he believed new clergymen, unlike the backward individuals already in the pulpits, would have to take a stand against slavery and put the church where it had always belonged — in the vanguard of the anti-slavery movement. But he was disappointed to hear two of the commencement speakers denounce the Garrisonian concept of refusing to participate in institutions that in any way tolerated slavery. He felt these young men were willing to compromise with evil just as much as the old clergymen with whom he had been feuding for years.

Then Charles Grandison Finney rose to speak. In the 1830's, Finney had led a great religious revival in Ohio and New York. He had converted people to Jesus in large, open-air meetings at which people had camped out for three-day stretches and had listened in rapture as he laid Christ upon them. Often people had become prostrate in their repentance and love for the Lord. His emotional preaching had won over Theodore Dwight Weld who had gone on to preach anti-slavery in similar fashion. As Garrison listened, Finney urged the graduates at Oberlin to support "all the reforms of the age." Then, in his familiar style, he told them to be "anti-devil all over!"

As much as Lloyd agreed with Finney, he knew from experience that being "anti-devil all over" was not conducive to advancement in the practical world. If the graduates followed Finney's advice, he thought, they would never find congregations and salaries. This was the essential conflict between institutions and a true moral conscience; this was why William Lloyd Garrison shunned institutions.

Following the graduation, Garrison and Douglass attended two days of anti-slavery meetings at the Oberlin meeting house.

Afterwards, they spoke at more gatherings in small towns around Oberlin, concluding with four meetings at Salem that were attended by five thousand people. With these exhilarating sessions stimulating his optimism, Lloyd wrote to Helen: "Our friends are in the best possible spirits. The tide of anti-slavery is rising daily. Everything looks encouraging." (24)

Finally, on September 11th, Garrison and Douglass reached Cleveland, a small but growing city on Lake Erie that was to be their last stop on the tour. As rain fell in intermittent showers, Garrison addressed a crowd in the open air and got chilled to the bone. No true abolitionist ever let a bit of rain put out his fire, however, and he continued on until he felt his heat had reached the people. The next day his brow was aflame with a high fever and he was put to bed in the home of some Cleveland abolitionist friends. For five weeks he was too weak to return to Boston where Helen was waiting and worrying.

Helen and Lloyd bore such troubles with stoic good spirits, for such was the life of a reformer. If the cost of bringing the abolitionist spirit to the West was five weeks of illness and separation for husband and wife, it was well worth it. They had dedicated themselves to a cause. Earthly pleasures had no meaning for them except in so far as they revitalized their bodies to fight for reform — to fight by speaking at meetings and publishing *The Liberator*, as Lloyd did, or by providing a stable and happy home base for the reformer, as Helen chose to do.

The Garrison home at this time was a happy, albeit struggling place. Helen managed the home with serene competence, never begrudging Lloyd his piles of newspapers on every available flat surface, his long absences from home or his abolitionist guests who taxed the food budget. Although Lloyd was a man of fiery passion for his cause, he was (as a true pacifist) opposed to all forms of punishment with his children (five boys and two girls by 1848), and a gleeful participant in romps about the house

Frederick Douglass

or through grassy fields. Friends often wished that people who thought of Garrison as a devil and a fanatic could see the happy man and gentle father.

Lloyd was a hypochondriac, always sure he had some new and rare disease that would carry him off. Sometimes he left the editorship of *The Liberator* in other hands for weeks at a time while he recovered from some sort of malady. As he knew all too well, life in the 19th century could be snuffed out very quickly and mercilessly. In April of 1848, his little sixteen-month-old daughter, Elizabeth Pease, died of a "lung disorder." As was customary at the time, Lloyd and Helen summoned a photographer to record the dead child lying in a little gingham dress on the couch. The parents were devastated.

Fearful of losing any more of his precious family, Lloyd was an easy prey for quack remedies. In 1849, his gullibility in this area had tragic consequences. When his seven-year-old son, Charles, became very ill, Lloyd took a friend's advice and subjected the boy to a special steam bath that the friend's wife had administered successfully to several others. Lloyd and the woman put Charlie into a scalding bath and, as the poor child screamed in pain, urged him to be brave. The bath seared off large areas of the poor child's flesh and so shocked his body that he died four days later. As Christians and believers in an afterlife, Lloyd and Helen took comfort in the knowledge that their son, like little Elizabeth, had gone to a better place. But, Lloyd never got over his responsibility for the tragedy.

Since *The Liberator* still had few subscribers — and many who never paid — the Garrison household was always on a tight budget. Fortunately, his wealthy abolitionist friends would send barrels of flour or cash to help ease the family through tough times. Through his entire abolitionist career, Garrison lived financially from day to day, but he never backed down from doing anything that would promote the cause because of lack of money. The Lord would provide, he believed, and so he traveled about as if he were a man of means. The Lord did, indeed, provide friendly abolitionists who offered food and shelter whenever Lloyd traveled.

A letter Lloyd wrote to Helen in 1848 stated his outlook on the world succinctly. He wrote from Northhampton, Massachusetts, where he had gone for a few weeks to restore his health at a secluded commune that Helen's brother had organized. The countryside was beautiful; city noises and smells were far away.

". . . I could well enjoy the solitude of a country residence where one is cut off from intercourse with society," he wrote, "but I see too many things on terra firma that need to be corrected or destroyed . . . to allow me to dwell in an ideal state, or to gaze upon imaginary rainbows in the clouds, pleasant as it might be under other circumstances. I want, first of all, to see the horrid system of slavery abolished in this country, and then, everything else that is evil." (25)

5. A POLITICIAN'S COMPROMISES

While Abraham Lincoln was in Congress, he felt the issue of slavery's extension into California and New Mexico was not urgent. The newly acquired lands would remain unorganized until some plan acceptable to the North and the South was adopted. But, the discovery of gold in California in 1848 made it imperative for Congress to make a decision quickly. Throughout the year 1849, thousands of people made their way to the California gold fields, filling the territory with settlers so rapidly that by the end of the year it had a population large enough for admission to the Union as a state. The territories were no longer seemingly endless stretches of deserts, peaks and valleys; the slavery question was no longer abstract; an actual state existed and one side or the other, pro-slavery or anti-slavery, was going to "get it."

The people of California wrote a constitution that outlawed slavery. They did so not because they had moral objections to slavery but because they did not want to compete for jobs with slave labor and they did not want black people living in their state, slave or free. Southerners in Congress refused to accept California into the Union with its new constitution. In fact, Southerners were outraged at the prospect of a free California. Another free state would leave them outnumbered in the Senate as they already were in the House.

Moreover, there were other grievances that some hotheaded Southerners felt were grounds for secession from the Union by the southern states. For one thing, there were too many slaves escaping to the North. On the "Underground Railroad," a system of way stations operated by people sympathetic to the slaves, thousands of African-Americans were following the North Star and making it to Canada. In some cases they simply settled down in a free state where they were protected by "personal liberty laws" that made it almost impossible for their masters to recover their "property." Another southern grievance was that there was too much talk in the North of closing all of New Mexico to slavery and reducing the size of Texas so that slave territory would be smaller yet. Southerners had done most of the fighting against Mexico, southern congressmen exclaimed, so the South's people should share equally in the spoils of the war.

Free soil men and northern Whigs were just as strong in opposing Southern demands. The people of California had the right to ban slavery if they wished, these men shouted, and Congress, which controlled territories, had the right to ban slavery from New Mexico if it so wished. As for Texas, its claim to a long arm of territory extending northward to the fortieth parallel was ridiculous. Finally, most northern congressmen were appalled at the sight of the slave auctions that were held almost daily on ground within sight of the Capitol Building.

As 1850 began, it appeared that war might erupt between the North and the South over these issues. Southern leaders were talking about a convention to organize the South's secession from the Union. Remembering President Andrew Jackson's threat in 1832 to lead an army into South Carolina when that state nullified the tariff, most people believed that secession meant war. If the Union were going to be held together, if peace were to be maintained, the men who sat in Congress in 1850 were going to have to bend a little bit, give in to one another, and reach some sort of an agreement.

Leadership in the Senate was still in the hands of three men who had been the guiding lights of that body for twenty years. John C. Calhoun, withered and dying of consumption (tuberculosis), was the leading spokesman for the South. Fierce looking, with white hair standing out all over his head, he sat in the Senate too feeble to speak. For years he had argued the righteousness of slavery and for the rights of slaveholders. Now, with his dying breaths, he would do it one last time.

Daniel Webster of Massachusetts, a dynamic and powerful man with a huge, domed forehead, represented the views of the North. Over the years he had stood for the banking and commercial interests of his section. He had always defended the Union, particularly in a dramatic speech in 1830 in which he had proclaimed, "Liberty and Union, now and forever, one and inseparable!"

Henry Clay of Kentucky was the third demigod. Elegant looking for his seventy-three years, he had twice before proposed compromises to settle differences between the North and the South. In 1820 he had gotten the two sections to agree to divide the Louisiana Territory into slave and free sections along the 36-

30 parallel, with Missouri the only slave state to be allowed north of that sacred line. In 1833, he had introduced a tariff that would gradually decrease over a ten-year period, thus satisfying South Carolina and the southern states that wanted a low tariff, and the northern states that wanted a high one. Like his home state, Clay was fixed firmly in the middle. He was a man who could see both sides — a slave owner who, nevertheless, hoped to see slavery end some day, and a high tariff advocate who hoped to use tariff revenues to build a better economy for rural areas. Now, people looked to Henry Clay to devise a way to save the Union again.

In January, Clay rose before a hushed Senate to introduce a compromise proposal he had worked out, "I know no South, no North, no East, no West to which I owe allegiance" he told the Senators. Then he proceeded to outline his plan. First, California would be admitted as a free state as it wished. Second, New Mexico would be divided into two territories, Utah and New Mexico, and these would be settled with no restrictions on slavery. When the time came to organize the governments of the territories, the settlers themselves would decide whether or not to allow slavery. Third, Texas would give up its land claims in return for ten million dollars from the United States Treasury. Fourth, the slave trade — but not slavery itself — would be abolished in the District of Columbia. Finally, Congress would enact a strong fugitive slave law requiring all Americans to return fugitive slaves to their owners or suffer prosecution by the Federal Government.

Clay was trying to give something to everyone. In effect, he was asking the South to give up California and a *guarantee* that slavery would be allowed in New Mexico, in return for a strong federal fugitive slave law. Northerners were being asked to accept the fugitive slave law as an evil necessary for the preservation of the Union. The deal was sweetened for the North by the elimination of the slave trade in the nation's capital.

But, extremists on both sides were not happy. William Lloyd Garrison excoriated the entire deal as an example of the death grip the slave power had over the government. Northern acceptance of the compromise with its horrid fugitive slave law, he declared, would prove that people in the free states had learned nothing from recent examples of northern subservience to the slave power.

John C. Calhoun would settle for nothing less than total recognition of the South's right to bring slaves anywhere, and firm guarantees of protection for the South's "peculiar institution." Sitting grimly stoic, wrapped in blankets, he listened as Senator Mason read his speech that he was too weak to deliver. The agitation of the slave question will drive the South out of the Union, the dying man declared, unless the South can be satisfied she can remain in the Union in safety. That satisfaction can only be effected by guaranteeing slavery in New Mexico and California.

Against this extremism Henry Clay needed an ally and he found one in Daniel Webster. On March 7th, Webster, nearly as imposing as ever though he was old, rose to speak to a packed Senate chamber. People had been anticipating this speech for weeks and had come from miles around to hear it. What position would the great Massachusetts orator take? Would he speak for the growing feeling in the North that slavery should be contained? Would he represent the wishes of his constituents in Massachusetts who were now against returning fugitive slaves?

"I wish to speak today not as a Massachusetts man, nor as a Northern man, but as an American, and a member of the Senate of the United States," Webster began. "I speak today for the preservation of the Union. Hear me for my cause." He went on for three hours, pleading with Northerners to accept the compromise, arguing that no Southerner would want to try planting in New Mexico and so, even with popular sovereignty, it would become a free territory. Why should the North want to risk a conflict over something it would achieve peacefully? He begged Northern men to understand that if the South seceded, there would be war.

It was the great man's greatest speech. It won several Senators for compromise; and it earned Daniel Webster the undying hatred of William Lloyd Garrison and many people in Massachusetts. In *The Liberator* Garrison condemned the "7th of March speech" as "indescribably base and wicked." Webster had completely surrendered to the slave power! The people of Massachusetts should show that he did not speak for them; they should subject him to official censure. Thereafter, he eagerly printed editorials from other papers that condemned Webster and watched with satisfaction as petitions poured in to the state legislature denouncing the speech and calling for censure. As Webster suffered this abuse, Garrison declared that he deserved it for shocking the "moral sense" and grievously insulting "the intelligence of the people." (26)

Yet many Northerners supported Webster, supported the compromise proposals, and were anxious to reach accommodation with the South. This was demonstrated to Garrison in May at the annual meeting of the American Anti-Slavery Society in New York. The compromise plan was still before Congress and northern businessmen especially were anxious to see it passed so that normal trade with the South could continue. James Gordon Bennett, editor of the New York *Herald*, a sensationalist paper filled with exaggerated stories and stinging editorials, began an effort to whip up sentiments against the abolitionists prior to the meeting. On April 30th his paper said, "The merchants, men of business, men of property in this city (should) come down on the meetings of these people, if they would save themselves. What business have all the religious lunatics of the free states to gather in this commercial city for the purpose which, if carried into effect, would ruin and destroy its property?" Other editorials called on New Yorkers not to allow their city to be represented by Garrison, whom Bennett described as a "mulatto man – mixed race." (27)

By the time the abolitionists convened their meeting in the Congregational Tabernacle, hundreds of men were ready to disrupt the proceedings. As Lloyd stood on the platform speaking, it was clear to him that the people in the seats that rose in tiers around the platform were not all members of the society. Jeers and catcalls interrupted him, and even some of his more mild anti-slavery remarks drew grumbles in the seats behind him. Suddenly, an angry group of men came charging out of the seats and onto the stage. Their leader was Captain Isaiah Rhynders, a former Hudson riverboat man, proprietor of the Empire Sporting Club and a powerful figure in New York City politics.

With Rhynders and his gang on the platform, the meeting became the most bizarre and hazardous anti-slavery gathering Lloyd had ever witnessed. Waving his fist, Rhynders shouted he would not allow Garrison to insult the president of the United States. The group behind him shouted its agreement. Lloyd offered to allow Rhynders to address the Society, even promising to keep order while he did so. With the whole place in an uproar, the Hutchinsons, a famous group of anti-slavery singers, tried to calm everybody with a hymn, but to no avail. Finally, when the noise briefly subsided, Rhynders agreed that he would speak after Garrison.

Lloyd finished his speech with the Rhynders gang standing unpleasantly nearby. When he turned the floor over to Rhynders, the gang leader surprised everyone by calling up a substitute "speaker" — a bedraggled looking man who called himself "Professor Grant." The "Professor" addressed the crowd on the subject of "Negro inferiority." He said black men were part of the "monkey tribe," and talked on so foolishly that even Rhynders and his followers had to laugh.

Unfortunately for Rhynders and the "Professor," the next speaker was Frederick Douglass. Powerful and imposing, he asked the crowd, "Am, I a man?" The crowd roared its agreement and laughed. Soon Rhynders and "Professor Grant" and their gang were fidgeting on the stage, trapped and forced to watch Douglass make fools of them. Douglass repeatedly asked the crowd to compare his own manhood with that of "Professor Grant," which they were happy to do with loud and raucous laughter.

When the Society met the next day, however, Rhynders and his gang were back again. This time they stormed onto the stage like legions from hell when Wendell Phillips denounced the Constitution and pretended to stomp the imaginary document under foot. Rhynders took over the platform and led his supporters through a mock meeting in which they passed a resolution opposing anti-slavery agitation. Lloyd, Frederick Douglass and Wendell Phillips, and the rest of the Anti-Slavery Society watched silently. Then Rhynders put his arm around Charles C. Burleigh, an eccentric abolitionist with a long, flowing beard. Earlier one of the rowdies had suggested that the beard be shaved to make a wig for Garrison, and now Rhynders stroked it with mock admiration.

Soon, the Tabernacle was a scene of ear-numbing confusion with Rhynder's gang running every which way and shouting, the Hutchinsons again trying to serenade the crowd, and no one able to be heard. An observer would have been hard-pressed to know what to look at next. The police finally arrived to break up the meeting, and Garrison reluctantly adjourned the annual convention of the American Anti-Slavery Society "under protest." (28)

For the rest of the year other Rhynders-type mobs disrupted abolitionist meetings in Boston and elsewhere. The spirit of the Union was strong; the desire to keep commercial contacts with the South was strong. Despite the progress that seemed evident in the formation of the Free Soil Party, and despite the outrage many people in Massachusetts expressed against Webster's pro-compromise speech, the North was still a long way from accepting Garrison's anti-slavery stand and his call for disunion.

In July, President Taylor, who opposed the compromise plan, died of food poisoning, and in September the compromise proposals passed Congress and were signed into law by the new president, Millard Fillmore. All across the North there was almost an audible sigh of relief that the Union had been saved. In the South, the talk of secession gradually subsided.

To William Lloyd Garrison, the compromise was an outrage. Under its terms, Northerners were going to have to return slaves who had escaped to freedom and to agree with the notion that the "slave power" had the right to extend slavery into New Mexico and Utah. Such was the sinful fruit of union with slaveholders. Soon, Garrison was convinced, Northerners would see that a tree that produced slavery (the Union) was evil, and they would chop it down.

Eight hundred miles to the west, in his law office in Springfield, Abraham Lincoln read of the events in Washington with renewed admiration for his idol, Henry Clay. The compromise had kept the peace. It had resolved the territorial issue between the North and the South in such a way that slavery would probably not be extended, and it had smoothed over the points of friction that could cause a civil war. It was true that Northerners were now under the terms of a strong, federal fugitive slave law. But, the fruit of the compromise was the preservation of the Union with no likely extension of slavery. Thus, to Lincoln, the compromise was good.

COMPROMISE OF 1850

Oregon Territory

Minnesota Territory

Unorganized Territory

Utah Territory 1850

California 1850

New Mexico Territory 1850

VT · ME · NH · MA · RI · CT · NJ · DE · MD

NY · PA

WI · MI · IA · IL · IN · OH

MO · KY · VA · NC

Indian Territory · AR · TN · SC

TX · LA · MS · AL · GA

FL

Free state or territory

Territory open to slavery under the principle of popular sovereignty

Slave state or territory

CHAPTER SIX

The "Slave Power Conspiracy"

1850-1859

As the 1850's advanced, the South seemed to be proceeding toward making slavery a national institution. Lincoln became a leader in the movement to stop slavery's spread. Garrison opposed making the debate over slavery a matter of territory rather than morality, but he was pleased to see northern opinion moving in the right direction.

1. FUGITIVES AND FANATICS

On February 18, 1851, the courtroom of Commissioner George T. Curtis in Boston was in adjournment during the case of the fugitive slave, Shadrach. As people milled about the room, twenty free black men clustered around the unfortunate Shadrach and, for a moment, he was lost from the view of the white marshals. When the crowd was dispersed and the officers attempted to resume their watch over their captive, he was gone. White men ran out the doors in a panic- stricken search, but Shadrach was out of sight, running down the back alleys of Boston. Soon he would be guided by friendly abolitionists from house to house and driven in wagons down dark country roads until he was safely in Canada.

"In Boston, all is activity . . . ," Wendell Phillips wrote to a friend a month later. "The rescue of Shadrach has set the whole public afire," he went on. "We have hundreds of fugitives among us. . . . Our vigilance committee meets every night. The escapes have been providential." (1)

The Fugitive Slave Law had activated Boston as nothing before had ever done — even twenty years of *Liberators*. Phillips' vigilance committee (formally known as the Boston Committee of Vigilance) was a group of famous and influential people including Theodore Parker, the Congregational clergyman, and Richard Henry Dana, lawyer and author of the popular book *Two Years Before the Mast*. Its members opened their homes to fugitive slaves who came to Boston. They rushed to rescue captives such as Shadrach and whisk them to Canada. Doing these things was illegal; some of the most respectable people in the city were openly breaking a federal law. But the sight of poor, frightened black people about to be seized by armed marshals and dragged back to the cruel plantations in the deep South was too much for respectable citizens to bear.

For months the Boston group was successful in every rescue it attempted. Several of those who participated in the Shadrach adventure were indicted for violating the Fugitive Slave Law and tried in federal court. Witnesses positively identified the defendants as those who had assisted the slave in his escape. But, the jury could not reach a verdict because one man held out for acquittal. Only years later did that juror tell Reverend Parker that he himself had been part of the rescue team — that he had driven

Shadrach from Concord to Leominster on the first leg of the journey to Canada.

Phillips told a friend how jovial and confident the Vigilance Committee was in spite of the fact that its members were outlaws. Their meetings were held in secret; they were constantly in fear that they would be arrested. Yet, Phillips reported, "We enjoy ourselves richly and I doubt whether more laughing is done anywhere than in anti-slavery parlors." (2) Of course they were all comfortable in the knowledge that they were fighting for a cause that was one hundred percent right.

The South was enraged at this cavalier disregard of the Fugitive Slave Act. Southerners came to Boston for the sole purpose of capturing a fugitive slave and returning him to his owner. Phillips described how one fugitive saw his master on the street and had to dive into a nearby cellar to avoid apprehension. "There have been several as close escapes as that," he wrote of the cellar diver, "and there are still a number of Southerners here. It is said privately that all they want is *one from Boston* to show the discontented (slaves) at home that *it can be done*; and our merchants groan at the trade they lose by the hatred the South bears us because she has not yet brought Boston under." (3)

Inevitably the slave catchers in the city and their local allies were bound to succeed in returning a fugitive, and they did in April, 1851. Thomas Sims, a luckless fugitive from bondage, was captured and guarded with extraordinary precaution by the city police and the state militia. Armed guards were stationed around the courthouse where Sims was held; the militia was barracked in Faneuil Hall and ready to spring into action with muskets and bayonets should a mob attempt to storm the courthouse and extricate the prisoner. When the time came to put Sims aboard a ship for the trip south, the militia, with bayonets fixed, escorted him before dawn past angry Bostonians to the wharf.

The South had its victory, but it was a costly one. The sight of armed guards leading the downcast Sims to the dock, and the images the scene aroused of the fate that awaited the poor black man on the plantation where he would be whipped and branded, awakened the consciences of many Bostonians and transformed them into abolitionists.

Disregard of the Fugitive Slave Law was endemic throughout the North after 1850. Even a few very conservative people who had always apologized for slavery considered the law obnoxious. If a northern state does not permit slavery within its borders, people reasoned, why should it lock up African-Americans as slaves? Furthermore, the law was a travesty of justice down to its smallest detail. For example, it provided that a commissioner received five dollars for a case in which he judged a captured African-American to be free, but ten dollars if he decided that the "Negro" should be turned over to the white man demanding his "property." Defenders of the law said the extra five dollars was payment for the paper work involved in returning a man to slavery. Most Northerners called the five dollars a bribe for deciding a case in the slave owner's favor.

In Syracuse, New York, a mob broke into the courthouse and carried the slave "Jerry" away to freedom in a triumphal procession. Although eighteen people were indicted for this crime, the town was so hostile to the Fugitive Slave Law that no trial was ever held. At Oberlin College in Ohio, students rescued the African-American, John Rice, and whisked him to safety. And, in Christina, Pennsylvania, someone in town killed Edward Gorsuch, a slave catcher, and the townspeople spirited away several fugitives.

William Lloyd Garrison was not involved in the work of the Boston Committee of Vigilance and never assisted in a smuggling adventure or a "break-out." His pacifist principles forbade him to use violence. Some of the committee members carried Bowie Knives and revolvers under their coats to fight it out with slave catchers or federal marshals if necessary. In the pages of *The Liberator*, however, Garrison gave full publicity to the famous cases, making special point of describing how Southerners were infuriated over northern violation of the offensive law, while they themselves were violating the freedom of the press and speech of every Northerner who dared to oppose slavery. He saw clearly the propaganda value of fugitive slaves, and especially, *unsuccessful* attempts to rescue them. He was ready to exploit each incident for all it was worth.

Yet, similar to his feelings on the "free soil" issue, Garrison's support for assisting fugitive slaves was tempered. Once again he felt that Northerners were dealing with a secondary issue and were salving their consciences too easily. In a speech in West-chester, Pennsylvania, in 1852, he revealed how he truly felt about the fugitive slave issue. "Many persons glory in their hostility to the (Fugitive Slave Law)," he said, "and upon this capital they set up an anti-slavery reputation. But opposition to that law is no proof in itself of anti-slavery fidelity. That law is merely incidental to slavery, and there is no merit in opposition which extends no further than its provisions. Our warfare is not against slave hunt-ing alone, but against the existence of slavery." (4)

Consequently, the pages of *The Liberator* continued to con-centrate on Garrison's central thesis: The Christian duty of all people to oppose slavery without compromise . . . and NO UNION WITH SLAVEHOLDERS! His attacks against south-ern spokesmen took on particular venom when they focused on Calhoun's successor in the Senate, Robert Barnwell Rhett. When Rhett, a radical pro-slavery man just as determined to secure southern rights as Calhoun had been, gave a speech threatening South Carolina's secession from the Union, Garrison blasted him. If South Carolina left the Union even for a single day, he proclaimed, her slaves (who outnumbered whites in the state) would rise in rebellion. South Carolina did not *dare* to secede. The whites of the Palmetto State depended on the Union for their beloved slave system. That was why the *northern* states should secede and watch slavery implode.

When *The Boston Commonwealth* stated editorially that Garrison was no different than Rhett since both men favored the break-up of the Union, Garrison had to deal with a charge that would haunt him until the outbreak of the Civil War. To him the difference between himself and Rhett was obvious. "All this would be extremely amusing were no principle at stake," he wrote in *The Liberator*. Garrisonian abolitionists were defending *liberty*; how could they be compared with southern disunionists who defended *slavery*? Then he went to the core of the issue: "But how can the dissolution of the Union at once strengthen and perpetuate slavery, as the Carolinians contend — and also tend to the speedy overthrow of slavery as the Garrisonians maintain?" It has been shown that the Union has been a boon to slavery. ". . . the PRESERVATION, PROPAGATION, and PERPETUATION of slavery has been the vital and animating principle of the national government." Therefore, he concluded, the destruction of the Union would be the destruction of slavery. (5)

Despite their negative feelings about the Fugitive Slave Law, most Northerners found these arguments unconvincing. On another speaking trip to the Midwest in 1853, this time to Michigan, he spoke to large and encouraging audiences as he had in Ohio in 1847, but once again he was harassed by mobs and damned in the local papers. Most Northerners were not ready to accept the logic of NO UNION WITH SLAVEHOLDERS! That certainly would not happen until their hearts were won over further to the cause of the slaves.

Garrison had been working on the people's hearts for over twenty years. In *The Liberator* and on the platform he had related story after story of slaveholders' cruelties and black peoples' sufferings. But the effect of all his efforts was but a single tear compared to the wailing for the slaves aroused by a tiny woman named Harriet Beecher Stowe. The daughter of minister Lyman Beecher and the wife of minister Calvin Stowe, this mother of six was a devout Christian. Living in Ohio she had seen many runaway slaves; she had visited slave plantations in Kentucky and had seen slaves in their quarters and at work in the fields. Now, living in Maine, she told the world about slavery in her novel *Uncle Tom's Cabin or Life Among the Lowly.*

Ms. Stowe's hero is a Christ-like slave named Tom. Owned at first by a kindly master – a man who fits the South's image of the typical father-figure slave owner – Tom is treated well. But, when the man falls into financial difficulties, he sells Tom to a slave trader and keeps Tom's wife and children with him. Even humane slaveholders sometimes treated their slaves cruelly. Tom tells his new owner that even though he feels secure as a slave, he yearns to be free and reunited with his family. Tom's final owner is Simon Legree – a complete villain – the kind of evil, violent heartless man at whose mercy any slave might one day find himself. Legree catches Tom helping other slaves escape and, in the climactic scene of the book, orders Tom whipped to death. As the poor slave submits to his fate and the lashes tear up his flesh, he begs God to forgive his tormentor.

Every southern state took action to ban *Uncle Tom's Cabin*, but the book became a huge best seller in the North. Millions of Northerners wept over the fate of the saintly Tom and raged at the cruelty of Simon Legree. The evils of slavery they had thought of in abstract terms became a real human tragedy as they identified with Ms. Stowe's fictional character. The story was brought to the stage where people could see wicked Simon Legree in person — dressed in black with a black, curled mustache and snapping a huge whip — and weep bitter tears as Tom succumbed to his wounds before them. For many Northerners, Legree was the typical plantation owner; his image burned in their minds during the next several years as new tensions developed with the South.

William Lloyd Garrison welcomed Ms. Stowe's contribution to the battle for northern hearts but, as usual, he had some reservations about the purity of her abolitionism. On March 26, 1852, he reviewed *Uncle Tom's Cabin* in *The Liberator*.

" . . . we confess to the frequent moistening of our eyes, and the making of our heart grow liquid as water, and the trembling of every nerve within us, in the perusal of the incidents and scenes so vividly depicted in her pages," he wrote. An agreeable feature of the book, he went on, was the personification of non-resistance in Uncle Tom. Yet, he wondered why Northerners advocated non-violence for blacks only — whether they found it correct for blacks to submit meekly to injustice while whites had the privilege of fighting for their rights. It seemed to him that if a man was willing to use violence — as he, Garrison, was not — then he should be glad to see violence used on behalf of the slave who was suffering the greatest denial of rights ever imagined. Perhaps Ms. Stowe was pandering to the comfortable northern image of the meek slave who would wait forever for freedom, when Northerners would be best advised that the black man was ready to fight for liberty, as *they* would be in the same circumstances.

A glaring impurity in the book, in Garrison's view, was Ms. Stowe's suggestion that black people would be best off living in Africa, far away from the prejudices of white Americans. "The work . . . contains some objectionable sentiments respecting African colonization, which we regret to see," he stated. (6) Even the lady who was winning thousands of converts to abolitionism every week did not fully meet the exacting standards of the editor of *The Liberator*.

Clearly the fugitive slave incidents and *Uncle Tom's Cabin* were shattering the calm that had settled over the nation after the Compromise of 1850. Then, in May of 1854, the tension reached new heights when, in one tumultuous week, the nation was convulsed by two incidents involving slavery: the capture of another runaway slave and the passage of a new, very controversial law.

The first incident centered on Anthony Burns, a black man who escaped from slavery and went to Boston in February, 1854. In May, he was recognized by his master, taken into custody, and guarded at the courthouse by the state militia. Richard Henry Dana, the attorney for fugitives from the Vigilance Committee, went to see Burns and advise him of his rights, but found the unfortunate man completely dejected and unwilling to prolong the proceedings for fear his master would take it out on him when they were back on the plantation.

Aroused citizens met at Faneuil Hall one evening to discuss how to set Burns free. From there, a group marched to the courthouse where they planned to storm the building and extricate the captive. At the courthouse doors, however, one member of the group was killed and several others were wounded when the officers opened fire. Wendell Phillips later compared this incident to the Boston Massacre, observing that in both instances the soldiers were defenders of tyranny shooting into the midst of liberty loving people.

When Burns had his hearing, the judge quickly decided he should return to slavery. On the day Burns was to be shipped to the South, crowds of people lined the street leading to the wharf just as they had when Thomas Sims made the tearful trek, only this time the crowd was much larger and much angrier. The President of the United States, Franklin Pierce, had ordered a full military guard to ensure a successful mission. Burns walked to the dock surrounded by four platoons of marines, while a sheriff's posse and twenty-two companies of state militia held the crowd back, threatening to shoot anyone who stepped forward. People hissed and shouted "Shame! Shame!" as Burns was led past. The only relief from the tension during the hour was Burns' droll comment to a guard, "There is lots of folks to see a colored man walk down the street." (7)

As word of Anthony Burns' heartbreaking return to slavery was sweeping the North, even more disturbing news arrived from Washington. Senator Stephen A. Douglas of Illinois had reopened the whole issue of slavery in the western territories.

Douglas, Lincoln's old opponent in the Illinois State House, had gone to Washington as a Senator about the time Lincoln was "retiring" from politics. In the Senate, just as he had in Springfield, Douglas quickly gained a reputation as a powerful and dynamic Democratic spokesman — a "Little Giant" reputation he hoped would some day make him president. He needed a big issue and he found it in the debate over a route for the proposed transcontinental railroad. Southerners, led by Senator Jefferson Davis of Mississippi, wanted a southern route across Texas and New Mexico and on to California. Northerners, particularly those in Douglas's home state of Illinois, wanted a route that would link Chicago and the Great Lakes to California. If Douglas could settle this issue, he would be the hero of the hour and the logical choice of his party for the White House.

For the northern route to have a chance, the territory west of Iowa would have to be organized and settled. Rather than finding this a liability, Douglas thought it was his chance to win southern support for the northern route. He introduced legislation to organize two territories, Kansas and Nebraska. Into those territories people could bring slaves, if they wished, until territorial governments were organized. At that time, the people would vote on whether or not to allow slavery. This was the great principle of "popular sovereignty" which was already in effect in Utah and New Mexico thanks to the Compromise of 1850, and which Douglas found eminently reasonable. Best of all, it enticed Southerners into voting for his bill because, prior to this time, they had been denied the right to take their slaves into the regions Douglas was organizing and unable to hope for any new slave states there.

The North was outraged! The land that made up Kansas and Nebraska had been closed to slavery ever since the Missouri Compromise of 1820. That supposedly hallowed agreement had made the 36-30 line of latitude the northern boundary of slavery in the Louisiana Territory (Missouri excepted). Now Douglas's bill was wiping it out and opening the gates to a new flood of slave migration. When the bill passed during the same week that Anthony Burns was returned to slavery, the wrath of many Northerners knew no bounds. William Lloyd Garrison reported in *The Liberator* that Congress had passed the Kansas-Nebraska Bill "against the laws of God and the rights of universal man . . . in utter disregard of the scorn of the world, and for purposes as diabolical as can be conceived of or consummated here on earth." (8) The Burns case and the Kansas-Nebraska Act together were incontrovertible proof that the union with the South was sinful and should be dissolved. After these outrages, Garrison intended to make a dramatic demonstration of his anti-Union sentiments.

His chance came at the annual Fourth of July Anti-Slavery gathering in Framingham, Massachusetts. The platform was decorated to suit what Garrison called a mournful occasion — no red, white and blue bunting here! White flags of surrender with the words "KANSAS" and "NEBRASKA" were hung above the words 'REDEEM MASSACHUSETTS." Above the platform was the American flag, hung upside down and draped in black.

Lloyd began his address, as he had every Fourth of July since his first speech at the Park Street Church in 1829, by contrasting the words of the Declaration of Independence with the existence of slavery in the United States. Then he announced he was going to give testimony to his feelings on the pro-slavery laws and deeds of the nation. He held up a copy of the Fugitive Slave Law, took a match to it and watched it burn to ashes. "Let the people say amen!" he proclaimed, and the people shouted AMEN! Next he burned a copy of the judge's decision to send Anthony Burns back to slavery. Finally, he held aloft a copy of the United States Constitution. This, he exclaimed, is the source of all the other atrocities; it is a "covenant with death and an agreement with hell." With that, he set fire to it saying, "So perish all compromises with tyranny! And let the people say 'Amen.'"

"AMEN!" shouted the audience and Lloyd stood before them, his arms outstretched, his head bowed in solemn conviction. (9)

2. AN AMBITIOUS, PRINCIPLED MAN

Abraham Lincoln spent the four years after the Compromise of 1850 working hard at his law practice and staying active in Whig politics as a non-candidate for any office. He watched his party lose the presidency in 1852 under a Democratic landslide for Franklin Pierce of New Hampshire, a "northern man with southern principles;" he delivered a eulogy for Henry Clay who died in 1852 believing he had saved the Union with his compromises; and he kept watch over national affairs, maintaining contacts with Whig leaders in the state. Every day found him in his law office, in court, or in his house with his wife and young boys.

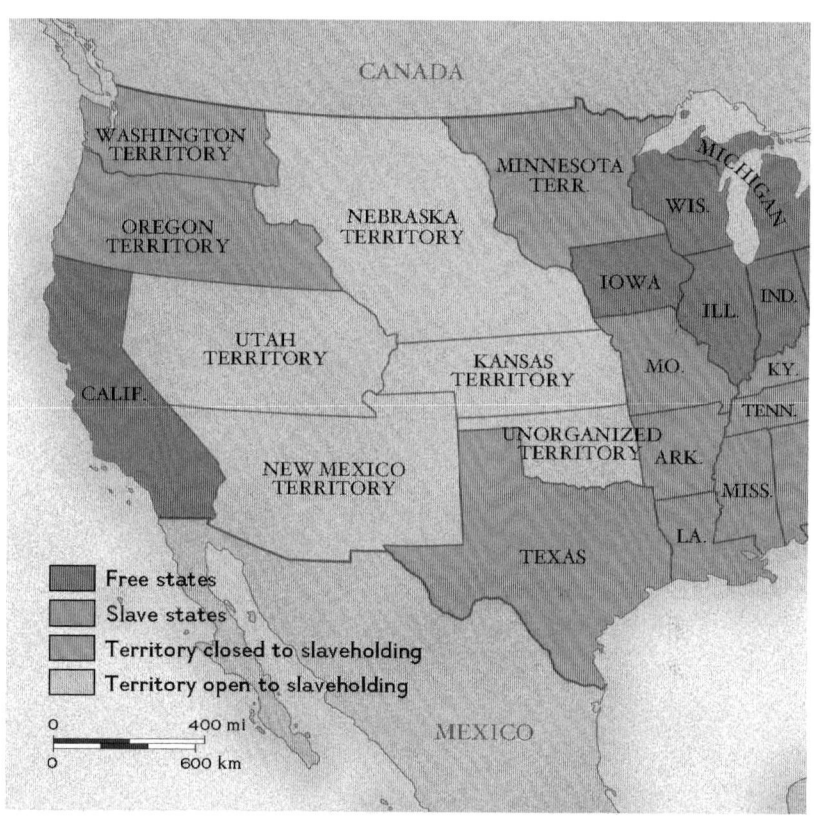

Map of Kansas-Nebraska Act

Stephen Douglas

The law partnership with Billy Herndon flourished as it never had before. Cases came aplenty, and Abe found himself speaking in court on suits ranging in the millions of dollars. He commanded high fees. He became an expert on railroad litigation — so much so that lines such as the Illinois Central and the Rock Island looked to him for legal help. Each fall and spring he rode the circuit as he had since the 1830's, sleeping at roadside inns and meeting people in their cornfields and kitchens.

In the late 1840's he had handled a case for a slave owner named Robert Matson from Kentucky who was trying to secure the return of his "bondsmen." They had run away claiming they were free when he brought them into Illinois. In court, Abe argued that Matson had not brought his chattels into Illinois permanently, that he had fully intended to return with them to Kentucky, and that the slaves, therefore, had no right to the protection of the anti-slavery laws of Illinois. People said that Abe's heart was not in his argument, and the judge ruled against Matson, probably to Abe's relief.

After that, Abe became known in northern Illinois as one of the few lawyers who would take the case of a fugitive slave. Many lawyers, with an eye to their political futures, turned away black people who came to their offices. But Abe took them in and handled their cases as best he could within the limits of the 1850 Fugitive Slave Law. On one occasion, he and Herndon put up the money themselves to secure freedom for the son of a black woman who had won their sympathy.

Herndon, as much an abolitionist as he was before Lincoln went off to Congress, continued to ply Abe with abolitionist papers and pamphlets. Perhaps to counter-balance his zealous partner, Lincoln subscribed to several southern newspapers such as the Richmond *Enquirer* and periodicals such as *The Southern Literary Messenger*. There was a southern point of view, he thought, and it ought to be known. He told Billy they would each have a place on the table for their respective publications so that both sides would have their "day in court."

In the 1850's, life in the Lincolns' frame house at the corner of Eighth and Jackson Streets went along with joys and sorrows. Robert Lincoln was seven-years-old when the decade began; he was a sturdy little fellow whom Abe adored. In 1850, little Edward took a fever and died before his fourth birthday. Abe looked down at the pale little boy and thought of the many other heart-breaking deaths he had known in his hard frontier life.

Other sons came to Mary and Abe. Willie was born in 1850 and Thomas, named for his grandfather, was born in 1853. Thomas had a large head when he was born and looked to Lincoln so much like a tadpole that he was ever after nicknamed "Tad." By the end of the decade, the Lincolns were a typical mid-western family of five.

Lincoln had once been able to stand in his yard and see the cornfields and grazing land. But, in the 1850's, there were many houses around him and he was living in the center of town. Springfield had grown from 1,500 people to 5,000. To the north, Chicago had over 60,000 people and was a big city, a focal point for railroads and farm products. The frontier had moved past Illinois and was now across the Mississippi and most of the way across Iowa and Missouri.

Mary and Abe would talk at the dinner table about the great things that were happening in Illinois and Abe was a part of them. Mary shared Abe's ambition and wanted very much that they should achieve wealth, power and "standing." Abe would leave their home on a workday morning and talk to the men in the square on his way to the offices of Lincoln and Herndon. People in Springfield liked Abe; everyone always had. Folks knew he had been a congressman, but few knew the heat of the ambition that burned in his soul.

To some people, Abe appeared to be anything but an ambitious man. He daydreamed a great deal. For hours at a time, even while handling a case in court, he might gaze off into space. But he wasn't dreaming; he was thinking. His mind told him that every problem, no matter how seemingly complex, had a core, and if your thoughts could penetrate to that core through the soft, useless matter around it, you could discern a simple solution. To penetrate, you needed reason and logic. Your thoughts needed to follow each other as if they were becoming a shaft, and they needed to hone to a hard, sharp point.

To develop this kind of thinking power, Abe studied geometry and practiced going from a set of known truths to a logical solution. He studied logic and practiced producing logical arguments — arguments that started at one truth and proceeded so inexorably toward another truth that they could not be refuted. Sometimes lawyers on the circuit would get up in the morning to find Abe sitting by the fire — now just ashes — where they had left him the night before. He would still be thinking, totally oblivious to time.

All of this self-training had a noticeable effect. People began to sense that Abe Lincoln was quite a brilliant man. His writing, which had always been awkward albeit with a touch of simplistic beauty, was becoming truly eloquent. His arguments in court were becoming masterpieces of deductive logic. Prior to a case, he would study all the facts; he would learn about the subject involved in the case by reading books. If it was a case involving bridge rights-of-way, he would learn all about bridges, and he would come into court prepared to devastate his opposition with a clear and forceful presentation. Often the opposition would be drawn into thinking they had the case won when they would see

Lincoln sitting half asleep all through the trial, conceding point after point to them. Only too late would they realize he was going after one crucial item — the "core" of the problem — which would be so obvious to the jurors, so easy for them to understand and remember, that Lincoln would win the verdict.

As Abe increased his reputation around Springfield and northern Illinois, he would sit in the law office of Lincoln and Herndon and savor his success, yet feel frustrated about his political life. Many of his old opponents, Democrats all, were in lofty elected positions. James Shields, whom he had almost dueled with broadswords, had been elected to the United States Senate. Stephen A. Douglas was not only a United States Senator, he was also a major aspirant to the presidency.

Then, early in 1854, word came to Springfield of Douglas' Kansas-Nebraska Act. The news touched a raw nerve deep within Lincoln. He was perplexed; he was chagrined; he was angry. The issue of slavery in the territories, which Henry Clay had so skillfully laid to rest in 1820 and 1850, was suddenly being agitated again. The confidence Abe — and many others — had felt that slavery would be forever confined to the regions south and east of Missouri and Texas, was severely shaken. He would have to re-enter politics to do what he could to stop this terrible new policy put forth by Douglas and the Democratic Party.

Douglas, full of confidence, returned to Illinois in the summer after his bill passed. His organization of Kansas and Nebraska Territories paved the way for a northern route for the "Transcontinental Railroad;" it would be a boon to Illinois, and Chicago in particular. For his achievement, the people of Illinois were bound to welcome him home as a hero. But, on a Saturday night, when he attempted to address a gathering in Chicago, Douglas awakened to a harsh reality. The sentiment of this group of people was "free soil." They loathed his reopening of the Louisiana Territory to slavery. They were not going to listen to him. The louder he tried to speak, the louder the crowd yelled and shouted him down. The story is told that Douglas finally looked at his watch, noticed it was after midnight, and shouted to the people, "It's now Sunday morning. I'll go to church, and you may go to hell!" More likely, he simply stomped off the stage in bitter frustration.

Other Chicago audiences and people in other towns were friendlier and Douglas regained his famous self-confidence. Finally, he came to Springfield to speak at the agricultural fair. With Lincoln sitting in the front row, he put on a dramatic display of oratory, his heavy features scowling in the dim lights. Able to project his booming voice to the rear of a large hall, he was a spellbinder. He began with the simple logic of his position as embodied in the Kansas-Nebraska Bill. The people in a territory should be left on their own to determine for themselves their territorial laws. This was "popular sovereignty" — the people in command — which was the fundamental principle of democracy. Then he took a swipe at those people, Whigs and Free Soilers, who opposed him. They were aligning themselves with "black abolitionists;" they were becoming Negro worshippers and advocates of Negro equality. He told the people flatly that the time had not come for Illinois to be a Negro worshipping, Negro equality state. Frequently the crowd interrupted the "Little Giant" to applaud. He had won them. If he was going to be answered effectively, it was going to take a mighty good speech to do it.

The "Anti-Nebraska men" in town had chosen Lincoln to answer Douglas. Throughout the senator's speech Abe sat, obviously amused, frequently leaning over to make comments to the men sitting next to him. An observer might have guessed that the reply to the speech he would make the next day would be silly and weak. At the conclusion of his speech, Douglas walked up the aisle as cheers engulfed him. Smiling with assurance, he was unafraid of what Lincoln might say the following afternoon. Abe, chatting amiably, walked up the aisle with Senator Douglas.

The next day, when Abe stood on the platform facing the same group of people and Douglas sat in wary watchfulness behind him, he was all business. He was determined to make a speech that would strip away the husk and get to the kernel of the Kansas-Nebraska matter.

He began with a short history of slavery in the United States. Congress had banned slavery in the "Northwest Territory," part of which was Illinois, in 1787. "Now," he went on, "the Northwest Territory is the happy home of teeming millions of free, white, prosperous people, and no slave among them." In 1820, the Missouri Compromise excluded slavery north of 36-30 in the same language as the Northwest Ordinance of 1787, and even Douglas once described that compromise as "a sacred thing which no ruthless hand would ever be reckless enough to disturb." The Compromise of 1850 settled the final territorial issue of California and the Mexican Cession, and people thought that the slavery extension problem had at last been laid to rest.

But now, Lincoln said, with a touch of sorrow in his voice, Douglas declares the Missouri Compromise line inoperative, allowing slaves to be brought into Kansas and Nebraska, and he claims not to care whether settlers vote slavery up or down when they form a territorial government. "This declared indifference, but, as I must think, covert zeal, for the spread of slavery," Abe lamented, "I cannot but hate." Douglas is fooling no one; he is really for the extension of slavery.

Then Abe went on to make his position clear on the subject of slavery itself, taking care to emphasize that he was not an abolitionist. "I have no prejudice against the southern people," he declared. "They are just what we would be in their situation. If slavery did not now exist among them, they would not introduce it. If it did now exist among us, we should not instantly give it up." He continued with a long discourse that was to be his attitude toward the South and slavery for the next ten years:

> When the Southern people tell us they are no more responsible for the origin of slavery than we are, I acknowledge the fact when it is said that the institution exists, and that it is very difficult to get rid of it in any satisfactory way, I can understand and appreciate the saying. I surely cannot blame them for not doing what I should not know how to do myself. If all earthly power were given to me, I should not know what to do as to the existing institution. My first impulse would be to free all the slaves and send them to Liberia, to their own native land. (But that would be impractical.) What then? Free them all and keep them among us as underlings? Is it quite certain that this would better their condition? What next? Free them and make them politically and socially our equals? My own feelings will not admit of this, and if mine would, we well know that the great mass of whites will not. . . . We cannot make them equals. It does seem to me that systems of gradual emancipation might be adopted, but for their tardiness in this I will not undertake to judge our brethren of the South. (10)

Not only did Lincoln feel that slavery could not be ended quickly, he also believed that the laws protecting slavery should be religiously observed. He recognized the South's constitutional right to own slaves and would give the South "legislation for the reclaiming of their fugitives."

None of this, however, furnished an excuse for slavery to go into a free territory. This was where Lincoln drew the line. Slavery should be confined where it was, as it always had been, with no chance of its going any further. Some people, he knew, argued that popular sovereignty would keep slavery out of Kansas and Nebraska because Southerners would not go to those territories where the climate was unsuitable for cotton growing. But Lincoln could not accept this. The entire eastern border of Kansas was up against Missouri, a slave state populated with slave owners who would be glad to move west with their slaves.

As he said all of this, Abe warmed to his audience, waved his arms for emphasis, and paced back and forth. He loved the Union, he insisted. He would keep it together at all cost. "Much as I hate slavery," he confessed, "I would consent to the extension of it rather than see the Union dissolved, just as I would consent to any great evil to avoid a greater one." But Douglas contends that the Nebraska law is a "great Union-saving measure," that it makes the South feel more at home when she can share equally in the territories. Far from it. "Could there be a more apt invention to bring about collision and violence on the slavery question than the Nebraska project is? . . . If (Congress) had literally formed a ring and placed champions in it to fight over the controversy, the fight would be no more likely to come off than it is. And if the fight should begin, is it likely to take a very peaceful, Union-saving turn? Will not the first drop of blood so shed be the real death knell of the Union?" (11)

Next, Lincoln called all men, Whigs especially, to his position and assured them they would not be radical if they stood with him. Some men, mostly Whigs, who condemn the repeal of the 36-30 line hesitate to oppose it actively for fear they will be associated with the abolitionists, he remarked. "Will you allow me, as an old Whig, to tell them good-humoredly, that I think this is very silly. Stand with anybody that stands right. Stand with him when he is right, and part with him when he goes wrong. Stand with the abolitionist in restoring the Missouri Compromise, and stand against him when he attempts to repeal the Fugitive Slave Law. In the latter case you stand with the southern disunionists.

What of that? You are still right. In both cases you are right. In both cases you oppose the dangerous extremes." (12)

Finally, Lincoln closed with an eloquent exposition of what the Kansas-Nebraska Law threatened to do to the nation. The law made the assumption that slavery was morally right — that it did not matter whether it was voted up or voted down. The founders of the country assumed slavery was wrong, so they "hemmed it in to the narrowest limits of necessity." People rested in the belief that slavery was on the road to extinction. But the Nebraska Act suddenly places slavery on the high road to extension and perpetuity. "Henceforth (slavery) is to be the chief jewel of the nation — the very figurehead of the ship of state." The spirit of 1776 that all men are created equal is giving way to the Nebraska spirit that it is right for one man to enslave another. (13)

He was finished. He was well satisfied with his effort because he believed that after weeks of thought he had distilled out the truth and taken a stand for what was right. Slavery had always been restricted to the South by a nation that believed all men were created equal. That was the truth from which he started. No moderate, peaceful, Union-loving man wanted to disrupt that situation and attack slavery where it already existed, or deny Southerners their right of "property." But moderation, peace and the preservation of the Union also demanded that slavery not be extended; no people who thought slavery was wrong could stand by and watch it voted into Kansas. Douglas' law was morally wrong because it saw no difference between slavery's extension and slavery's containment, and it was dangerous because it brought pro-slavery and anti-slavery people into Kansas in competition — competition that almost surely would lead to violence. Thus, the law should be repealed and the 36-30 Missouri Compromise line restored.

The crowd roared its approval. Here was the man who could answer Douglas; here was the man who could express in words what they were thinking and feeling. He was not an abolitionist. What sane man was? Yet, he thought it was wrong to open up new areas for slavery and, although they could not express it as well as he did, they thought so, too.

Twelve days later Lincoln made the same speech in Peoria and received another tumultuous ovation. Anti-Nebraska Act men in the state began to think about Lincoln. Abe began to think, too. Perhaps he could take his anti-Kansas-Nebraska stand to the United States Senate. Senator Shields was going to have to stand for re-election that year. Abe could go for that seat. Quickly making his decision to go for it, he began writing letters to Whig party leaders.

In February the state legislature met to choose the U.S. Senator from Illinois. Shields was in the running for his own seat, and so was Governor Matteson, a pro-Kansas-Nebraska Act Democrat. Then there was Lyman Trumbull, a Democrat who had left his party to stand *against* the Kansas-Nebraska Act. And, there was Lincoln. He sat in the gallery among the spectators and watched himself get forty-seven votes in the first ballot, three short of the majority needed for election. Then, he watched his total in succeeding ballots dwindle to a paltry fifteen. Men who had supported him at first were switching either to Trumbull or Matteson. It was apparent to Lincoln that Matteson, the Democrat, would win unless he acted fast. Sadly, he told the fifteen legislators who were still voting for him to switch their votes to Trumbull so that an anti-Nebraska man would be elected. Thus, Trumbull went to Washington and Lincoln remained in the law office of Lincoln and Herndon.

3. ABE THE REPUBLICAN

This time Lincoln was not out of politics. The issues at stake were too great, and he had too many firm ideas on those issues to drop out now. He was thinking much more about the slavery question than he ever had before. Events in Kansas were causing most people to think and re-evaluate. Thousands of people were moving into Kansas, many of them not to settle but to win Kansas for their side of the slavery issue. Pro-slavery men from Missouri and the Deep South were going with guns and Bowie Knives, determined to make Kansas a slave state. Anti-slavery men from Illinois and as far away as New England traveled, armed with rifles, to make Kansas free. On the grassy plains people were dying; Northerners and Southerners were shooting each other in a bloody civil war. In 1855, Kansas was becoming known as "Bleeding Kansas."

Lincoln began to believe that the slave question was soon going to reach a climax. It was becoming more obvious to him every day that the slave and free sections of the country were going to come to blows. There was a story that Lincoln, when he was on the circuit, sat up all one night thinking about the Union. When the lawyer, T. Lyle Dickey, with whom he was sharing a bed, woke up, Lincoln looked at him solemnly and said, "Dickey, I tell you this nation cannot exist half slave and half free." Dickey turned over sleepily and replied, "Oh, Lincoln, go to sleep!" (14)

Abe could not dismiss the problem from his mind. In August, 1855, he wrote a letter to George Robertson of Kentucky, who had been a member of Congress in 1820 when the Missouri Compromise was passed. Abe lamented that the spirit of slavery was growing so strong that Robertson's once expressed dream that slavery would be gradually abolished had very little hope of ever coming true. The principle "All men are created equal," Abe wrote, was once a self-evident truth but is becoming a "self-evident lie." The Fourth of July is dwindling in meaning, he continued, until it is now only a day for "burning firecrackers!!!" (15) He concluded with what was becoming his constant thought: The political problem facing the nation is, can it exist permanently — forever — half slave and half free?" Lincoln thought not.

A week later he wrote to Joshua Speed, his old friend in Kentucky. He assured Speed, a slave owner, that he was perfectly willing to guarantee Speed's right to own slaves even to the extent of supporting the Fugitive Slave Law. "I confess I hate to see the poor creatures hunted down and carried back to their stripes and unrequited toil," he went on, "but I bite my lips and keep quiet." "You . . . ought to appreciate," he continued, "how much the great body of northern people do crucify their feelings in order to maintain their loyalty to the Constitution and the Union." (16)

Speed had written to Lincoln asking where he stood in politics. Lincoln answered: "I think I am a Whig; but others say there are no Whigs, and that I am an abolitionist. I now do no more than oppose the extension of slavery." (17) Lincoln's problem was that the Whig Party was virtually dead in 1855. Shocked by its defeat in 1852, it had split in two over the Kansas-Nebraska Bill — many northern Whigs opposing it, many southern Whigs standing with the Democrats in favor of it. If there was no Whig Party, where could a man such as Lincoln go?

There was a movement afoot in the North to create a new political party that would have as its major credo the non-extension of slavery. Its membership would draw from the defunct Free Soil Party, anti-Nebraska Whigs, and northern Democrats. In 1854 there had been some early meetings of this new "Republican Party" in Wisconsin and Michigan. In 1855 the movement was growing. Abe had to decide whether or not to give up his old Whig loyalties and join the new group. He agonized over the decision because he saw many abolitionists joining the Republicans. He did not want to connect politically with any man who believed slavery could be or should be immediately abolished. Events, as they so often do, were about to force his hand.

In 1856, the news from Kansas worsened. Pro-slavery settlers had organized their own government at Lecompton; anti-slavery men had set up a government in Topeka. Each claimed to be the legitimate government of Kansas. Meanwhile, the bloodshed continued. Pro-slavery men rode into the anti-slavery town of Lawrence, burned down the "Free State Hotel," wrecked two printing offices and killed five people. John Brown, an anti-slavery fanatic, avenged those five deaths by marauding one night with several armed men. At Pottawatomie Creek they hacked five Southerners to death. "Popular Sovereignty" was staining the Kansas prairie with blood.

As the stories were told of Lawrence and John Brown, Abraham Lincoln turned into a Republican. He abhorred the violence committed by both sides and strongly believed that only closing the territories to slavery would end the bloodshed. When Illinois Republicans met in Bloomington in May to organize the state party, Lincoln was there. There were some abolitionists there, too, but Lincoln was pleased to see in attendance men he knew were as conservative as he was.

After the men at the meeting had voted to establish an Illinois Republican Party, the men in attendance began shouting for Lincoln. He modestly took the platform and began a little speech. A few minutes into his extemporaneous remarks, the Republicans realized they were hearing a beautiful and powerful oration. After expounding again on the theme that was becoming his mantra — that slavery was wrong and should not be extended into new territories — he took on a new cause. Rising up to his full 6'4" height and waving his arms emphatically, he shouted, "Southern disunionists, we won't go out of the Union and you shan't!" (18)

THE AGITATOR AND THE POLITICIAN

As Abe spoke, the delegates cheered and waved handkerchiefs. Reporters put down their pencils to listen; even Billy Herndon, always a faithful recorder, forgot to take notes. It may have been the greatest speech Abe ever made. Some said it was. But, since everyone was so swept along by it, only its highlights were ever written down. It became known as Lincoln's "lost speech," but it was a speech that put him in the front ranks of Illinois Republicans.

A few days later the Republican National Convention met in Philadelphia. Old free soil men, anti-slavery Whigs, and a few anti-slavery Democrats were there. They adopted a platform that proclaimed it was the right and the duty of Congress to ban slavery from the territories. For president they nominated John C. Fremont, "The Pathfinder" who had explored California, and they devised the slogan: "Free soil, free speech, free men and Fremont!"

Word came to Lincoln that he had received 110 votes for the vice-presidential nomination, although the prize had gone to William L. Dayton. Abe humbly responded, "I reckon that ain't me; there's another great man in Massachusetts named Lincoln and I reckon it's him." (19) But it *was* Abraham Lincoln of Illinois, and he had received the votes of all the delegates from Illinois and Indiana. He was becoming known nationally.

The Democrats nominated James Buchanan of Pennsylvania, a man flabby in principles as well as physique. For twenty-five years he had tried for the Democratic nomination and now, because he was a Northerner who looked kindly on southern claims to the western territories, it was his.

Through the summer of 1856, Lincoln campaigned up and down Illinois for the Fremont ticket and even went to Kalamazoo, Michigan, for a speech. Reports were coming from the South that the Republicans were considered abolitionists down there, and that the election of the "Black Republican" Fremont would drive the South out of the Union. The Republicans were called a sectional party, able to draw votes only in the North, while the Democrats, led by Buchanan, could get votes nationwide.

Lincoln answered the charges. "No one in the Republican Party is an abolitionist, the supporters of Fremont are not abolitionists," he said, somewhat disingenuously (some of them *were* abolitionists!). We simply oppose slavery in the territories, he went on, and we wish to keep them open for free white people. Our stand is not disunionist; we do not want to dissolve the Union. If the South insists on dissolving it, we will not let her.

The election gave Buchanan the White House. All the southern states plus Pennsylvania, Illinois, New Jersey, and Indiana went for him. But Fremont won the rest of the North and received 1,340,000 popular votes to Buchanan's 1,838,000. It was a very impressive showing for a party waging its first presidential campaign. Significantly, all but 1,200 of the people who voted Republican lived in the free states. Even more significantly, the candidate of the Free Soil Party, Millard Fillmore, collected 873,000 votes, mostly in the North. His votes combined with Fremont's amounted to 55% of the total, a figure certain to alarm every Southerner who was paying attention.

In December, the Republicans of Illinois held a banquet at the Tremont House in Chicago to celebrate. Fremont had lost Illinois, but they had elected a Republican governor and, as Abe reminded his friends, Fremont had collected a lot of votes in the state. There was a solid base on which to build.

After dinner, Abe spoke to the rows of cigar smoking men. The central idea of our country has always been the equality of men, he said. The Democrats are changing that to "slavery is right," the result of which will be the extension of slavery everywhere. They have won this time, he conceded, but "the human heart is with us; God is with us." (20) Soon, he predicted, the Republican Party will re-establish the principle "all men are created equal." He was beginning to sound almost Garrisonian!

4. KANSAS PRELUDE

In Boston, the struggle for control of Kansas became something of a crusade. Some people said that a man could do a great anti-slavery duty by going to the new territory, settling there for a few years, and voting for a free state constitution. The "Emigrant Aid Company" was organized to provide money — and rifles — to people willing to make the journey. Some of Garrison's followers were caught up in the excitement.

As always, Garrison had deep-rooted doubts about the territorial cause, and the whole idea of attacking a peripheral issue of slavery without crusading against the "monstrous injustice" of slavery itself. Moreover, he was not convinced that the people going to Kansas were always motivated by anti-slavery zeal. His suspicion seemed to be confirmed by a letter he received from Charles Stearn, an abolitionist who had gone to Kansas. Stearn's letter, which Lloyd published in *The Liberator*, said in part:

> (Northerners who come to Kansas) are desperately opposed to slavery entering here — and why? . . . Because they don't want the "niggers" about them. . . . Now I feel quite certain that the very people who vote against the introduction of slavery will also vote for a "black law" (a law banning Negroes). . . . I can find a few who dare to say that they are in favor of allowing the colored man to come here and buy land on an equality with the white man. The common cry is "We want no slavery and no niggers." . . . I am much disappointed in the character of the New England emigrants. They come here as men go to California, mainly after money. (21)

Familiar as he was with northern racial attitudes, Lloyd was not surprised by this letter. He had seen the people in Oregon declare their territory free and then ban Negroes from it; he knew that some northern states banned African-Americans from the voting booth and from public facilities used by whites; he knew that even in Boston, a city that was now, twenty years after it mobbed him, beginning to take pride in being an abolition center, much of the anti-slavery activity was hypocritical. Very few Bostonians favored racial equality.

As a pacifist, Garrison could not condone the violence perpetrated by Northerners who went to Kansas. He agreed that the settlers in Kansas were subjected to many insults and outrages and that they were in a dangerous situation. But, he wrote, "When Christ said 'Love your enemies,' he did not mean 'kill them if they go too far.'" Garrison was also annoyed that the Kansas settlers were not acting on principle or contending for equal rights for all. They were fighting for their own rights and their own wealth. He believed the way to a truly free and prosperous world was down the path of peace. If all Americans were true pacifists there would be no slavery, and therefore no wars over slavery. (22)

As the fighting in Kansas went on, Garrison repeatedly criticized those who were making the fight against slavery a question of "who gets Kansas?" In *The Liberator*, at anti-slavery meetings, and in letters to friends, he went to great lengths to emphasize that the real battle had to be against slavery itself where it already existed. At the New England Anti-Slavery Convention in May of 1856, he introduced a resolution on the territorial issue that received the usual near-unanimous approval of the delegates. It said: "We deplore the moral blindness and inconsistency of those who are seeking to transform the anti-slavery cause into a mere territorial struggle . . . making it no longer a question as to the liberation of four millions of imbruted slaves at the South, but only one of latitude and longitude." (23)

The Republican Party, with its platform of banning slavery from Kansas by restoring the 36-30 line, came increasingly under Garrison's fire as it became evident that the party was going to have some strength in the 1856 election. Like all political parties, he said, the Republican Party was not "pure" on the moral issue of slavery. Writing to his old friend and early follower, Samuel May, he said: "The tone of the Republican Party is becoming more and more feeble and indefinite, in order to secure a larger vote in the coming presidential struggle. At Pittsburgh they resolved to vote for admission of Kansas to the Union as a free state! Wonderful. Put not your faith in politicians." (24) He warned other abolitionists to stay away from the Republican Party, to keep their hands clean, not to dilute their pure abolitionism with territorial issues.

Yet, as he had in the Free Soil Party, Garrison saw in the Republican Party signs of progress towards a true anti-slavery position. He heard some Republican politicians in his part of the country actually speak of the *moral* wrong of slavery. In May of 1856 he was particularly impressed with a speech given by Republican Charles Sumner of Massachusetts on the floor of the United States Senate. Sumner had become an opponent of slavery during the 1830's partly as a result of reading *The Liberator* and had been elected to the Senate by the Massachusetts Legislature in 1851. During his early years in Washington he had been criticized mercilessly in *The Liberator* for not standing strongly enough against slavery. But, now, on the Senate floor, he delivered an oration titled "The Crime Against Kansas." Although his focus was the Kansas issue, he attacked the slave system itself, the South in general, and slave holders with such venom that Lloyd was full of admiration.

Three days later, Sumner became the ultimate anti-slavery man in Lloyd's eyes when he was beaten nearly to death by a Southerner. Preston Brooks, a member of the House of Representatives from South Carolina, angered over Sumner's speech and the slurs it contained against his uncle, Senator Butler, marched right into the Senate chamber, walked up to Sumner's desk where the Senator was busy writing, and proceeded to pummel him on the head with a heavy cane. For the next several months, descriptions of Sumner's severe wounds (it took him three years to recover) and of the hero's welcome Brooks received when he returned to South Carolina, were prominent features in *The Liberator*.

Thus, Garrison tempered his anti-Republican remarks with admissions that the party was favorable to the cause of freedom. At one point he wrote, "In general intelligence, virtuous character, humane sentiment and patriotic feeling — as well as the object it is seeking to accomplish — it (the Republican Party) is incomparably better than the other rival parties; and its success, *as against those parties*, will be a cheering sign of the times." Then, very uncharacteristically, he made what seemed to be an endorsement of the Republican candidate in 1856. "As against Buchanan," he wrote, "it seems to us, the sympathies and best wishes of every enlightened friend of freedom must be on the side of Fremont; so that if there were no moral barrier to our voting, and we had a million votes to bestow, we should cast them all for the Republican candidate." (25)

Horace Greeley, the famous editor of the New York *Tribune*, promptly wrote to Garrison asking if this statement was an endorsement of Fremont. Lloyd replied that he would not vote for Fremont, that he was urging all true abolitionists not to do so, that he only favored Fremont because of his non-extension of slavery stand, and that he still upheld the motto, NO UNION WITH SLAVEHOLDERS!!

By 1857, with the South continuing its aggression in Kansas and continuing to insist that Northerners return fugitive slaves and uphold the slave system in every way, Garrison felt it was time to push for the idea of disunion harder than ever before. On January 15th, a "disunion Convention" of New England abolitionists met in Worcester, Massachusetts. Although the group was small, Lloyd spoke with confidence and vigor. The people of the North will gradually come to accept the idea of breaking away from the Union, he predicted, just as the colonists gradually adopted the idea of breaking away from Britain.

Then he answered a question commonly put to him by people who opposed disunion: Wasn't he forsaking the slave if he "got out?" No, he answered; he was freeing the slave. He had no doubts that the South wanted the Union and needed the Union to uphold slavery. Without the Union, the South's economy would suffer, her slaves would escape to the North — which would no longer be obliged to return them — and slavery would die. True, he admitted, Southerners threatened to break up the Union if certain things happened, but those were just threats to frighten the North into conceding to the South even more than it already had. (26)

As the 1850's drew to a close, Garrison was pleased with the progress he perceived in the anti-slavery struggle, but still fighting to maintain "pure" abolitionism in the face of events. He was pleased that the South was proving that it really did control the Union. With the Fugitive Slave Act and the Kansas-Nebraska Act as evidence, how could any Northerner deny that there was a slave power conspiracy to make the country a slave republic? But, he was struggling to keep peoples' minds on the true issue — the equality of human beings and the right of all races to be free. He was struggling to make Northerners see that, as a moral duty to the slaves, they must give up the Union. And, he was struggling with the spirit of violence abroad in the land. He may have begun to realize that liberation of the slaves might require violence — many Americans were coming to that conclusion — but, in his heart, he wanted peace and believed that only peaceful abolitionism could have real force.

In a soul-baring speech before the New England Anti-Slavery Society in May of 1858, he told his followers that a solution to the slave question was probably going to be bloody, but he deplored the growing war-like spirit among abolitionists such as those who were sending guns to Kansas. " . . . a sad change has come over the spirit of anti-slavery men . . . ," he said. "We are growing more and more warlike, more and more disposed to repudiate the principles of peace . . . Just in proportion as this spirit prevails, I feel that our moral power is departing and will depart. I say this not so much as an abolitionist but as a man. I believe in the spirit of peace, and in sole and absolute reliance on truth and the application of it to the hearts and consciences of the people. I do not believe that the weapons of liberty ever have been, or ever can be, the weapons of despotism."

"I pray you, abolitionists," he went on emotionally, "still to adhere to the truth. Do not get impatient; do not become exasperated; do not attempt any political organization; do not make yourself familiar with the idea that blood must flow." (27)

Lloyd was unaware that some of the very people he was talking to were plotting violence. He did not know that the "slave power" that he had crusaded against for thirty years and the North that he had been trying to "abolitionize" peacefully, were going to soon engage in the most terrible violence the world had ever seen. In Washington, in Kansas, in plantation drawing rooms and in northern political meetings, ideas that had been partly set in motion by Garrison himself were rushing towards violence with a force far greater than his power to stop them.

5. MODERATE ANTI-SLAVERY

Dred Scott was a slave who had been taken by his master first to Illinois, then to the territory of Louisiana north of the 36-30 line (prior to the passage of the Kansas-Nebraska Act), and finally back home to Missouri. He sued his master for his freedom on the grounds that he had been a resident on free soil. On March 6, 1857, the Supreme Court under Chief Justice Roger B. Taney published its findings in the case of *Dred Scott v Sandford*. In a 7-2 decision, Taney, writing for the majority, declared that Scott, as a slave, had no right to sue. Furthermore, as a resident of the territory north of 36-30 Scott had not been free anyway because Congress had no right to exclude slavery from a federal territory. In essence, the Court was declaring the Missouri Compromise line unconstitutional and stating categorically that slavery could not be banned from Kansas, Nebraska, or any other United States territory. The Court ruled that the Fifth Amendment to the United States Constitution clearly prohibits Congress from taking a person's property without "due process of law."

The decision exploded like a bomb, sending shock waves to every corner of the country. The South, of course, was overjoyed. Here was its long-held position finally written into law. Garrison, of course, was outraged, but not surprised. Here was just further proof that the "slave power" controlled the government. Would the North *now* consider disunion?

The Republican Party was thrown into turmoil. The Court had declared its platform (exclusion of slavery from the territories) unconstitutional. Republicans could only hope to elect a Republican president who would appoint Republican justices to the Supreme Court and wait for a new ruling *upholding* Congress's right to exclude slavery from the territories.

The party needed strong voices to speak out against the threat of slavery's unrestricted expansion. In Illinois, it had that spokesman in Abraham Lincoln. He had answered Stephen Douglas on the Kansas-Nebraska issue. Now he would carry on the battle in the face of this new setback.

In June of 1857, two weeks after Douglas had spoken in the Illinois state house defending the Dred Scott ruling, Lincoln took the podium to attack it. Gesturing with his large hands he denounced Douglas and Taney for their assertion that the Declaration of Independence did not mean African-Americans when it said, "All men are created equal." It did not say "all were equal in color, size, intellect, moral development or social capacity," he exclaimed. It defines with "tolerable distinctness," however, in what respects they *were* equal. They were equal in their unalienable rights to "life, liberty and the pursuit of happiness." Thus, it meant that no man should be a slave to another.

Lincoln then launched into what he had long considered to be the ideal solution to the slavery and race problems in the United States — colonization. "The enterprise is a difficult one," he admitted, but "'where there is a will there is a way,' and what colonization most needs is a hearty will." "Let us be brought to believe it is morally right," he concluded, "and at the same time favorable to, or at least not against, our interest to transfer the African to his native clime, and we shall find a way to do it, however great the task may be." (28)

The crowd responded well. There were some who had heard that Lincoln was a radical, that he favored not only the abolition of slavery, but also blacks living with whites. They were won over by his plea that the Republican program would be the best plan for keeping the races apart. Under the Republican roof, Lincoln was uniting those who had a moral aversion to slavery and those who did not like African-Americans and wanted to keep them in the South or send them to Africa. Although Abe was personally fond of all of the black people he had ever met (indeed, he was fond of all people), and although he was morally opposed to slavery, he was not above thinking white people were superior to black. Nor was he in favor, as he had said before and would say again, of setting them free quickly without arranging for a place for them to go.

The Illinois Republican Convention in 1858 nominated Lincoln to be its candidate against Stephen Douglas, who was up for re-election. The voters would decide the winner of the debate that Lincoln and Douglas had been waging for four years. In a speech that would be eternally remembered, Lincoln delivered a complete expression of the things he had been contemplating for a long time. He began with a paragraph as strikingly prophetic as any ever spoken by an American political leader:

> A house divided against itself cannot stand. I believe this government cannot endure permanently half slave and half free. I do not expect the Union to be dissolved — I do not expect the house to fall — but I do expect it will cease to be divided. It will become all one thing or all the other. Either the opponents of slavery will arrest the further spread of it and place it where the public mind shall rest in the belief that it is in the course of ultimate extinction; or its advocates will push it forward till it shall become alike lawful in all the states, old as well as new, North as well as South. (29)

This seemed to be the core of the question facing the country. The South was determined to extend slavery; the North was determined to contain it. As events in Kansas were proving, neither side was going to give in no matter how violent the struggle became. Lincoln went on to charge that because the Dred Scott decision so neatly fit into the plans of Douglas and the recent presidents to extend slavery, there must be some agreement — indeed a conspiracy — between Douglas, Pierce, Buchanan, and Taney to extend slavery. Ultimately, Lincoln concluded, unless the power of this southern political dynasty is met and overthrown, a Supreme Court decision will come down denying the right of a *state* to exclude slavery. Then the "slave power conspiracy" will have a complete victory; the United States will be a slave republic!

Lincoln hoped these remarks would not be considered too radical. A week after the speech, he wrote to John Scripps, a Chicago journalist, assuring him that he did not intend to interfere with slavery where it already existed. "I believe," he told Scripps, "that whenever the effort to spread slavery . . . shall be fairly headed off, the institution will then be in a course of ultimate extinction; and by the language I used, I meant only this." (30) Lincoln believed that if slavery were kept within its 1858 limits, it would gradually die. Southerners would realize it was unprofitable and, with world opinion against them, finally agree that it was immoral. He did not think the South would leave the Union or fight a war over the extension of slavery, despite their loud threats. For his own part, he had no intention of advocating northern secession as some of the radical abolitionists in the east were doing — even if slavery did go national. Rather, he would campaign and run for office to see that the extension of slavery did not happen.

As the campaign against Douglas began, Lincoln followed his Democratic opponent from place to place, speaking to the same crowds Douglas had regaled the previous day. Soon, Republican leaders began to doubt the effectiveness of this strategy, and they proposed a series of face-to-face debates between the two candidates. Douglas accepted the challenge; he was extremely confident of his platform speaking ability. Furthermore, the "Little Giant" relished the thought of calling Lincoln a "Negro lover" and "racial amalgamist" in front of large audiences.

Douglas's and Lincoln's advisors arranged seven debates to be held in towns scattered throughout the state. At each confrontation, both men would have an hour to speak. Then, each would have time to rebut the other's remarks.

Of all the political campaigns ever waged, nothing has equaled the excitement, color and drama of the Lincoln-Douglas debates. With little else to entertain them, especially in rural areas, the people followed politics even more passionately than they do in our own time. The day before a debate was to occur, the citizens of the host town would cluster by the hundreds at the railroad station to welcome their respective heroes. When Douglas's train arrived, the Democrats would cheer mightily, a brass band would begin to play, and the "Little Giant" would be carried to his hotel on the shoulders of his adoring followers. Later, Lincoln would receive a similar welcome from his Republican admirers. Through the night, as the candidates prepared themselves in their hotel rooms and tried to rest, the partisans debated the merits of Lincoln and Douglas in crowded taverns and on dimly lit street corners.

In the morning, wagons would roll into town from all over the countryside. By the time of the debate, hundreds of people would be sitting on benches, standing in wagons, or perched in trees all around the flag-draped platform. Everyone was ready to watch mighty Stephen slay the rustic stick man, or to cheer as "Long Abe" crushed his tiny opponent beneath his huge boot. Throughout the speeches, people would shout, "That's right, Abe!"or "You tell 'im, Stephen!" whenever they thought their man had made an important point.

At Freeport, each candidate attempted to ask the other politically embarrassing questions. Douglas asked Lincoln if he favored the repeal of the Fugitive Slave Law, if he opposed the admission of new slave states to the Union, if he was pledged to abolish slavery in Washington, D.C., and if he was pledged to abolish the slave trade between the states. Lincoln answered "No" to all of these and repeated his stand that he did not intend to interfere with slavery where it already existed. He was not going to let Douglas brand him a radical.

Then Lincoln asked Douglas a question that he had thoughtfully prepared. How, he asked, in light of the Dred Scott decision, do the people of Kansas or any other territory really have a choice? Didn't the Court rule that slavery could not be excluded from a federal territory? This appeared to put "The Little Giant" in a bind, but Douglas was prepared for the question because he had been thinking about the issue for quite a while. With confidence, he asserted that the people could, if they wished, effectively ban slavery by simply not passing any laws providing for its protection. No slave owner would bring his "property" into a territory that did not provide "night patrols" around plantations to stop slave escapes and rebellions. This answer kept Douglas's concept of popular sovereignty alive and found a receptive audience in Freeport, Illinois. He had effectively parried Lincoln's question and won a debating point.

However, as word of what Douglas had said spread through the South, the people reacted quite differently. Douglas had been a hero in Dixie when his Kansas-Nebraska Act opened the lands north of 36-30 to slavery. The Supreme Court had cemented the idea that slaves could, indeed, be brought into the territories with no interference because they were property. Now Douglas was concocting a way for slavery to be excluded in spite of the court's ruling, and Southerners were enraged.

Lincoln's response to Douglas at Freeport was to remark that Douglas's scheme was a very weak reed on which to rest northern hopes that slavery would not go into the territories. He continued to charge that Douglas was part of a conspiracy to make slavery national and that Douglas was morally blind if he did not view slavery as a wrong that should be contained.

At every stop, Douglas read Lincoln's "House divided speech" to the crowds. So often did he read it that Lincoln said at one point that he should have it memorized. Ignoring Lincoln's quip, Douglas charged that Lincoln did not believe in differences and did not believe that each state should have its own institutions. Lincoln says we must be all one thing or all the other and then proposes to deny the rights of Southerners to own slaves. This is dangerous talk, Douglas shouted. Lincoln is saying we will have civil war! The divisive nature of Lincoln's platform is proved by the fact that he cannot speak it in the South. "Popular Sovereignty," on the other hand, can be expounded up and down the land and accepted by reasonable men everywhere as the best answer to the slavery problem.

At Alton, in southern Illinois, the town in which Elijah P. Lovejoy was killed defending his abolitionist press, Douglas whipped up the anger of the pro-slavery audience by charging that at heart Lincoln was an abolitionist. In reply, Lincoln spoke with fervor and conviction. He did not banter or exchange quips with Douglas as he did in other debates. These people in Alton, many of whom were Southerners, had to know how he stood. He proceeded as logically and unemotionally as he could.

He began with what he thought was an irrefutable fact. The founding fathers had placed slavery on what they thought was the road to ultimate extinction, he said. They banned slavery from the Northwest Territory, part of which was Illinois, in 1787; they cut off slave imports from Africa in 1808. These acts were designed to hem slavery in from all sides and leave it to die a natural death. They did not even use the word "slavery" in the Constitution because they did not want it recorded on the great charter that such a thing had ever existed among us. For years, Americans accepted this decision by the founding fathers to restrict slavery. The house really did not become divided over slavery until Douglas opened up the territorial issue with the Kansas-Nebraska Bill. Now, we Republicans merely want to place slavery back where it always was — enclosed in the South.

Republicans, he went on, think slavery is wrong and hope to see it end some day. But, no man is a true Republican who wants to destroy it without regard to the constitutional difficulties such as the guaranteed right of property. I stand by the Fugitive Slave Law. I have no taste for running and catching Negroes, but I do not believe the constitution can be supported without my doing so.

Finally, in an appeal to the personal interests of the white men before him, he pointed out that closing the territories to slavery would make it easier for white men to find homes in the West. As he said this, tanned faces nodded in approval, and work-hardened hands clapped together in applause. Many agreed; this man understood a farmer's homesteading instinct. Many more, however, sat on their hands and scowled. The Republican platform opposing slavery was a hard sell in southern Illinois, where many of the inhabitants had emigrated from the slave states.

At last the speeches, the parades, the noise and the arguments were over. It was time for the voters to make known whom they favored in more sober fashion. Because the state legislatures, in those days, elected the U.S. Senators, voters indicated their preferences by voting for the legislator of their candidate's party.

Lincoln's arguments had turned many heads. Folks liked him personally, and they liked that much of what he said about slavery made sense. When the votes were counted, Republican candidates for the state legislature had 4,085 more votes than the Democratic candidates. However, because the populations of the districts were imbalanced, Democrats won more seats in the legislature and Douglas was re-elected when the legislators voted in the State House.

On a cold evening in January, 1859, Lincoln sat in his law office contemplating the vote: Douglas 54, Lincoln 46. Once again his political career seemed over. His only consolation, he wrote to loyal friends, was that he had waged a good campaign and had made some important points for people to consider. "Though I shall now sink out of view and shall be forgotten," he wrote, "I believe I have made some marks which will tell for the cause of civil liberty long after I am gone." (31)

Only his streak of superstition kept Lincoln from believing completely that he was through. As he walked home on the night of his defeat he slipped on the ice; one boot knocked the other from under him. He barely managed to fling his long arms, twist his body and shuffle his feet to remain upright. "A slip and not a fall," he said to himself, and then, taken with the concept, repeated, "A slip and not a fall." (32)

6. CLOSER; STILL APART

In several respects, Abraham Lincoln, in Illinois, and William Lloyd Garrison, in Massachusetts, were as far apart on the subject of slavery in 1859 as they were geographically. Although both men thought slavery was a moral wrong, Garrison believed it must be purged from the land immediately, without regard to "property rights," without regard for the constitution, and without regard for any other artificial roadblocks. The issue of slavery in the territories, he believed, was a fake one put forth by white racists who wanted the new lands free of African-Americans. He believed the black man should be given rights completely equal to the white man's, with no consideration given at all to the idea of deporting the black race to Africa. Finally, he was convinced that the only action that was going to force the South to give up slavery was the withdrawal of the North from the Union.

Lincoln thought that slavery would best be ended by confining it to the southern states where it already existed. He was fully prepared to wait a long time for the South to give up slavery on its own. His quarrel with Douglas and the Democrats was that they were for allowing slavery growing room and making it unlikely slavery would *ever* end. His speeches tended to prove, at least partially, Garrison's claim that the Republicans were racists interested in land — "land for free white men." Lincoln believed that black people were equal to white people in the right to be free, but he was not about to extend full social, economic and political equality to them. He was convinced that the only way to avoid the racial conflicts that would inevitably follow emancipation was to make the prodigious effort to send the African-Americans to Africa. Above all, Lincoln was for preserving the Union, even if he had to accept slavery as part of it.

The philosophy of each man, while honestly held, was also a brilliant strategy to advance his career. Certain parts of each man's philosophy were possibly adopted for just that reason. By maintaining an ultra-abolitionist stance, Garrison was ensuring that he would be the most notorious of all the abolitionists. Also, he was setting up an ultimate standard — a lodestone of anti-slavery — toward which people would be drawn as they gradually perceived the evils of the slave system. Furthermore, he was provoking Southerners and their allies into committing outrages that did nothing but draw more support for the anti-slavery cause. Lincoln was collecting votes for himself by tempering his anti-slavery attitude and appealing to the people's self-interest and their racial prejudices. Perhaps, in his heart, he was more anti-slavery than he let on; perhaps he really did believe in racial equality. He knew, however, that he could do nothing for the African-American if he were never elected, and he would never be elected if he said too many radical things.

In spite of everything, there were some significant ways in which the two men agreed. Both realized that the Union could only be held together if the North agreed to the South's constitutional right" to keep its slaves — its property. Each believed there was a "slave power conspiracy" at work to extend slavery and that it should be exposed and stopped. Garrison proposed to solve both of these problems by dissolving the Union. Lincoln hoped to control them by electing Republicans to office. In an ironic turn of events, each was going to have his way, and they were going to come together at last in a common purpose.

CHAPTER SEVEN

Radicalism Breeds War

1859-1861

John Brown's raid into the South to free slaves and the reaction to it by southern pro-slavery "fire-eaters" set the stage for the South's rage over Lincoln's election in 1860. Southern secession and Lincoln's stand against it brought about the long-dreaded civil war.

1. TRIALS OF A PACIFIST

As William Lloyd Garrison looked about him in 1859, he could assess what his thirty years of anti-slavery activity had helped achieve, but he had no way of knowing what advances were specifically his responsibility. He knew that across the North there were thousands of people who favored the immediate abolition of slavery, but how many of them had reached this radical position by reading *The Liberator* or hearing his speeches? Very few of them were "ultra" abolitionists favoring immediate break-up of the union with slaveholders; his band of followers was very small. He also knew the Republican Party was a powerful new force in American politics and stood a chance of winning the presidency in 1860. But, again, he did not know how much of a role Garrisonian agitation had played in bringing Republican politicians as far along the anti-slavery path as they had come. Furthermore, it was by no means certain that most Republicans thought slavery was wrong. Many of them were openly saying that if it became a choice between stopping the spread of slavery and saving the Union, they would choose the Union. What true moralist would make *that* choice?

In Boston, Garrison could certainly notice a significant change. Where he once would have been killed if he had been recognized, he could now stroll along Washington Street on his way to the anti-slavery offices and receive warm smiles from passing citizens. The events of the last thirty years had shown the people that this "raving fanatic" was sometimes right and should at least be given a hearing.

Lloyd's "radical agitator" instincts told him that the conversion of people to abolitionism – or even to Republicanism – and his respectability in Boston were largely due to the reactions of the Southerners to his radical positions. Southerners saw him as a symbol of slave insurrection and a growing northern impulse to destroy the southern way of life. To stop him, they had incited mobs to attack all abolitionists, they had burned abolitionist literature and gagged Congress, and they had insisted that Northerners support slavery as a positive good by returning fugitive slaves and allowing the western territories to be open to slavery. These extreme reactions to Garrison's little movement had convinced Northerners that the slave owners and their friends in the South — and in the North — were a "slave power conspiracy" to take over the Union. Southerners, not Garrison, had convinced Northerners that Republicanism — if not abolitionism — was necessary to preserve the *North's* way of life.

Southerners had over-reacted to Garrison and his allies. Failing to notice his pacifism, they had taken his uncompromising language to mean that he favored the violent destruction of slavery. In 1859, they over-reacted yet again to what they thought was the logical result of Garrison's anti-slavery crusade — the violence of a man who had already killed five Southerners in Kansas, John Brown.

Contrary to what most Southerners thought, Garrison talked to John Brown only once. The two men met in January, 1857, at the home of Reverend Theodore Parker and spent several hours discussing pacifism. Garrison quoted Jesus in an attempt to convince the lanky man with an inflexible mouth that violence was truly unchristian. Brown responded with quotations from the Old Testament on the need for fire and blood to wipe out sin. Neither man changed his position, and Lloyd left feeling discouraged that an abolitionist could be just as violent as a slave owner.

Two years later, Brown attended the annual meeting of the New England Anti-Slavery Society where he saw Garrison speak and was reported to have left the meeting muttering, "These men are all talk; what is needed is action — action!" (1)

Brown was right then planning a very dramatic action — an invasion of Virginia to liberate slaves. Through the summer of 1859 he met secretly with several New England benefactors and rounded up an army of eighteen followers, including three of his sons. In October, he and his men crossed into Virginia to raid the federal arsenal at Harper's Ferry, a town on the Potomac River. Their purpose was to seize guns either for use in a slave revolt (as Southerners believed) or for defending several hundred slaves as they escaped to the North (as Brown later implied). For two days they held Harper's Ferry in siege. Finally, the Virginia militia and a detachment of marines under Robert E. Lee managed to kill or capture all of them and take Brown himself into custody.

Lying on a cot, his wounded head swathed in bandages, Brown was tried for treason. Without remorse, he faced his accusers and calmly accepted the verdict of guilty and the sentence to hang by the neck until dead. He was led to the gallows in Charlestown, Virginia, on December 2nd, but before he died, he handed a note to a guard on which he had written:

> I, John Brown, am now quite certain that the crimes of this guilty land can never be purged away but with blood. (2)

News of John Brown's raid sent a chill through the South akin to that caused by Nat Turner's rebellion in 1831. The very thought of slave rebellion made Southerners lose all sense of reason. Nearly every southern newspaper condemned the raid on Harper's Ferry and claimed it was the direct result of anti-slavery agitation. Garrison was behind the whole thing, some Southerners said; others believed it was not just Garrison but the Republican Party. Anti-slavery agitation must stop, Southerners screamed, or secession would be the South's only salvation.

Initially, Garrison was shocked at the news from Harper's Ferry. As a pacifist, he was appalled at the acts of violence. In previous years he had always been unhappy whenever the crusade against slavery took violent turns. But, he never fully condemned his friends' violent disobedience of the Fugitive Slave Law or the violent occupation of Kansas by anti-slavery men. He had always said that *he* was opposed to the use of force, but those who were willing to use it should be willing to see it used on behalf of the slaves. Would he, in the end, give public approval to what John Brown had done?

Soon after the news of the raid reached Boston, Lloyd printed a brief statement in *The Liberator*. "Our views of war and bloodshed, even in the best of causes, are too well known to need repeating here," he told his readers, "but let no one who glories in the revolutionary struggles of 1776 deny the right of slaves to imitate the example of our fathers." (3)

On the day Brown was executed, Garrison spoke in Tremont Temple. To a crowd gathered to commemorate the deeds of the man who was being hanged that day, Lloyd gave his finest speech on the place for violence in a society that held slaves and also repudiated the principles of non-resistance. "I am a non-resistant, ' he said, proudly. "I am a believer in the inviolability of human life, under all circumstances; I therefore, disarm John Brown and every slave at the South. But I do not stop there; If I did I should be a monster. I also disarm, in the name of God, every slaveholder and tyrant in the world." He paused to ask how many non-resistants there were in the audience. One voice shouted, "Here!" "There is one!" Lloyd exclaimed sarcastically. Those who are NOT non-resistants, he continued, speaking to everyone before him but that one man, have no right to call John Brown a traitor by their own standards. He went on:

> I thank God when men who believe in the right and duty of wielding weapons are so far advanced that they will take those weapons out of the scale of despotism, and throw them into the scale of freedom. It is an indication of progress and positive moral growth; it is one way to get to the sublime platform of non-resistance; and it is God's method of dealing retribution upon the head of the tyrant. (4)

In a sense, Garrison was trying to have it both ways. He was a pacifist, yet he applauded those who believed in violence if they used violence on behalf of the slaves. Whether this makes sense and is consistent with pacifism is a subject for debate. Some historians say that if Garrison were truly a pacifist, he should have condemned *all* acts of violence. It is worth noting that Garrison was consistent; he said virtually the same thing about anti-slavery violence from Nat Turner on: that he, himself, never supported violent acts and always counseled non-violence for all Americans – including, or especially, slave owners. If violent men were unwilling to listen to his advice, could he be blamed for cheering when they at least used it in the right cause?

With no pacifist principles to burden or confuse them, most abolitionist Northerners sympathized with John Brown more readily than Garrison did. In some northern homes he became a martyr to the noble cause of freedom. The Republican Party, however, joined with Democrats in denouncing John Brown. Republicans were afraid their party would be identified with the violent man at Harper's Ferry and that this would cost them the presidential election in 1860. Abraham Lincoln was speaking in Kansas — scene of Brown's earlier violence — when the old man was led to the gallows. Lawless attacks on slavery are indefensible, Lincoln told his audiences, and the North could only agree that Brown's trial and execution were justified. Abe's long-held adherence to the law was unshakeable and, besides, he was on the campaign trail again and he was not about to be associated with a fanatic.

2. A SECTIONAL PRESIDENT

After his loss to Stephen Douglas, Lincoln hoped to make yet another try for a Senate seat in 1860 or in 1864. His aspirations, at least in public, went no higher than that. Thus, he reacted with a modest chuckle when Jesse Fell, an old friend, suggested that he run for president. Fell, founder of the Bloomington *Pentagraph* and a skilled Republican politician, had been on a trip to the East where people had repeatedly asked him about Abraham Lincoln, the man who so ably opposed Douglas. In those conversations, he had become convinced that Lincoln could get the Republican nomination in 1860. Other prominent Republicans who were definitely in the race, such as Senator William Seward of New York and Salmon Chase of Ohio, had made too many radical statements, he argued. Lincoln could appeal to the conservative instincts of the people. Lincoln shunted the idea aside, saying that his place was in Illinois running for the Senate.

Yet Lincoln was paying close attention to the Republican Party outside Illinois, writing to other Republicans and influencing Republican politics whenever he could. He wrote to Salmon P. Chase warning him that a plank in the Ohio Republican platform calling for repeal of the Fugitive Slave Law was too radical and would alienate conservative voters. He contacted Republican leaders in other states emphasizing the need to be as inoffensive as possible so the party could stay together in 1860. Lincoln was keeping his name before the party so that he *could* run if conditions looked favorable, while all the time denying that he harbored any presidential ambitions. This is a common political tactic that allows the "candidate" to be available, yet avoid the attacks and close scrutiny that often overwhelm a candidate who commits himself too early.

In the fall of 1859, Lincoln went on several speaking trips outside of Illinois. Before Republican groups in Ohio, Wisconsin and Kansas, he gave his views on Republican policies and made statements that he hoped would help him become acceptable to most Republicans. Typical of his approach was the speech he made in Columbus, Ohio, on September 16th. He emphasized that the party was essentially conservative; it was only trying to return the country to its original position regarding slavery, and it was only opposed to the popular sovereignty doctrine of the Democrats because it led inevitably to the extension of slavery.

The next day, in Cincinnati, he pretended to be speaking to Kentuckians just across the Ohio River and told them that if they wanted the extension of slavery they should vote for Stephen Douglas because that was what he wanted, also. Then he launched an attack on the Southerners' notion of secession. "What will secession gain you?" he asked. "Do you think you can better yourselves on that subject (slavery) by leaving us here under no obligation whatever to return those specimens of your movable property that come hither? You have divided the Union because we do not do right with you, as you think, upon that subject; when we cease to be under obligation to do *anything* for you, how much better off do you think you will be?" (5) In a sense he was espousing Garrison's notion – that disunion would spell the doom of slavery – but, he was pleading for the continuation of the Union rather than the dismembering of it.

In Wisconsin, he spoke at the state fair in Milwaukee. After looking over the hogs, cattle and produce, he spoke to the Agricultural Society and gave them a new, more positive account of Republicanism than they had heard before. Besides *opposing* the spread of slavery, Republicans were *for* free labor and the right of a man to earn his own bread and rise in stature in a capitalist economy. The Republican ideal was a man, similar to Lincoln himself, who began as a penniless worker and rose through his own hard work to a position of wealth in which he employed others. Abe made it sound very doable: "The prudent penniless beginner in the world labors for wages for a while, saves a surplus with which to buy tools or land for himself, then labors on his own account another while, and at length hires another new beginner to help him. This, say its advocates, is free labor — the just, and generous and prosperous system, which opens the way for all, gives hope to all, and energy, and progress and improvement of conditions to all." (6) The contrast between this and a slave labor system was self-evident.

When Abe returned to Illinois in the fall of 1859, he was finally convinced that the presidency was not an unreasonable goal. The crowds in Ohio, Wisconsin and Kansas had been exceptionally warm. Many Republican leaders all over the country (the North, at least) were mentioning him as a "dark horse" candidate.

On December 20th he sent Jesse Fell a short autobiography to be used for campaign purposes. Overjoyed, Fell immediately circulated it among newspapers around the country. Lincoln also told the Illinois Republican Committee that he was a candidate. His purpose in entering the race, he was quick to point out, was to keep his name before the public so he could win that Senate seat in 1864. The Republican leaders in the state were less coy. They had secured Chicago as the site for the Republican National Convention and were making plans to use their "home team" advantage and any political tricks they knew to get Lincoln nominated.

Lincoln was not going to sit on his hands and let others do all the work. In fact, in spite of his Senate talk, he had made the decision to go all out for the presidential nomination. It is easy to imagine him sitting with Mary on New Year's Day, 1860, discussing the possibility of winning the highest office in the land that year. They liked to scheme together, and Mary was thrilled that the goal was so lofty. Abe prepared to make a speaking trip to the East where his name was, as yet, the least known of all the potential candidates.

The Young Men's Central Republican Club of New York City had invited him to address their organization at the Cooper Union Hall. Recognizing that this was his chance to make an impression on Republicans in the home state of his most potent rival, Senator William Seward, Lincoln intended to make the finest speech of his career.

During the wintry days of January he poured over records of the United States Constitutional Convention. He read the proceedings of the early sessions of the United States Congress as recorded in the *Annals of Congress* and the *Congressional Globe* (forerunners of today's *Congressional Record*). He also dug through old newspapers. His purpose was to find detailed *proof* of what he had been saying all along in his debates with Douglas and other speeches. He wanted to be able to prove to a sophisticated New York audience that the Founding Fathers really did intend to confine slavery and really did hope for its eventual demise. When he left for New York in February he was fully armed with strong evidence that the Republican Party was actually very conservative — that it was simply trying to restore public policy to what it had always been, and that it was a party worthy of the allegiance of business-minded men who deplored disruptive social change.

On the night of February 27, 1860, a large crowd of people forsook other entertainments on this unseasonably balmy winter's night to pay twenty-five cents admission into Cooper Union Hall where Abraham Lincoln of Illinois was going to speak. In the *Tribune*, Horace Greeley called the group a gathering of "culture and intellect." And indeed some of the city's most celebrated social figures, businessmen and journalists were in attendance. Abe was escorted to the platform by David Field, a well-known New York lawyer, and William Cullen Bryant, editor of the New York *Post*.

The applause was warm and the audience clearly favorable, but Abe was nervous. His throat felt tight and his legs a bit wobbly. Would the people laugh at this frontiersman's accent? Did his suit look all right, or was it loose fitting and wrinkled as his clothes often were? As he looked over the rows of well-dressed people, he saw many upturned faces, most of them smiling and receptive. They wanted to hear what he had to say. He had heard that some of them were lukewarm toward Seward and were looking for an alternative candidate. Encouraged, he grasped his coat lapel with his powerful right hand and began.

He started shakily, but soon he was effortlessly placing before them the facts he had accumulated in his many hours of research. It was very satisfying to be fully prepared, to go to the core of the issues and build an impregnable argument from known facts. The audience began joining the fun, applauding the telling points and sometimes laughing at the speaker's clever way of making them.

Of the thirty-nine men who signed the Constitution, Abe pointed out, twenty-one specifically showed that they believed it was permissible for Congress to control slavery in the territories. They did it by voting in Congress for the Ordinance of 1787 that outlawed slavery in the Northwest Territories, or by voting for the Missouri Compromise in 1820, or by doing both. Sixteen of the others were noted anti-slavery men who probably would have voted to restrict slavery in the territories if they had ever served in Congress. Thus, it was likely that at the most only two of the Founding Fathers felt that Congress did not have the right to keep slavery out of the territories.

Furthermore, Abe continued, Taney and Douglas claim that the Fifth Amendment (protecting the right of private property) prohibits Congress from outlawing slavery in the territories, but the very same First Congress that passed the Fifth Amendment also passed the legislation providing for the enforcement of the Ordinance of 1787. Certainly those men saw no contradictions in their actions. And so, it is Taney and Douglas, not the Republicans, who are putting forth new ideas that deviate drastically from the wishes of the Founding Fathers.

The founders marked slavery "as an evil not to be extended," he said, and they believed it should be "tolerated and protected only because of and so far as its actual presence among us makes that toleration and protection a necessity." Lincoln emphasized that if the Republican Party was a purely sectional (northern) party, that fact was of the Southerners' own making. They were rejecting the party that was standing for the Union as it had always been. It was not the Republicans' desire to exclude Southerners, and it was not the Republicans' fault that Southerners could not support a truly conservative platform.

Assuring the Republicans before him that their cause was correct, Abe pointed out that while they were doing their best to placate the South, the only way they could truly satisfy Southerners was to call slavery "right," return fugitive slaves with "greedy pleasure," and pull down "free state institutions." The essence of the issue was that Southerners thought slavery was right and Republicans thought it was wrong. Thinking it right, Southerners could not be blamed "for desiring its full recognition as being right." But, he asked, "Thinking it wrong, as we do, can we yield to them?"

The crowd was hanging on every word. This man from the West spoke with such clarity and good sense. Speaking firmly and without distracting arm waving, Abe looked into the faces of his audience, trying to reach each person as an individual. "Let us stand by our duty fearlessly and effectively," he pleaded. ". . . Let us have faith that *right* makes might, and in that faith let us, to the end, dare to do our duty as we understand it." (7)

The crowd rose to its feet as one and applauded in a prolonged ovation. Lincoln smiled and bowed his head slightly toward them as he unconsciously folded his manuscript. Men rushed onto the platform to congratulate him, to shake his hand, and clap him on the back. People milled about talking with Abe and discussing in small groups the magnificent speech and the man who had made it. The next morning, as New Yorkers went about their bustling lives, the name "Lincoln" was on many lips.

His spirits soaring, Abe planned to take the train from New York to New Hampshire where he would visit his son, Robert, who was attending Phillips Exeter Academy. Since Republicans in several of the towns along the route were anxious to have him speak, he prepared to address several more groups while he was in the East. As it happened, such large crowds turned out in New Haven, Hartford, Providence, Manchester, Concord, and several other towns that his trip to see Robert turned into a triumphal political tour of New England.

At each stop he gave a somewhat abbreviated version of his slavery remarks at Cooper Union, but also took a few occasions to emphasize other features of Republicanism. At New Haven, he commented on a shoe workers strike in progress at the time. He noted that it was refreshing to see a system of free labor in New England where workers were not forced to toil under all circumstances or to work whether they were paid or not. He noted that in a free labor society a man could start out poor, work hard, and one day be rich. And then he segued into the slavery issue. If you New Englanders find it too "thick" here, he said, "you may (if Republicans are elected!) have a chance to strike out and go somewhere else, where you may not be degraded, nor have your family corrupted by forced rivalry with Negro slaves." (8) Lincoln the politician was expressing his position on slavery in terms of white self-interest, and the audience loved it.

When he finally returned to Illinois, Lincoln had given up all trace of thinking of his presidential candidacy as a prelude to an 1864 Senate race. He felt he could be the first choice of some delegates to the Chicago convention and that others might turn to him if Seward or Chase failed to win on the first ballot. He began writing letters to men who would be in the various state delegations stating his views and suggesting that he might be an acceptable alternative to one of the leading contenders. He explained his strategy to friend and supporter Samuel Galloway: "Our policy, then, is to give no offense to others — leave them in a mood to come to us if they are compelled to give up their first love." (9)

The strategy was also to promote Lincoln's common man image and generate excitement over the Lincoln candidacy as the Whigs had done with their "log cabin and hard cider" campaign for William Henry Harrison in 1840. There were no presidential primaries in 1860, so potential candidates had to appeal to party leaders from each state who would lead their state delegations to the party's national convention. When the Illinois Republicans met in Decatur on May 9th and 10th, Lincoln waited until the hall was full before he walked in, thus assuring himself a vigorous ovation. Later, John Hanks, Abe's cousin, led a troupe of Lincoln men into the hall carrying two fence rails covered with streamers and a large banner that read "Abraham Lincoln: The Rail Splitter Candidate for President in 1860; Two rails from a lot of 3,000 Made in 1830 by Thomas Hanks and Abe Lincoln — Whose Father Was the First Pioneer of Macon County." Although the rails were surely fake, and although Thomas Lincoln was *not* the first settler in Macon County, the banner was a sensation. Lincoln was thereafter hailed as "The Rail Splitter," a man of humble beginnings who understood the workingman.

Abe's "rail splitter" image and his emphasis on the Republican ideals of free labor and free land for white men in the West were bound to attract some Democratic votes in a general election. The Democratic Party of Andrew Jackson had long been the party of the common man, but if Lincoln were nominated, the Republicans would have a solid platform and the right man to deliver it to the factory worker and the dirt farmer. This would be a signal achievement because the Republicans were mainly ex-Whigs, the so-called party of wealth and privilege.

The Decatur convention was so impressed with Lincoln that it unanimously adopted a resolution instructing its delegates to the National Republican Convention to cast Illinois's twenty-two votes for Abraham Lincoln. The national convention was set to open in Chicago just a week later.

In the 1830's, when Lincoln moved to Springfield, Chicago held barely 4,000 people. Now, in 1860, it was a bustling metropolis of over 110,000 people. Hugging the southern shore of Lake Michigan, it was a center for the farm products of the Midwest and a hub of fifteen railroads. In many ways it was a symbol of the emerging United States, an amalgam of urban and agricultural interests located in the fastest growing section of North America.

The city had built a large convention hall that seated ten thousand people. Called the "Wigwam," it was so hastily constructed that some of the rafters still sported foliage that the workmen had not trimmed. Those beams were to reverberate with the shouts of thousands of Republicans who, in the days before May 16th, were filling the streets of the city, parading up and down with banners proclaiming their favorites. Besides Lincoln, those banners advertised the acknowledged front-runner William Seward, Senator from New York, Salmon P. Chase, Senator from Ohio, an avowed abolitionist, and dark horses Simon Cameron of Pennsylvania, Montgomery Blair of Maryland, and Edward Bates of Missouri. All of these men had their campaign managers in town plotting strategy in their hotel rooms and looking for ways to get enough delegate votes to put their man "over the top." None of the candidates was there personally; it would be unseemly to be actively seeking the honor of the nomination.

Lincoln's manager was rotund David Davis, judge of the eighth Illinois circuit with whom Lincoln had traveled and shared hotel rooms for many years. Davis was so large that it is doubtful they ever shared a bed on the circuit. The judge set up headquarters at the Tremont House and began sending out representatives to the other state delegations to promote Lincoln and, if necessary, make deals.

The other candidates had weaknesses on which Davis could capitalize. Seward, because he had once proclaimed that there was an "irrepressible conflict" between the North and the South, was considered by some to be too radical. Lincoln, in his "House Divided" speech, had said virtually the same thing, but Davis ignored that. Chase, the only other formidable candidate and a man who truly lusted to be president, was considered even more radical than Seward. Thus, Davis was able to put Lincoln forth as the conservative alternative to both of the leading contenders. Furthermore, Abe was the "rail-splitter" candidate, the man who could get the votes of the common man — the man who could bring victory to the party in November.

As the delegates jammed into the Wigwam during the first two days of the convention, Davis moved his wheeling and dealing into high gear. Hardly a delegate got any sleep for two nights as the bargaining went on. Indiana finally agreed to give its votes to Lincoln in return for a promise that their own Caleb B. Smith would be Secretary of the Interior in a Lincoln cabinet. Pennsylvania agreed to vote for Lincoln on the third ballot if Simon Cameron would be guaranteed a cabinet post.

In the midst of all this wrangling, a telegram arrived from Lincoln who was waiting it out in Springfield. The telegram said, very simply, "I authorize no deals and will be bound by none."

Davis tossed the paper aside, said "Lincoln ain't here," and went on bargaining. (10) Lincoln was most likely acting in a fit of conscience or with an eye to history when he sent the message, because no one was more aware than he was of the political realities at nominating conventions. When he later formed his cabinet, Smith and Cameron got their rewards.

The day before the balloting, Davis and his men busily prepared for a manipulation of the crowd in the hall. Besides the usual "Rail Splitter" banners and demonstrations, they concocted an ungentlemanly maneuver to pack the Wigwam with Lincoln supporters. They printed phony convention tickets and distributed them to Lincoln men, some of whom were reputed to be the loudest shouters in the West. They told these men to present their tickets at the Wigwam early so they would be inside taking up seats when supporters of the other candidates arrived.

The ploy worked. While hundreds of Seward and Chase men raged outside, the Wigwam exploded in cheers every time a speaker mention Lincoln's name. On the first ballot, Seward polled 173.5 votes to Lincoln's 102, Cameron's 50.5, Chase's 49 and Bates' 48. No candidate had the majority necessary for the nomination. On the second ballot, Seward gained 11 but Lincoln gained 79 as delegates began switching to their second choice. In succeeding ballots, Lincoln picked up more votes while Seward began to fade. Davis had done his work well. When Lincoln reached 231.5, two short of a majority, Joseph Medill, an Illinois Lincoln man who had gone to sit with the Ohio delegation, whispered to David Cartter, the Ohio chairman, that if some Ohio votes would go to Lincoln, Chase (from Ohio) could have anything he wanted. Recognizing the inevitability of Lincoln's nomination, Cartter immediately rose to change four Ohio votes from Chase to Lincoln, and the Wigwam broke into pandemonium.

For over half an hour the cheering went on for Abe Lincoln, the "Rail Splitter" candidate of the Republican Party.

At the office of *The Sangamo Journal*, Lincoln got the message on the telegraph that the convention had voted to make his nomination unanimous. Elated, he walked through the streets of Springfield to go home and tell Mary the good news. On the way, people clustered about him. At home, he could not have a moment alone with his wife because of all the well-wishers who came by. The town was up all night celebrating the nomination of its "favorite son."

Lincoln's running mate was to be Hannibal Hamlin of Maine, an anti-slavery Senator chosen by the convention to give the ticket geographic balance and to energize the abolitionist vote. Always ready with a witty quip, Abe noted that the choice of Hamlin was destined because the last three letters of Abraham and the first three letters of Lincoln spelled HAMLIN. Besides pointing that out, Abe had no comment on his running mate because he had only a slight idea who Hannibal Hamlin was.

The Republican platform called for admission of Kansas to the Union as a free state, and it denied the right of Congress or a territorial legislature to sanction slavery in a territory. The platform went on to broaden its appeal to people who were unconcerned about slavery. For businessmen it promised a high protective tariff; to farmers and wage earners it promised a homestead law under which people who wished to move west would be given free land if they promised to live on it and farm it. Since this platform offered so much to so many people, Lincoln was confident he could win.

Following the custom for presidential candidates at the time, Abe stayed home in Springfield during the campaign and allowed Republican Party workers to carry the Republican message to the people. They used every technique available to them —

barbeques, parades, rallies in halls festooned with "Rail Splitter" banners — and they tailored their speeches and their literature to suit their audiences. In abolitionist areas such as New England and Ohio, they spoke of the moral wrong of slavery. In factory towns they often played down the slavery issue and spoke instead of the tariff and free land in the west.

Lincoln's election was virtually assured because the Democratic Party was in turmoil and split down the middle. In its April convention in Charleston, South Carolina — hotbed of southern radicalism — the party had imploded over slavery. William Lowndes Yancey, an Alabama secessionist, told Stephen Douglas that his notion of popular sovereignty was offensive to the South because it did not recognize that slavery was morally right. Poor Douglas! During the debates, Lincoln had been harping on him for refusing to call slavery morally *wrong*! By standing for popular sovereignty and ignoring the moral element in the slavery issue, the "Little Giant" was losing support in the North and the South! When he pushed a "popular sovereignty platform" through the convention, Yancey and fellow "fire-eater" Robert Barnwell Rhett led the Southern Democrats from the hall. Douglas was left with a truncated Democratic Party short of the two-thirds majority of the whole needed to nominate him. There was nothing left to do but adjourn and try again in Baltimore six weeks later.

But in June, when the Democrats met in Baltimore, they were still unable to unite behind a candidate. The party split. The Northern Democrats nominated Douglas on a popular sovereignty platform; the Southerners bolted and nominated their own candidate, John C. Breckinridge of Kentucky on a platform asserting the absolute right of Southerners to bring their slave "property" into the territories. With two candidates splitting the Democratic vote, the prospects for the party carrying very many states were grim indeed.

Further complicating matters, another candidate was in the field. Meeting in Philadelphia, a group of men mostly from border states met to form the "Constitutional Union Party" — a party that took no stand on the slavery question and proposed to rally support for simple enforcement of the laws and the United States Constitution. Obsessed with fear that the South would leave the Union and a civil war would erupt, these men hoped to poll enough votes to show there was strong Union sentiment around the country. Their candidate was John Bell of Tennessee. He and his followers were soon to discover that people in the North and South had become too agitated over the slavery issue to vote for a man who ignored it.

Despite the break-up of his party, Stephen Douglas still believed he could win if he could make Northerners see that popular sovereignty would give them what they wanted without antagonizing any but the most extreme Southerners. He was helped by word coming from the South that a Republican victory would be interpreted to mean that the North had decided to dominate the country and the South, to protect its way of life, would have to secede. Ignoring custom, Douglas campaigned in every corner of the Union. He even carried his campaign into the South, telling Southerners they would have a better chance of protecting their way of life with him rather than with secession. But, he was fighting a losing battle. Northerners saw too much advantage in voting Republican; Southerners had to express their pro-slavery sentiments by voting for Breckinridge.

On election night, November 6, 1860, Abe waited for the returns at the telegraph office in Springfield. Late at night the totals started to show a trend: Lincoln was carrying almost all of the free states and would collect enough electoral votes to win the election. Friends crowded around Abe, and with each encouraging ticker tape the pandemonium in the office grew louder.

Finally, the throngs spilled out into the streets and the town of Springfield began another long night of celebration.

The final results showed Lincoln with 1,866,452 votes to Douglas's 1,376,957, Breckinridge's 849,781 and Bell's 588,879. Lincoln had received less than forty percent of the popular vote and had not tallied a single vote in ten slave states. Nevertheless, in the electoral vote count — the only one that mattered — Lincoln won all of the northern states except New Jersey and had an electoral majority of 173 to 72 for Breckinridge (who won all the deep southern states), 39 for Bell (who won four border states), and 12 for Douglas. Douglas's scattered appeal over the entire country won him many popular votes, but the electoral votes of only Missouri and part of New Jersey.

Abe's victory was exciting and gratifying. He had risen from a log cabin birth and a hardscrabble upbringing; he had suffered nothing but political defeat in the last ten years. However, it was a bittersweet victory because it was purely sectional — purely northern. The nation and president-elect Abraham Lincoln waited anxiously to see what that would mean.

3. THE SHADOW OF WAR

As the presidential election of 1860 unfolded, William Lloyd Garrison's views of the Republican Party remained mostly unfavorable. Indeed, in some of his statements and resolutions he was more contemptuous than ever. Yet, he continued to leaven his criticisms of the party with comments allowing that Republicans were on the right track and that their numbers were hopeful signs.

At the Massachusetts Anti-Slavery Society meeting in 1859, Garrison called the Republican Party "time serving" and "cowardly," and charged that it never professed to be truly anti-slavery. He told his abolitionist friends to give credit where credit was due — to praise Republicans for holding fast to their opposition to the extension of slavery. But, he continued, the Republican Party's "awful guilt, consists in giving its consent and support to the existence of slavery in fifteen states of the Union under the constitutional pro-slavery compromises." He hoped for better things in the future: "(The party will) I trust, take a much higher position and give, at last, a firm support to the only rational, consistent, and victorious doctrine in the conflict with the demon of slavery — No union with slaveholders. . . !" (11)

The following year, when the Massachusetts abolitionists gathered again, he lashed out at the Republicans in less charitable language: "O, was there ever a party so lacking in self-respect, true courage and moral consistency, as the Republican Party? — knowing, as it does, that at the last presidential election no man could express his preference at the South for Fremont without being compelled . . . to flee to the North to save his life — yet still shouting 'Our glorious Union forever!' Was ever fatuity like this?" (12)

In May of 1860, as Lincoln was receiving the unanimous support of the Illinois Republicans, Garrison was warning abolitionists at the American Anti-Slavery Society meeting in New York not to lower their anti-slavery standards and to avoid all compromisers such as those in the Republican Party. In a long, powerful speech, he fired his strongest anti-Republican salvo ever concluding, in stark disagreement with the majority of Americans, that *union* with the South rather than disunion would result in violence:

I see no hope for the peaceful emancipation of the slave in our country while the North is willing to carry out . . . slave- holding guarantees and compromises – none whatever. I see nothing before us but fire and blood while the North is resolved to remain in connection with the South. (13)

As part of his critical view of Republicans, Garrison had a clear perception of his relationship as a radical agitator to them and the process that was at work between himself and the party. At the annual Fourth of July picnic, he told his followers: "Our mission is to regenerate public opinion. . . . We are for the honest, fearless, impartial proclamation of God's everlasting truth to the consciences of men — to parties and sects — to constitutions and laws — as we find them — never yielding one jot or tittle, though glad to observe the slightest signs of progress in any direction." (14)

Candidly, Lloyd had to admit that the growth of the Republican Party was more than a slight sign of progress. In *The Liberator* in January of 1860 he almost said as much when he wrote, "Though the end is not yet, surely it cannot be far distant — for the battle waxes to the gate, and all the signs of the times are indicating a great revolution is at hand." (15) In spite of what he might say in his darker moments, Lloyd recognized that slavery would have to be jeopardized by the unity the North was achieving under the Republican Party against the slave power.

Prior to the November election, Garrison had very little to say about Abraham Lincoln. The Cooper Union speech, while a sensation in Republican circles, went unnoticed in *The Liberator*. After the Republican convention, Garrison continued to say very little about "The Rail Splitter," except to note sadly, after examining the candidate's record and a few speeches, that Lincoln would probably do little to offend the South.

When Lincoln won the election, however, Garrison sprang to life. He was pleased with the number of northern votes cast for a candidate who opposed slavery's extension, but he was *elated* with the South's reaction to Lincoln. Southerners scream and rant and rave as if Lincoln were another John Brown, he thought, which appears truly ridiculous when one considers Lincoln's conservative position on "every critical issue." (16)

The South's reaction proved to be more than just talk. For several years they had threatened to leave the Union if a Republican were ever elected president, and many of them were ready to act. In December the leaders of South Carolina met in convention at Charleston and voted to secede from the Union. By early February, 1861, Mississippi, Florida, Georgia, Alabama, Louisiana and Texas had also seceded. Representatives from those states met in Montgomery, Alabama, to organize "The Confederate States of America," write their own constitution guaranteeing slavery, and choose Jefferson Davis of Mississippi as their first president.

The men at Montgomery explained their bold revolution. It was absolutely necessary, they said. Lincoln's election showed that power in the national government had passed permanently into the hands of the North — a North hostile to southern interests. Policies favoring northern business and harmful to southern agriculture were inevitable; restrictions on slavery would be imposed; eventually Lincoln, or some future Republican president, would abolish slavery altogether. Before any of these disasters happened, the South needed to leave the Union, form its own confederacy and control its own destiny. We will succeed, the leaders believed, because the North lacks the will to bring us back. And even if the North fights, southern boys, experienced at outdoor life and hunting, could lick ten times their number of soft, citified northern boys. Yes, the Union was dissolved forever!

Garrison was ecstatic! Shortly before the election he had asked in sardonic fashion, if Lincoln were elected would "the South be so obliging as to secede from the Union?" He had doubted it. "Perhaps they will," he had written, "Probably they will not! By their bullying and raving, they have many times frightened the North into a base submission to their demands — and they expect to do it again!" But, now the deed was actually done. "At last the covenant with death is annulled and the agreement with hell broken," he gloated. (17)

As it had done so often before, the South was doing for Garrison what he could not do for himself or his cause. He had been unable to convince the North to break up the Union . . . but now the *South* was doing it! The North is *free*, he told his readers, and the South has the responsibility on its own head. In that case, "She cannot long uphold her tottering slave system — speedy emancipation will follow. " (18)

Garrison's one fear was that the North, in a panic, would compromise with the South to hold the Union together. In January, 1861, he was ill and unable to attend the annual meeting of the Massachusetts Anti-Slavery Society, but he heard that non-abolitionists crowded into the hall and disrupted the proceedings by cheering for the South. All over the North, some people were making efforts to show the South they had good will toward her and had no intention of abolishing slavery. One good way to do this was to hound the abolitionists. Mob violence against abolitionists became almost as fashionable as it had been in 1835 and 1850.

For a while, Lloyd felt it was wise to leave Boston lest he be murdered by some misguided individual who thought he could save the Union by killing the primary symbol of abolitionism. Wendell Phillips, unencumbered by pacifist principles as Garrison was, stayed in town but began carrying a loaded revolver under his coat as he walked Boston's streets.

In Washington, desperate politicians tried to cobble together some sort of compromise that would pull the country back together. While James Buchanan sat in the White House waiting anxiously for March 4th when he could hand the problem over to the newly elected Abraham Lincoln, congressmen — particularly those from Border States — feverishly concocted Union-saving plans. Senator John J. Crittenden of Kentucky, heir to Henry Clay's mantel as "Great Compromiser," drew up the proposal that was most seriously considered. Among other things, it called for a constitutional amendment guaranteeing slavery forever and re-established the 36-30 line all the way to the Pacific Ocean as the boundary line between slave territory and free. Congressmen from slave states that had not yet left the Union thought the plan might be workable and believed they might use it to entice the representatives from the seven seceding states back into the Union. Everything depended on whether the Republicans and, most importantly, president-elect Lincoln, agreed to it.

"All Union-saving efforts are simply idiotic!" Garrison proclaimed in *The Liberator*. (19) He was greatly annoyed at the pandering to the South by some people in northern states and some politicians in Washington. Even some Republicans, such as Senator Seward, Garrison noted with dismay, were ready to compromise. All they needed was affirmation from the man in Illinois. How would Lincoln react to the crisis? Garrison feared the worst.

In Springfield, Lincoln — besieged every day by well-wishers and office-seekers — watched the developing crisis closely. At first he did not believe secession would actually occur; too many Southerners loved the Union for that to happen, he thought. He wrote letters to Unionists in all the southern states offering encouragement and reminding them that his policy was simply non-extension of slavery, nothing more. "Do the people of the South really entertain fears that a Republican administration would, directly or indirectly, interfere with the slaves, or with them about the slaves?" he asked Alexander Stephens, an old Whig friend from Georgia. "If they do, I wish to assure you, as once a friend, and still, I hope, not an enemy, that there is no cause for such fears. The South would be in no more danger in this respect than it was in the days of Washington," he assured his Union-loving friend. (20)

When secession became a reality in December and January, Lincoln decided on a two-part policy. First of all, he would make no public statement until he took office. Anything he might say would be misconstrued by men ready to read into his words what they wanted to hear. His positions on the issues facing the country were well known and could be found in any of his earlier speeches. Secondly, he would privately advise Republican congressmen that he would accept guarantees of slavery where it already existed — including the Fugitive Slave Law and the interstate slave trade — but he would oppose any measure that would allow slavery to expand. Containment of slavery was the Republican Platform on which he had been elected, and he would stand by it.

He wrote to Senator Trumbull of Illinois: "Let there be no compromise on the question of extending slavery. If there be, all our labor is lost and, ere long, must be done again. . . . Have none of it. Stand firm. The tug has to come, and better now than any time hereafter." (21) Later, he wrote to his old friend Congressman Elihu Washburne, "Whether it be a Missouri line or . . . popular sovereignty, it is all the same. Let either be done, and immediately (the extension of) slavery commences. On that point stand firm, as with a chain of steel." (22)

To Republican congressmen in Washington the message was clear. Most of them stood against Crittenden's plan, and all attempts at compromise failed. Frantic Northerners wrote to Lincoln begging him to make some sort of conciliatory remarks to the South — to say something that would bring the seven seceding states back into the Union. But Lincoln would say no more than he already had. From Springfield came only silence, and rumors that the new president was growing a beard.

As had become his habit, Abe was focusing on what he saw as the core of the issue. Southerners thought slavery was right and ought to be extended; he thought it was wrong and ought to be contained. That was the basic conflict. He was the president-elect, fairly chosen on a platform clearly stating his views for the voters. As such, he had the right — indeed the obligation to those who voted for him — to take office without changing or diluting his position.

Thus, on February 11th when he bade farewell to the people of Springfield and began the long trip by rail to Washington, the Union was still divided. Jefferson Davis was setting up his Confederate Government in Montgomery; Alexander Stephens, Abe's Unionist friend from Georgia, was the new vice-president; those slave states that had not already left the Union were considering whether or not to join the Confederate States of America.

On the way to Washington, Lincoln stopped at several cities across the North to speak to crowds that had turned out to see the new president. His remarks were non-committal and, to the South, totally unsatisfactory. He repeated his intention to enforce the Fugitive Slave Law and protect slavery where it existed; he expressed confidence that once he had taken office and had proven to Southerners that he meant no harm to their way of life, they would happily rejoin the Union. He expressed the importance of the Union and the need to keep it together; he seemed confident that it *would be* kept together without force.

In Philadelphia, Detective Alan Pinkerton told him there was a group of secessionists in Baltimore plotting his assassination. Traveling through the city in daylight and on schedule would be extremely dangerous. At first Abe was not inclined to change his plans. His policy was to carry on as the newly elected president as if nothing were wrong. He did not think it would create a good impression if he slithered into the city under cover of darkness. But finally his advisors convinced him that assassination was a real possibility in pro-slavery Baltimore, and that he should take a late-night train to get him through the city earlier than expected.

The decision was probably a wise one even though the image of the president sneaking into the capital was ridiculed in the press during the next several days. In Baltimore, the railroads were so poorly organized that the trains to Washington had to be taken off the tracks and drawn slowly through the streets by horses to another set of tracks. The city was full of violent, pro-slavery, anti-Lincoln men who could easily have mobbed the presidential car on the streets and killed Lincoln. Whether a plot to do so actually existed has never been determined. Lincoln went through Baltimore at 3:30 A.M., his car observed only by a few staggering drunks, one of whom sang "Dixie" in a slushy voice.

When Lincoln arrived in Washington at 6:00 A.M., he was met only by Congressman Washburne and a few others. The need for such cloak and dagger activity depressed Abe but, secession notwithstanding, he was determined to take office and begin administering the government and executing the laws just as all other presidents had.

On March 4th throngs of people crowded Washington. Some of those who lined Pennsylvania Avenue or gathered around the Capitol Building were hoping that Lincoln would be violently prevented from taking office. General Winfield Scott, hero of the Mexican War and now U.S. Army Commander, had ordered sharpshooters stationed on rooftops along the presidential route. The president-elect rode with retiring president James Buchanan in an open carriage past the crowds en route to the Capitol. Mounted soldiers clopped about on the cobblestones keeping the crowds in line and watching for assassins. Lincoln removed his stovepipe hat to acknowledge cheers and stoically ignored hateful stares.

At noon, heavy clouds moved slowly overhead as Lincoln walked out onto the special platform erected on the Capitol steps. Behind him rose the half-finished Capitol dome surrounded by scaffolding. In the midst of its construction, it stood as a symbol of the truncated Union. The crowd of ten thousand, gathered below the platform, cheered as Lincoln took his seat and Senator Baker of Oregon stepped forward to introduce the president-elect. When Baker finished, the crowd cheered again as Lincoln stepped to the podium, adjusted his spectacles, and waited for silence. When the noise had dwindled to a few voices in the rear, he began.

Almost immediately he assured the South, as he had so many times, of his moderation. "I have no purpose directly or indirectly to interfere with the institution of slavery in the states where it exists. I believe I have no lawful right to do so, and I have no inclination to do so." Going even further, he referred to the constitutional amendment passed in Congress with Republican support a few days before that guaranteed slavery in the states forever. He promised to support this proposed 13th Amendment right through to its ratification by the states. He believed such a guarantee was implied by the Constitution anyway, and he had no objection to "its being made express and irrevocable."

Then he went on to make clear what he would do as president in the days and weeks ahead. He would enforce the laws. "I shall take care, as the Constitution expressly enjoins upon me, that the laws of the Union be faithfully executed in all the states." He would do this only in so far as it could be done without violence, hoping the South would realize its happiest place was in the Union and would re-submit to federal authority.

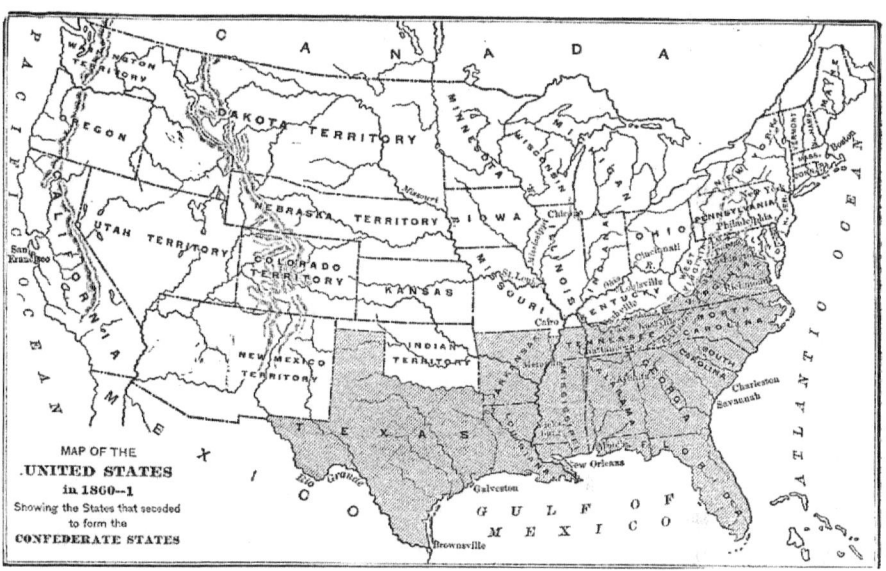

Seceeding states (Confederate States of America) in gray

Having implored Southerners to recognize his kindly disposition toward them, and having insisted that he would enforce the laws but with patience and forbearance, he knew not what else he could say. He simply issued a pledge that if there were to be a war over secession, the South would be the one to start it: "In your hands, my dissatisfied fellow countrymen, and not *mine*, is the momentous issue of civil war. The government will not assail *you*. You can have no conflict without being *yourselves* the aggressors. *You* have no oath registered in heaven to destroy the government, while I shall have the most solemn one to preserve, protect and defend it."

"I am loath to close," he went on in a final attempt at good will. "We are not enemies but friends. We must not be enemies. Though passion may have strained, it must not break our bonds of affection. The mystic chords of harmony, stretching from every battlefield and patriot grave, to every heart and every hearth stone, all over this broad land will yet swell the chorus of Union, when again touched, as surely they will be, by the better angels of our nature." (23)

The leaders of the Confederate States of America read this speech, rejected it, and went right on establishing their new country. Lincoln's words were friendly, perhaps, but his intentions were evil. They were glad to be rid of him. Once again they called on their sister slave states in the border regions to join them.

Upon reading the speech and the South's reaction to it, William Lloyd Garrison breathed a sigh of relief. In *The Liberator* he praised Lincoln's strong stand against the Confederacy. Then he denounced Lincoln's support of the proposed thirteenth amendment and his promise to return fugitive slaves. "He promises to give slavery more guarantees than it has ever had before," Garrison said in wonder, and yet he is the man "whose election causes seven of the slaveholding states to revolt, and in hot haste withdraw from the Union! Surely they must be desperately hard to conciliate!" (24) He hoped they would remain hard to conciliate, and that the other slave states would join them. Then "NO UNION WITH SLAVEHOLDERS! would be a reality – brought about, ironically, *by the slave owners themselves* — and the end of slavery would be at hand.

4. WAR AND THE PACIFIST ABOLITIONIST

When the seven seceding states left the Union, their state militias seized all symbols of the authority of the United States Government. Armed young men, brashly waving their state flags, forced federal officials to turn over post offices, arsenals and fortifications. By the time Lincoln took office, the Confederacy had control of all the Union installations except two forts: Pickens, in Pensacola, Florida, and Sumter in Charleston Harbor, South Carolina. In his inaugural address Lincoln had said that, in accord with his constitutional duty, he would maintain federal authority existing in the South. Thus, in the first weeks of his administration the country waited to see what he would do to keep Forts Pickens and Sumter from falling into rebel hands.

Lincoln did not have the luxury of time. The day after his inauguration he received word from Robert Anderson, Commander at Fort Sumter, that since the Confederates regarded his force as a foreign invasion of the sovereign state of South Carolina, they were refusing him the right to purchase supplies in Charleston. This meant that he could hold the fort only six more weeks; after that he would have to be re-supplied or starved out.

Aware that the supply ship "Star of the West," which Buchanan had sent to Sumter in January, had been fired upon by Confederate shore guns and forced to turn back, Lincoln knew that attempts to provision the fort might mean war. However, failure to provision it would mean surrender to the Confederacy. With

April 15th fixed firmly in his mind as the day by which he had to get food to Anderson, Lincoln struggled to find a policy. Foremost in his thinking was the need to maintain federal control of Sumter. But, he also had to consider those slave states — eight of them — that had not yet seceded. They were watching what he would do and would likely secede if he used force against South Carolina. His hope was that if it had to come to arms, he could force the Confederates to fire the first shot.

Time passed, and it seemed to the country that Lincoln was befuddled, that he had no idea what to do and was drifting aimlessly. There was very little truth to that. His policy, for the moment, was to wait. He was employing a strategy he had learned as a lawyer: take time to gather all the facts, wait until the last minute when all the facets of the problem are as clear as they are ever going to be and your opponents have had a chance to commit themselves, and *then* act.

He sent observers to South Carolina to check out the situation. They reported that the harbor was ringed with guns and the fort was almost impossible to re-enforce peacefully. He talked with a Unionist named John Baldwin from Virginia, the most important slave state still in the Union, and asked if Virginia would remain loyal to the United States if he gave up Fort Sumter. Baldwin could not promise anything.

The damp, cold days of March slogged on. Abe stood at the windows of the Executive Mansion, looked out across the Potomac River into Virginia, and wondered what to do. He comforted himself with the thought that, for the moment, waiting was good strategy. Give the "Union men," many of whom were old friends of his, time to convince the hotheads to calm down and draw back from drastic action.

On April 1st William Seward, whom Lincoln had appointed secretary of state, decided to take matters into his own hands. He felt that Lincoln was a bumbling fool who had somehow managed to steal the Republican nomination from him. Now, as a member of the cabinet, he, William Seward, would take charge of the administration and tell the inept president what to do. He sent Lincoln a note entitled "Some Thoughts For the President's Consideration" in which he outlined his plan to save the Union: Evacuate Fort Sumter to show good will toward the South, and then engage the country in a war against England or France or both. The South would then reunite with the North in the face of the common danger. Whatever the policy, Seward concluded, it must be carried out vigorously and decisively either by the president or by some member of his cabinet. In effect, Seward was asking Lincoln to become a figurehead and turn the direction of the government over to the secretary of state.

Abe was amazed at the note. In a less tense situation he might have considered it a good April Fool's Day joke. Clearly Seward was not thinking clearly under the strain; he could not stand the suspense of waiting for the proper moment before making a move. But Abe could not allow the challenge to go unanswered, nor could he afford to lose a good man such as Seward from his group of advisors. He wrote back to the secretary of state that the policy, as announced in the inaugural address, was to hold all federal property, that Seward had agreed with that policy, and that it would be maintained. He did not mention Seward's plan for a foreign war and concluded that *he* would run the government with advice from *all* the cabinet members.

Lincoln told no one about the secretary of state's message and left it to Seward to accept his proper role in the cabinet. Seward did. Because of Lincoln's note back to him, and because of what he observed as he watched the man, Seward began to see that Lincoln was a man in charge who only appeared indecisive because he had the strength to wait. Two months later he wrote to his wife, "Executive force and vigor are rare qualities. The President is the best of us." (25) Part of Abe Lincoln's greatness was his ability to have men such as Seward in his cabinet, make full use of their talents, and yet remain in control.

Determined not to fire the first shot of a civil war, yet also determined not to back down, Lincoln ordered ships readied to sail to Charleston Harbor loaded only with "food for hungry men." He sent a messenger to Governor Pickens of South Carolina to inform him that Sumter would receive provisions only and that no attempt would be made to re-enforce the fort unless it was attacked. On April 9th the relief expedition left New York to sail to Charleston, and Lincoln waited.

Governor Pickens, in constant contact with Jefferson Davis in Montgomery, decided that Sumter must not be provisioned. That would mean the continued presence of a "foreign fort" in the territorial waters of the Confederate States of America — a situation not to be tolerated. Pickens ordered General Beauregard, the commander of the Confederate garrison at Charleston, to demand Anderson's surrender. Anderson told Beauregard's messengers that he could not honorably surrender, but in just a few days he would be starved out. Beauregard replied that Anderson must set an exact date for his evacuation; Anderson sent word that it would be April 15th, unless he received supplies or orders to hold on from Washington. Pickens and Jefferson Davis, aware that supply ships were on their way, could not abide Anderson's conditional promise. They ordered Beauregard to open fire with his shore batteries.

Early on the morning of April 12th the men inside Fort Sumter saw a red ball of fire arc overhead from the shore and explode. Although it had the appearance of a Fourth of July firework, it was followed almost immediately by a full-scale artillery bombardment. Cannons flashed all along the waterfront; shells exploded in the fort sending showers of dirt and bricks into the air. Anderson's men fired back, grimly determined to uphold their honor. At the entrance to the harbor, the men on the unarmed relief ships that had just arrived watched helplessly. All day and into the night, the shooting continued. Smoke filled the fort and fires broke out everywhere.

Finally, after two days of bombardment, Anderson surrendered on April 14th. His grimy company of ninety men lowered the battle torn American flag and boarded one of the supply ships to sail in defeat to New York. Cannon boomed for several hours as Charleston celebrated its great hour of victory. Ironically, only one man died in the first battle of what was to become the bloodiest war of the 19th century.

When news of Sumter's fall reached the Executive Mansion, Lincoln knew what he had to do. The Confederates were now in armed rebellion against the United States Government. As president, he had to use the military power of the government to put the rebellion down. After an emergency cabinet meeting, he issued a call to the nation for seventy-five thousand military volunteers and summoned all citizens loyal to the government to "suppress (the rebellion), and to cause the laws to be duly executed." (26) It was significant at this moment that he considered the rebellion an act of individual people, not states. For Abraham Lincoln, the Confederate States of America, in a legal sense, did not exist. He maintained that concept through the war and into its aftermath.

In Virginia, Lincoln's call was greeted with anger and dismay. A state convention, which had been meeting in Richmond for weeks trying to decide on a course of action, voted to secede from the Union. Men at the convention saw Lincoln as the aggressor at Fort Sumter; they were not about to join his war against their sister slave states. Preparations began to move the Confederate capital from Montgomery to Richmond as a symbol of Virginia's solidarity with the Confederate States of America. During the next few weeks North Carolina, Tennessee, and Arkansas followed Virginia out of the Union. By June, eleven states were sending their representatives to the Confederate Congress in Richmond while their congressional seats in Washington sat empty.

Missouri, Kentucky, and Maryland, all slave states, wavered. In all three, men marched south to fight for the Confederacy, and men marched north to answer Lincoln's call to save the Union. Secessionists in each state threatened to take their states out of the Union violently; Union men in each threatened to be just as violent to keep their states in. Armed men in Baltimore mobbed a train during the dangerous trek across town and shot several soldiers of the Massachusetts Sixth Regiment, which was on its way to defend Washington. In St. Louis, riots erupted as Union and Confederate sympathizers battled over supplies and ammunition. In Louisville, Kentucky, Unionists marched up one side of Main Street exchanging angry looks and curses with secessionists marching down the other side.

If these border states left the Union, invasion of the South would be much more difficult for Union armies, among other problems, so Lincoln watched events there closely. He was particularly concerned lest he offend the sensibilities of men who were willing to stay with the Union as long as they were left alone to manage their own affairs — such as owning slaves! To avoid incidents, Lincoln ordered troops coming to Washington to avoid Baltimore for the time being. He established recruiting headquarters for Kentucky in Cincinnati, Ohio — just across the river from Kentucky, but discreetly off the "blue grass."

In contrast to the border region, almost all the people in the northern states responded to Lincoln's call for troops with supercharged patriotism. State legislatures and town councils from Iowa to Massachusetts passed resolutions of support for the president. Men rushed to enlist, and soon the railroads were hard pressed to carry all the volunteers to Washington and other rallying points in the North.

By June, Washington was an armed camp. All along the Potomac, men and boys from every northern state lived in tents and waited for the order to march south and defeat the rebels. Soldiers guarded the bridges connecting the capital with Virginia and stood lookout on the hills around Washington where they could see the Confederate soldiers in Virginia preparing for war. Most of the Union soldiers had enlisted with visions of flags and glory filling their heads. War was going to be a great adventure! More than a few, however, must have had sobering thoughts as they fired musket balls through dummies in practice and watched the shredded straw fly out of large holes.

Lincoln, along with Secretary of War, Simon Cameron, and Army Chief of Staff, Winfield Scott, organized the army and ordered military supplies from northern manufacturers and Europe. Lincoln instituted a naval blockade of all the southern ports to prevent the largely agricultural Confederacy from getting arms and supplies from foreign sources. Because the Union outnumbered the Confederacy three-to- one in men and nearly monopolized all the railroads and manufacturing capacity in the country, Lincoln was sure the Union cause would prevail in a long war. But, he hoped the conflict would be short and decisive, that a quick march on Richmond by the Union forces would capture the Confederate capital and snuff out southern will.

To the surprise of many, Lincoln received staunch support in his war to save the Union from William Lloyd Garrison. Immediately after the Confederate attack on Fort Sumter, Garrison began calling on his followers to support the government. He even postponed the annual meeting of the American Anti-Slavery Society so that nothing would divert attention or energy away from the Union war effort. People at the time — and historians later — were confused, unable to comprehend how a man who had been urging disunion for so many years and was a confirmed pacifist could suddenly support a war to reunite the South with the North. There had been no mention of emancipation of the slaves in Lincoln's call for volunteers to put down the rebellion.

The explanation for Garrison's behavior was simple, if a bit tortured. He believed that even if this war fever was a great departure from his principles, it was impossible for a man who had been fighting to destroy slavery for over thirty years not to back a great undertaking that had a good chance of quickly achieving his life-long goal. Furthermore, he could explain how supporting the war was not inconsistent with his former positions. He had always believed that *abolitionist* disunion was right, and *southern* disunion was wrong. The revolutionary right to secede belonged only to those with a moral right to do so. While the North had always had a monumental reason to secede — the fact that its connection with the Union involved it in the terrible guilt of slavery — the South had none. Legally, the South's property was protected by the Constitution and by the new president, who had repeated many times his intention to preserve Southerners' property in slaves. Thus, the South had no moral or legal reason to secede. The Declaration of Independence, Garrison reminded his readers, proclaimed that men had the right to revolt and form a new government whenever their present government became destructive of their right to life, liberty and the pursuit of happiness. In what way could the South claim that this right had been violated by the Union?

Because the Union was now free of the slave interests, Garrison now felt he could support it. (He chose to ignore the continued presence in the Union of the slave states Maryland,

Delaware, Kentucky and Missouri.) In a speech at the Cooper Institute eight months after the war began, he was asked why he now supported the Constitution. He drew laughter and applause when he responded: "Well, ladies and gentlemen, you remember what *Benedict* in the play says: 'When I said I would die a bachelor, I did not think I should live till I were married.' And when I said I would not sustain the Constitution because it was a covenant with death and an agreement with hell, *I had no idea that I would live to see death and hell secede.* Hence it is that I am now with the government, to enable it to constitutionally stop the further ravages of death, and to extinguish the flames of hell forever." (27)

Perhaps the most important reason for Garrison's support of the government, however, was not any philosophical argument — which can always be skewed to suit any purpose — but rather the scent of victory. He was overwhelmed by the enthusiasm in the North for a war against the southern slaveocracy. It warmed his soul to see his neighbors in Boston, who had always spoken highly of the Christian slave owners and had even mobbed abolitionists on the streets a few months earlier, suddenly turning on the Southerners and calling them the "meanest of scoundrels and the vilest of robbers." In *The Liberator,* when he called off the American Anti-Slavery Society meeting he wrote: "Let nothing be done at this solemn crisis, needlessly to check or divert the mighty current of popular feeling which is now sweeping southward with the strength and impetuosity of a thousand Niagaras, in direct conflict with the haughty and perfidious slave power which has so long ruled the republic with a rod of iron for its own base and satanic purposes." (28) All the abolitionists needed to do, he assured his friends, was stand aside and let the superior might of the North crush the slave power.

Some of Lloyd's fellow abolitionists had misgivings. They noted that Lincoln was not making it a war against slavery; he had called for volunteers to put down the southern rebellion, presumably with slavery intact. At the Anti-Slavery picnic on July 4, 1861, Stephen Foster, a hot-headed abolitionist who had a reputation for being even more radical than Garrison, offered a resolution opposing abolitionist support of the government which would not place itself openly and unequivocally on the side of freedom.

Garrison rose to answer Foster. In the same place where he had burned the United States Constitution seven years before, he spoke in support of the United States Government and the president. The flag (which now hung prominently and right-side-up on the platform) no longer symbolized the old state of things, he said. Since it was now "trampled upon by the dealers in human flesh," it looked handsome in his eyes! Lincoln, who was perhaps not as fervently anti-slavery as abolitionists might like, was not to be criticized as long as he made himself an outlaw south of the Mason-Dixon Line in company with William Lloyd Garrison! The government could not have the success it was seeking in the struggle, Garrison concluded, unless it freed the slaves. Indeed, the war would be idiotic if it did not end with the total elimination of its major cause — slavery. While Lincoln had not yet announced that he would free the slaves, Garrison urged patience. If the government conquered the South and returned to the old constitution with its pro-slavery compromises, *then* he would condemn it. (29)

The society overwhelmingly rejected Foster's resolution. In July of 1861, the Garrisonian abolitionists went on record in firm support of the Union war effort. Garrison, like Lincoln, hoped and believed the war would be short and bloodless. As a pacifist, he had always prayed slavery would end non-violently; as a pacifist, it was indeed difficult for him to support a war. But, repeating a theme he had stressed before, he said: "If (my peace principles) had long since been embraced and carried out by the people, neither slavery nor war would now be filling the land with violence and blood." Since the majority of the people were now resorting to arms to resolve their differences, he could only stand back and support the side fighting for justice. In *The Liberator* of June 14, 1861, he had written: "I thank God when men who believe in the right and duty of wielding carnal weapons, are so advanced that they will take those weapons out of the scale of despotism and throw them into the scale of freedom." (30)

During the next year, the "weapons in the scale of freedom" were to be almost inadequate. Moreover, Garrison was going to have doubts whether Abraham Lincoln had placed them in the "scale of freedom" after all.

CHAPTER EIGHT

Slavery and the Tactics of War

1861-1862

Abolitionists were dismayed that Lincoln did not free the slaves when the civil war began. But Lincoln had several reasons for delaying such a radical action: He knew the Border States were crucial to the Union war effort, so he abstained from an emancipation policy to avoid driving those slave states into the arms of the Confederacy; he was reluctant to seize private property in defiance of the Constitution; he had grave doubts that four million newly freed African-Americans would survive in a white society that held strong prejudices against them. So, Lincoln waited and Garrison and his allies fretted.

1. HOLDING THE BORDER STATES

The Union Army assembling in Washington in the spring and early summer of 1861 was a motley group of raw recruits, some of whom had never fired a gun. General Irwin McDowell was doing his best to equip and train them, marching them up and down within sight of the Executive Mansion, but he knew he had a long way to go before they would be worthy of the name

"Army of the Potomac." Time was running short, however, since the three-month enlistments of most of the men would be over at the end of July. All over the North, impatient newspaper editorials called for the army to take action and put down the rebels. The cry on many lips was, "On to Richmond!"

Bowing to expediency, and anxious himself to get started, Lincoln ordered the army to advance toward Manassas Junction where the Confederate Army was stationed. On the morning of July sixteenth, General McDowell led thirty-five thousand raw troops out of Washington. The men marched in ragged formation, and because they were in poor physical condition and had to stop for rest frequently on the hot, dusty roads, they made slow time. It was not until late in the day on Saturday, the twentieth, that they made contact with the enemy near the sluggish creek called Bull Run. Early on the morning of the twenty-first, the Union troops moved to engage the forces of the Confederate States of America.

Word of the impending fight got back to Washington. On that Sunday morning dozens of people, including several members of Congress and scores of newspaper reporters were with the Union troops hoping to see them whip the upstart rebels. Men and ladies in carriages brought picnic lunches with them to enjoy while they watched the young men from each side kill each other.

In the initial fighting the Federal troops seemed to be on the attack and the rebels retreated on several fronts. The spectators, watching through binoculars at a safe distance, sent news back to Washington that everything was going well and that a great victory was in the making. President Lincoln went for his usual afternoon carriage ride calm in the belief that the rebels were being routed. When he returned to the White House, however, he was confronted with the news that is the nightmare of all commanders-in-chief. The tide of battle had turned. The Union soldiers had begun retreating in panic, refusing to take new positions and face the advancing Southerners. The spectators had joined the retreat, and in fact had caused a traffic jam on the road back to Washington. Men, women, horses and carriages were scurrying in disarray, leaving discarded muskets and picnic baskets in their wake. Terrified men were rushing into the White House to warn that the city itself was in danger.

During the next day, as a drizzly rain fell, exhausted and frightened men staggered into the city. Through windows streaked with rivulets of water, President Lincoln watched his defeated army. As the hours wore on he pondered what to do; as usual he tried to get to the core of the problem and develop solutions that addressed it. Essentially the army lacked dynamic leadership and the government lacked a plan that went beyond killing rebels and capturing the Confederate capital.

First of all, he would call General George B. McClellan to Washington to take command of the army and organize the defense of Washington. Thirty-five-years-old, handsome and dashing, McClellan had won some impressive victories in small battles in western Virginia's Shenandoah region. He was a good organizer and an inspiration to his men. He could get the defeated army back on its feet.

Secondly, Lincoln decided he would have to prepare for a long war. There was to be no quick and decisive march on Richmond. He ordered the navy to tighten its blockade of southern ports so that, over the long haul, the Confederacy would get few imports and suffer for its lack of manufacturing. And he called for longer enlistments for Union soldiers — three years. The army was going to have to be much larger and capable of sustained action.

Finally, Lincoln hardened the overall strategy of the war that he had been contemplating, with the advice of the aged General Winfield Scott, since the attack on Fort Sumter. Besides block-

THE AGITATOR AND THE POLITICIAN

ading the South and advancing on Richmond, the Union would secure the Border States and then begin an advance down the Mississippi River that would split the Confederacy in two. Simultaneously, another advance through Tennessee would further divide the enemy. Gradually, the Union forces would squeeze and confine the Confederacy to increasingly smaller areas; Union forces would squeeze the life out of it, just as an Anaconda envelops its prey. In time, the Union strategy would be dubbed the "Anaconda Plan."

An essential ingredient in the Union plan was the need to secure the Border States. After Bull Run, Lincoln believed Missouri should be handled with military action. A Union army was in St. Louis under General John C. Fremont (the 1856 Republican candidate for President), and Lincoln was optimistic that Fremont could bring the state under control by the end of the year.

Kentucky, however, was another matter. Kentuckians had made it clear that an invasion of their state would drive them into the Confederacy, so Lincoln had carefully kept Union forces north of the Ohio River. Kentucky had also emphasized that she would not side with the North in a war against slavery. It was largely with this in mind that Lincoln was avoiding references to slavery and emphasizing that the war was only being fought to restore the Union.

It should be noted at this point, that the desire to avoid offending the Border States was only part of Lincoln's motivation for avoiding the slavery issue. He actually *did* want to win the war without touching slavery. He believed that an immediate grant of freedom to four million largely uneducated African-Americans would be an economic and social disaster. Moreover, his constitutional duty as president was to enforce the laws — including those securing slavery.

In practice, Lincoln left the handling of the slave problem to generals in the field whose forces often came into contact with runaway slaves. Many slaves took advantage of the wartime confusion and ran off their plantations into Union encampments. Generals McDowell and McClellan ordered fugitives who came into the Washington area returned to their masters. The city's jails became crowded with African-Americans waiting to be shipped back to their "masters." For the first five months of the war, the Lincoln administration scrupulously guarded the slave system and enforced the Fugitive Slave Law.

Congress made the first small crack in this "hands off" policy in early August when it passed the Confiscation Act, which allowed the Union Army to seize slaves owned by Southerners who used them in the service of the Confederacy. Thus, any master who sent his slaves to dig trenches in the Confederate lines or who brought his "man servant" with him into the army, as many of them did, ran the risk of losing his "property" should "it" choose to run away or should "it" be captured by Union troops. Lincoln felt that Congress, goaded by its more radical Republican members, had acted too soon in passing this act; he was especially concerned that Kentucky would react adversely; but he signed it into law on August 6th rather than veto it. A veto, he reasoned, would encourage Southerners to use their slaves for military purposes.

By signing the Confiscation Act, Lincoln knew he was only temporarily appeasing the Republicans in Congress who were anxious to strike a blow against slavery. In the future, he knew he could expect more anti-slavery pressure from Republicans on Capitol Hill. He was completely unprepared, however, for a challenge to his slavery policy from one of his generals.

On August 30th General Fremont in St. Louis, fearful that the bands of Confederate guerillas in Missouri would gain control of the state, imposed martial law and issued an edict emancipating all slaves owned by disloyal masters. Lincoln was appalled at Fremont's taking matters so boldly into his own hands, at his wanton disregard for private property, and at the damage Fremont's policy might do to the government's efforts in the Border States. In a series of letters, Lincoln ordered Fremont to modify his proclamation so that it conformed to the Confiscation Act that freed only slaves in actual military service and then only after a court hearing. A few weeks later, as Fremont resisted Lincoln's policy, the president removed the insubordinate general from his command.

Lincoln explained his actions regarding Fremont in a private letter to his friend Oliver Browning. Property (such as a farm) may be seized for military purposes, he wrote, but it must be returned when the need for it has passed. "Can it be pretended," he asked, "that it is any longer the Government of the United States — any government of constitution and laws — wherein a general or a president may make permanent rules of property by proclamation?" (1)

Lincoln recognized that Fremont's order was popular among some Northerners, but he had to think always of the crucial Border States. Reports were coming from Kentucky of whole companies of Union men throwing down their arms upon hearing news of Fremont's order. Lincoln was sure that if he had let the order stand, Kentucky would have joined the Confederacy. That would have been a disaster. "I think to lose Kentucky is nearly the same as to lose the whole game," he wrote. "Kentucky gone, we cannot hold Missouri, nor, as I think, Maryland. These all against us and the job on our hands is too large for us." (2)

Convinced that, for the moment at least, he had no choice on the slavery issue, Lincoln stood by his legalistic, hands-off policy for the rest of 1861. In September, when some friends of Senator

Sumner visited the Executive Mansion and urged him to free the slaves, he told them that it would do no good to proceed any faster than the country would follow. "I think Sumner and the rest of you would upset our applecart altogether," he told his guests. "We'll fetch in, " he added cryptically, Just give us a little more time. We didn't go into the war to put down slavery, but to put the flag back." (3) His implication may have been that if it would help save the Union he would free the slaves, but Sumner's friends left the office quite dissatisfied.

Lincoln was succeeding in holding the Border States with his policies, but he was losing support of abolitionists in the North. When General Fremont's proclamation was announced, William Lloyd Garrison heralded it as "the beginning of the end," but when Lincoln ordered the edict revoked, Garrison was dismayed. He printed Lincoln's final letter to Fremont surrounded by black, funereal borders. He charged Lincoln with "serious dereliction of duty" in not making Fremont's order *national* policy, and called Lincoln's letter "timid, depressing and suicidal." (4) Throughout the fall of 1861 he reprinted editorials from other newspapers praising Fremont's courage and damning the president's subservience to the Border State slave interests.

At the end of the year, Garrison vented his frustration and anguish in a letter to fellow abolitionist Oliver Johnson. "(Lincoln) has evidently not a drop of anti-slavery blood in his veins; and he seems incapable of uttering a humane or generous sentiment respecting the enslaved millions in our land. . . . In fact, I shudder at the possibility of the war terminating without the extinction of slavery, by a new and more atrocious compromise on the part of the North than any that has yet been made. . . . A curse on that (Border State) 'loyalty' which is retained only by allowing it to control the policy of the administration." (5)

Lincoln believed he could afford to let Garrison and the other radical abolitionists wring their hands, at least for a while, as he left slavery alone in order to save the Union. The abolitionists *had* to remain loyal to the Union because they would otherwise give aid to the slave power Confederacy. In this belief he was correct, at least as far as Garrison was concerned. Although he editorialized in *The Liberator* that Lincoln's failure to free the slaves was "tantamount to the crime of their original enslavement," (6) he continued to support the war effort and speak out for Lincoln in abolitionist gatherings.

At the annual meeting of the Massachusetts Anti-Slavery Society in 1862, Wendell Phillips, Stephen Foster, and several others whose patience was exhausted waiting for Lincoln to strike a blow against slavery, spoke in discouraging tones about Lincoln's shortcomings, particularly his lack of moral conviction. Garrison responded with a cheery speech in which he told his friends they should be grateful for the war because it spelled the end of southern domination of the North. No matter what might be said about Lincoln, he argued, at least he has made the North unendurable to the South. Moreover, Garrison was sure that sentiment in the North — and in the Executive Mansion — was moving gradually in the right direction. Then, in a remarkable display of tolerance and empathy for politicians, Lloyd said to his friends:

> Supposing Mr. Lincoln could answer tonight, and we should say to him, "Sir, with the power in your hands, slavery being the cause of the rebellion beyond all controversy, why don't you put the trump of jubilee to your lips, and proclaim universal freedom?" Possibly he might answer; "Gentlemen, I understand this matter quite as well as you do. I do not know that I differ in opinion from you, but will you assure me the support of a united North if I do as you bid me? Are all parties and all sects at the North so convinced and so united on this point that they will stand by the

government? If so, give me the evidence of it and I will strike the blow. But gentlemen, looking over the entire North, and seeing in all your town and city papers representing a considerable, if not a formidable portion of people, menacing and bullying the government in case it dare liberate the slaves, even as a matter of self-preservation, I do not feel that the hour has come that will render it safe for the government to take that step.

Garrison assured his listeners that he would urge the president to stand with God and freedom on his side "come what may," but concluded, " . . . men in high office are not apt to be led by such lofty moral considerations." (7)

In essence, Garrison was restating what he had always said about politicians —that they were unlikely to take moral action — only now he was counseling understanding rather than rebuke. He knew he had no choice other than to rely on the president. He also may have had a feeling that Lincoln's heart was in the right place, that only practical politics stood in the way of his doing the right thing, and that gradually the political climate for emancipation would become more favorable.

Garrison knew that protracted war was essential if Lincoln were to find it politically and strategically advantageous to free the slaves. The longer the South held out, the more likely it was that the people of the North would favor depriving the South of its greatest resource — slaves. Northerners would see emancipation as righteous punishment for the South and a weapon to use to bring the South down to defeat. Moreover, Garrison knew from his contacts with George Thompson, the British abolitionist, that the British government favored the Confederacy because of the economic ties between the cotton planters of the South and the textile mill owners in Britain, *but* it would switch to supporting the *North* if Lincoln made it a war against slavery. Thus Lloyd was not altogether unhappy with the Northern military failures of 1861 and early 1862. Those defeats put pressure on Lincoln to take radical action or risk losing support at home and abroad.

2. A CRAWL TOWARD EMANCIPATION

By February, 1862, George McClellan had been in command of the Army of the Potomac for over six months. During that time, his force had grown to over 300,000 men and he had been fully supplied with rifles, cannon, mortars, ammunition, and everything else needed by a modern army. But, he had made no move to do anything except drill and parade and make ready for a battle that never came. As the Confederates strengthened their defenses around Richmond and boldly operated as an independent nation within sight of Washington, McClellan staged large military reviews and held staff meetings at his headquarters. Lincoln grew more vexed by the day, saying at one point that if McClellan had no use for the army, he'd like to borrow it.

When McClellan was at last ready, his plan was to advance on the Confederate capital from the east. This involved loading the entire army onto ships, transporting it down the Potomac River into Chesapeake Bay, and landing it on the tip of the Yorktown Peninsula. He carried out the initial maneuvers effectively but, as he approached Richmond, he continually — and mistakenly — believed he was outnumbered and thus advanced slowly. The commander of the Confederate defenses, Robert E. Lee, used brilliant diversionary tactics, outflanked McClellan, and finally drove him back from his most advanced positions, which at one point were only ten miles from the city.

In the meantime, General Stonewall Jackson was leading successful Confederate raids in the Shenandoah Valley of Virginia and threatening at any moment to attack Washington itself. In June, Lincoln felt compelled to order McClellan back to Washington to defend the city. Thus, another attempt to end the war quickly with the capture of Richmond had failed.

All of these military setbacks occurred just as Abraham and Mary Lincoln were suffering through the worst nightmare parents can experience. In February, just as McClellan's "Peninsula Campaign" to take Richmond was about to get underway, their son, Willie, came down with typhoid fever. After steadily declining for several days, he died in his White House bedroom. Mary was inconsolable and went into a period of deep and profound mourning that was to last for over a year. Abe could barely find the spirit and energy to carry on his presidential duties. The year ahead was to be the most consequential year in American history since 1776; Abe was going to have to dig deep into his soul to meet the challenges he was to face.

The only bright news for Lincoln in the first half of 1862 came from the West. In February, General Ulysses S. Grant captured Forts Henry and Donelson at the mouth of the Tennessee River and began a drive south into Tennessee. At Shiloh in April he was surprised by a Confederate attack and lost 10,000 men, but he still kept moving south. Meanwhile, Admiral David Farragut sailed a naval squadron up the Mississippi River, laid siege to New Orleans, and then captured that important city. Thus, by the middle of 1862 some important first moves had been made toward gaining control of the Mississippi River and dividing the Confederacy in the West.

As the war dragged on, Lincoln at last believed some moves against slavery would enhance the war effort. Some of the moves were initiated by Congress as the previous summer's "Confiscation Act" had been, but some were his own ideas. His thinking had evolved over the year because the Border States now seemed securely in the Union, and the war was proving to be a costly undertaking requiring utilization of all available weapons against the South. Also, Lincoln was becoming increasingly aware that a growing number of Northerners favored some sort of action against slavery and that, indeed, many would cease to support the war unless they could fight for the slaves as well as for the Union. Of course, Lincoln did have a moral aversion to slavery, but he now felt it was possible, without jeopardizing the war effort, to strike a few harmful, if not deadly, blows against the "peculiar institution."

From the day he took office, Lincoln had been working to snuff out the slave trade from Africa. Although the practice of hauling shiploads of chained Africans across the Atlantic had been illegal since 1808, profiteers still carried on highly profitable smuggling, and Lincoln considered the whole business nefarious. He and Secretary of State Seward negotiated a treaty with Great Britain under which the two nations agreed to cooperate in efforts to seize slave vessels, some of which were British. Lincoln ordered the navy to be on special watch for "slavers," and he was pleased to see the slave trade nearly wiped out during 1862.

To show how much he meant business in this fight against slave importation, Lincoln refused to pardon Nathaniel Gordon, a slave trader captured in 1861 with over eight hundred Africans on board his ship. Gordon's sentence was execution and Lincoln, who was known to spare many a soldier who had fallen asleep during guard duty with a presidential pardon, merely postponed Gordon's hanging for two weeks to give the condemned man time to prepare for death.

On April 11, 1862, Congress passed a bill to abolish slavery in the District of Columbia. It allowed masters loyal to the Union to be paid for the loss of their "property," it scheduled emancipation to take place gradually, and it encouraged freed "Negroes" to emigrate to Haiti or Liberia. Lincoln signed the bill on April 16th saying he had "ever desired to see the national capital freed from the institution in some satisfactory way." (8)

Most pleasing to the president were the compensation and colonization features of the new District of Columbia law. As a man of the law — and as the president sworn to uphold the law — he could not tolerate the government's taking people's property without payment. As a man who knew the racial prejudices of the people, he believed both races would be better off if the black people went to their "own land" far away.

As he signed the District of Columbia Act, Lincoln was at work on a far more extensive emancipation proposal. On March 6, 1862, he sent to Congress a message recommending federal government support for compensated emancipation. Under his plan, which proposed gradual emancipation, Border States would receive financial aid from the United States Government so that owners could be paid for their "property." In arguing for the idea, Lincoln emphasized not the *humanitarian* goal of freeing black human beings from their chains, but rather the *military* goal of winning the war more quickly. If the Border States began to free their slaves, he reasoned, the South could no longer hope that those states would join the Confederacy in order to protect slavery.

A further, unstated, political goal of the plan was to stall off the abolitionists — particularly those in Congress such as Charles Sumner — who were growing increasingly restive and vocal in their demands for emancipation. This goal was partially achieved on April 10th when Congress voted overwhelmingly to support the idea, Sumner and most of the other radicals voting "aye," even though they gagged at the idea of compensation.

Lincoln was chagrined, however, when it became clear that the Border States were not interested. Meetings with Border State congressmen went nowhere. In an attempt to change people's minds, the president wrote letters to the plan's opponents and tried to convince them that his plan was practical as well as moral. It even made financial sense. Eighty-seven days of the war cost $174 million, he pointed out. Paying for the freedom of all the slaves in Missouri, Kentucky, Maryland and Delaware at $400 per head would cost $173 million. Surely compensated emancipation in the Border States would shorten the war more than eighty-seven days, he argued — so, was it not a good bargain?

In July, with McClellan back in Washington after his failure to take Richmond, and the war likely to go on interminably, Lincoln called all the Border State congressmen to the Executive Mansion. Looking weary from the unending frustrations of the war and the mounting casualties, Lincoln read them a statement on the need for compensated emancipation. If their states had taken this step in March, he declared rather overly optimistically, the war would be over. He stressed that he was getting a great deal of pressure to free the slaves from people in the North whose support he could not afford to lose. The abolitionists and the "Radical Republicans" in Congress would cease to support the war to save the Union unless he took some steps toward emancipation soon.

As proof of the pressure he was under, Lincoln reminded the congressmen of the events of the previous May. General Hunter, commander of the Department of the South, had proclaimed freedom for all slaves in Georgia, Florida and South Carolina. As he had done with Fremont the year before, Lincoln had revoked Hunter's order immediately. However, this time he had warned that the "signs of the times" were that emancipation was coming unless some more moderate policy could be adopted.

The Border State men listened to Lincoln with distinct coolness. They left the White House making no pledges of support, promising only to check with their constituents to see how they felt about the idea. Lincoln expected nothing to come of these promises and nothing did.

Pacing the White House floors night after night, the president turned thoughts over and over in his mind. Rational arguments for various slavery strategies must have become jumbled in his head with images of bloody corpses on the battlefield, letters to grieving mothers, and meetings he was having with outraged people storming about his office demanding action and quick victory. He tried to sort things out, to eliminate the outer layers and get to the core.

It had been a year since the disaster at Bull Run. Since then, the Army of the Potomac had suffered several more great defeats and was not a bit closer to taking Richmond. In the West, the Border States were pretty much secure, Grant was advancing into Tennessee, and Union forces had occupied New Orleans. But many lives had been lost and the people of the North were discouraged. Slavery was the key. Favorable reaction to Fremont's and Hunter's orders showed that many people would cheer an edict that turned the war into a struggle against slavery. Yet, there were many who would throw down their weapons at such an announcement. Still, the South would certainly be struck a blow if the slaves were freed, and Great Britain would cease thinking about recognizing the Confederacy as a nation.

It all seemed to indicate that some direct action against slavery might be necessary as a war measure, especially since indirect proposals such as compensated, gradual emancipation were not getting support from the Border States. But, what a disruption emancipation would be! If only it could be done gradually, he mused, so that all Americans, white and black, could adjust to the idea.

A few days after Lincoln's meeting with the Border State congressmen, Congress passed a second confiscation bill that was more radical than the previous year's. This one freed all slaves of rebels and people who committed treason, not just those helping the Confederate war effort. Abe wrestled with whether or not to sign this. It involved government seizure of private property; it would set uneducated "Negroes" free into a society that was not ready to accept them. But the rebellion had been going on for a year and a half; congressmen were getting impatient. He signed the bill.

In the Confiscation Act and the District of Columbia Act, Congress appropriated money for the purpose of finding a place overseas where the freed African-Americans could be sent. Lincoln wanted very much to research the various possibilities. He invited Ambrose V. Thompson to the White House to discuss Thompson's plan to set up a "free Negro colony" in Panama. However, because the Central American countries objected to the scheme as a violation of the Monroe Doctrine, Lincoln decided to give it up. But, he continued to look for other places to send the black man after freedom came because he fully believed the two races could not co-exist.

Lincoln was twisting on the horns of a dilemma. Emancipation was presenting itself to him as a logical and effective action to win the war, but for him it was such a radical step! In Boston, William Lloyd Garrison understood the inner conflict the president must be experiencing and continued to support Lincoln, while at the same time attempting to call the reluctant chief executive to his duty. He was confident that if the war dragged on — as it appeared it would — Lincoln would have no choice but to free the slaves.

When Lincoln proposed compensated emancipation, however, Garrison reacted strongly. "Why wait for the dealers in human flesh to determine when they will deem it advisable to cease from their villainy as a matter of pecuniary advantage and cunning speculation with the government . . . ?" he wrote. (9) He was afraid, for a while, that the border congressmen would accept Lincoln's plan. Emancipation would be left to the states and thieves would be paid for the lives they had stolen. When the Border States did not respond to Lincoln's plan, Garrison was relieved.

After Lincoln repealed Hunter's order, Garrison denounced the deed at abolitionist meetings in Boston. He reminded the president of the responsibility he bore of speaking or withholding the word that would free millions. Yet, at the same meetings, he introduced nineteen resolutions outlining the gains made against slavery so far, including the abolition of slavery in the District of Columbia and the crushing of the African slave trade. Although men such as Wendell Phillips had grave doubts, Garrison was convinced that the country and the president were headed in the right direction. "Those who hold office by the will of the people cannot be judged wholly like private men." He reminded his brethren. (10) Lincoln had many factors to take into account, Lloyd explained. Give him more time, he prophesied, and Lincoln would free the slaves whether he wanted to or not!

3. PARTIAL EMANCIPATION

Through the summer of 1862, the pressure on Lincoln to free the slaves intensified. A delegation of Quakers from Pennsylvania arrived at the White House with a memorial they had drafted with William Lloyd Garrison's help. It reminded Lincoln that he had once said "a house divided against itself cannot stand," and implored him to free the slaves "as a measure imperatively demanded by a due regard for the unity of the country." (11) Charles Sumner came to see Lincoln every day, and so did many other radical Republicans in groups of two or three, all of them urging emancipation.

In August, Horace Greeley printed an editorial in the New York *Tribune* called "The Prayer of Twenty Millions." In it he asked Lincoln to make it clear to the people of the North (twenty million of them), many of whom favored emancipation, what his policy was on slavery. Greeley regarded it as absurd that Lincoln was trying to put down the rebellion without destroying its cause.

Lincoln responded on August 22nd with a letter stating as simply and clearly as he ever had what he thought about the relationship of slavery to the war and the conflict between a politician's moral beliefs and his legal duties:

> My paramount objective in this struggle *is* to save the Union and is *not* either to save or destroy slavery. If I could save the Union without freeing *any* slave, I would do it; and if I could do it by freeing some and leaving others alone, I would also do that. What I do about slavery and the colored race, I do because I believe it helps save this Union; and what I forebear, I forebear because I do *not* believe it would help save the Union. I shall do *less* whenever I believe what I am doing hurts the cause, and I shall do *more* whenever I shall believe doing more will help the cause. . . . I have here stated my purpose according to my view of *official* duty, and I intend no modification of my oft-expressed personal wish that all men, everywhere, could be free. (12)

After Greeley published this letter, William Lloyd Garrison's confidence in Lincoln fell. Most ominous to the abolitionist was the president's assertion that he might free some slaves and not others if that would be enough to save the Union. Such halfway measures had always annoyed him. On September 9th he wrote in exasperation to his abolitionist friend Oliver Johnson: "I am growing more and more skeptical as to the 'honesty' of Lincoln. He is nothing better than a wet rag!" (13)

Garrison was soon to discover, however, that Lincoln's letter was an effort to prepare the country for what was soon to come.

He had already decided to free most of the slaves and he was assuring conservatives – and posterity – that he was taking action against slavery as a military necessity for the purpose of saving the Union.

On July 22nd Lincoln had called his cabinet together and had read them a proclamation freeing all the slaves in the states rebelling against the Union. Secretary of State Seward had advised postponing the announcement until the Union Army had won a victory. Otherwise, he said, the world, and the South, would think that Lincoln was making a last desperate attempt to mortally wound the Confederacy after the armies had failed. Lincoln had agreed and had put the proclamation away ready to be produced as soon as the Union had a victory.

The Union military success Lincoln was waiting for did not come for many weeks. In July, he replaced General McClellan with General John Pope who led the Army of the Potomac on another march toward Richmond. He met Confederate forces at familiar Bull Run Creek and, in an agonizing re-run of the battle the year before, came slogging back to Washington covered with defeat. The men were completely disorganized, tired, frustrated and ready to quit.

In desperation Lincoln turned again to General McClellan. Despite his faults, McClellan did have the ability to inspire confidence in the soldiers and lift up their spirits. Moreover, he could quickly organize the defeated army and prepare it to meet an anticipated advance northward by General Lee.

During the first weeks of September, McClellan took command and rallied the troops as Lincoln had hoped. The army was back on its feet just in time to meet Lee's hardened veterans as they marched into Maryland with hopes of encircling Washington and winning a stunning victory that would bring foreign recognition to the Confederate States of America. As historical fate would have it, an observant corporal in McClellan's army spotted a small bundle of papers wrapped around a few cigars in the grass near his campsite and realized the papers contained the battle plans of the Confederate force. With this in hand, McClellan was able to confront Lee's army at Antietam Creek. What followed was one of the bloodiest battles of the 19th century. Casualties mounted as each side threw in everything it had for two days. Twenty thousand men fell in the fighting before Lee finally realized he could no longer carry on and prepared to withdraw.

As had become his habit when a battle was in the offing, Lincoln waited anxiously with the telegraph operators at the War Department for news dispatches. On September 19th he was delighted that Lee had been stopped, but he hoped for even more. "God bless you and all with you," he had wired McClellan. "Destroy the rebel army if possible." (14) McClellan took a pessimistic view of what was "possible." He considered it enough that Lee was retreating back into Virginia. His own men were tired. He would wait. Lee's army forded the Potomac and went into hiding in Virginia to lick its wounds, defeated, but still able to fight another day.

The Battle of Antietam was, then, only a partial victory. But, Lee and Jefferson Davis had been denied the chance to prove to Great Britain that they could win and that they were a viable nation. The people in the North would begin to see that the Union superiority in manpower and military supplies would eventually wear the South down. Lincoln considered Antietam enough of a victory to warrant announcement of his emancipation plans.

On September 22nd, he called a cabinet meeting. Around the table sat William Seward, whom Abe had come to trust as a close friend and advisor, Salmon P. Chase, treasury secretary who believed he could handle the presidency better than Lincoln and hoped to steal the Republican nomination from him in 1864, Edwin Stanton, a sour man with a long, gray beard who ran the war department with an iron hand and thought the president was soft on slavery, Gideon Welles, the kindly, white bearded secretary of the navy whom Abe nicknamed "Neptune" and who was often available for consultation and advice, Edward Bates of Missouri, the attorney general, and Montgomery Blair, postmaster general. They all knew the president was about to announce an important decision.

To break the tension Abe began by reading a selection from *A High Handed Outrage at Utica*, a humorous essay by Charles Farrar Browne. Abe chuckled as he read and Seward joined in, but the others, less able to mix humor with serious business, either sat in stony silence or smiled meekly. Stanton, particularly, seemed annoyed, his mouth a tight line above his scraggily beard. At last, the president was relaxed and ready to proceed with one of the most significant presidential decisions in the history of the United States.

He reminded the cabinet of the decision he had made in July and the strategy he had adopted, at Seward's suggestion, of waiting for a Union victory before announcing it. While Antietam was not the sort of victory he had hoped for, he felt the time had come to make his decision public. He would announce through the newspapers that on January first, 1863, all slaves in areas still in rebellion against the Union would be declared forever free. If a state returned to the Union by January first, which it could do by renouncing secession and electing representatives to Congress, that state would not be subject to the emancipation. Lincoln was hoping, futilely he knew, that some southern states would return quickly to the Union in order to keep their slaves. He emphasized that the policy was motivated by a desire to save the Union.

As Lincoln finished, the men of the cabinet nodded their approval. Chase and Seward, avid foes of slavery for years, felt relieved that the waiting was over and the time for action had finally come. Even Stanton, also an anti-slavery man, managed a tight smile. There was unanimous agreement that this was the right action at the right time. Only Blair of Maryland and Bates of Missouri felt trepidation over what the reaction would be back home. The proclamation left Border State slave owners still holding their "property," but clearly, if the South lost the war, slave property in the Border States would be jeopardized, to say the least.

When news of the "Preliminary Emancipation Proclamation" reached the country, the reaction was predictable. Southerners were enraged and contemptuous. They intended to win the war, so it made no difference that this "foreign" president had issued his edict. Wasn't it fortunate, many Southerners asked, that they had left the Union because Lincoln had, indeed, turned out to be a "black abolitionist?!"

Border State people and many conservatives in the North reacted negatively. As Lincoln had feared, some soldiers refused to fight any longer now that the war was for freeing the slaves. Others denounced the proclamation as an unconstitutional seizure of private property. There were enough of these conservatives that Republican congressmen who supported Lincoln did poorly in the November elections of 1862. The party lost thirty-one seats in Congress, although it still kept its majority.

Yet, many Republicans and most abolitionists were dismayed that Lincoln had not gone far enough. Garrison, while not dismayed, was only mildly pleased about the proclamation at first. On September 25th he complained in a letter to his daughter, Fanny: "The president can do nothing for freedom in a direct manner, but only by circumlocution and delay. How prompt was his action against Fremont and Hunter?" The next day *The Liberator* called the proclamation "a step in the right direction," but stressed the nature of the times required the government to do more. Lloyd expressed disappointment that the South had one hundred days' grace, and that the proclamation mentioned the possibility of colonizing the freed African-Americans. (15)

Still, Garrison believed all abolitionists should continue to stand by the government. While a much more far-reaching emancipation was necessary, and all abolitionists should continue to demand it, they should support the president through the completion of this important step. The angry reaction of conservatives and the desertion of a fair number of Union soldiers showed that the president was pushing things as fast as they could go. The immediate concern was whether Lincoln would maintain his resolve and actually announce the proclamation on January first.

Lloyd was beset with doubts that Lincoln would come through. During the fall he waited anxiously, looking for signs that might reveal how determined — or how vacillating — the president was. In *The Liberator* office, in his parlor at home, and at anti-slavery meetings, he discussed with his friends the disheartening possibility the president might back down. Certain signs were ominous, such as Lincoln's emphasis on compensated emancipation and his only casual reference to the proclamation in his December annual message to Congress. In the December 26th edition of *The Liberator*, with the great day close at hand, Garrison seemed to be preparing himself for the worst. " . . . It seems to be the general conviction (that Lincoln will stand by his proclamation)," he wrote, "though we should not be greatly surprised if he substitute some other project for it. A man so manifestly without moral vision . . . cannot be safely relied upon in any emergency." (16)

This proved to be the last time Garrison ever underestimated Abraham Lincoln. "I may advance slowly," Lincoln once said, "but I don't walk backward." He was ready to accept any representative from a rebel state — and he did accept two from districts in Louisiana under Union control that had special elections — but he would free all slaves in areas still out of the Union on January 1st just as he said he would. As New Year's Day approached, he became more convinced than ever that his course was correct. Most important to him was the fact that he was not acting hastily and that he was acting within the law. He had given the South nearly two years to return to the Union with slavery still intact; he had given the South one hundred days' notice of his intentions; he had given the North enough time to accept emancipation as a war aim; he had waited for the proper military situation before he acted; and, very significantly, he was acting as commander-in-chief seizing property as a war measure.

Congressman John Covode reported that during the last week of December he found Lincoln walking back and forth in his office mumbling: "I have studied the matter well; my mind is made up . . . it must be done. I AM DRIVEN TO IT. There is no other way out of our troubles. But although my duty is plain, it is in some respects painful, and I trust that people will understand that I acted not in anger but in expectation of a greater good." (17)

To make emancipation as painless as possible, Lincoln was secretly planning ways to send many liberated slaves from the country. In August he met with several black spokesmen in the Executive Mansion and urged them to promote the idea of colonization among African-American people. He was blunt with them, saying that their presence in the United States was the cause of the war, and that the white and black races would never be able to live happily together. Naturally annoyed at the president's remarks, they refused to help him achieve black support for his scheme. Nevertheless, he moved ahead on it, still hoping to accomplish this quixotic dream.

On December 31, 1862, the day before he was to sign the Emancipation Proclamation, Lincoln signed a contract with a business adventurer named Bernard Koch who promised to settle five thousand "Negroes" on "Cow Island" in the Caribbean. Koch promised that the settlers would have employment, a school with "a New England teacher," and a church with "a New England minister!" (18) Lincoln hoped that this would be the prelude to other similar projects and possibly a great national program to deport large numbers of the black race.

At least one member of the cabinet believed Lincoln was able to go ahead with the proclamation because he had high hopes for colonization. Gideon Welles wrote: "I sometimes wondered if he would have hesitated longer in issuing the decree of emancipation had he been aware that colonization would not be accepted as an accompaniment." (19) More than likely, Welles was overstating the case. The forces pushing for emancipation — including Lincoln's own, sincere abhorrence of slavery — were strong enough to make him stick firmly to his proclamation, even if he had known the Koch scheme and all others like it were destined to fail. But Lincoln did feel somewhat comforted by the hope that some of the disruptions of emancipation, for both races, would be alleviated by the deportation of some African-Americans. He at least felt it was his duty to try to relocate as many as possible.

On New Year's Day, having mulled over the arguments for emancipation a thousand times, Lincoln felt fully prepared for what he was going to do. The weather was calm and sunny, at odds with the tumult that many people thought would result from what the president was about to do. From eleven in the morning until two, Abe and Mary held their usual New Year's Day reception, shaking hands and talking to an endless stream of callers. At three o'clock he was finally free to go to his office and sign the Emancipation Proclamation.

Only a dozen people — cabinet members and high government officials — were on hand as Lincoln sat down at his desk. William Seward, the secretary of state, part of whose job is to oversee the security of public documents, put the proclamation before the president. As Abe dipped his pen in the ink bottle, he noticed that his hand was swollen and quivering from the hours of hand shaking. I have never been more certain that I was doing the right thing, he told the gathering, but I am afraid that a trembling signature might be taken to mean that I had some doubts. "But anyway," he said with conviction, "it is going to be done!" As legibly as he could, he wrote out his full name (not the usual "A. Lincoln") at the bottom of the paper.

As the last awkward letter appeared on the document, the Emancipation Proclamation was official. But it did not free a single slave. As Lincoln had promised in September, it freed only those slaves in areas still in rebellion against the Union — in other words, in areas where the federal government had no ability to enforce presidential edicts. Lincoln had been careful to exclude from its provisions the Border States and even several areas of the South already occupied by the Union Army, such as northern Tennessee, New Orleans, and certain sea islands off the coasts of Virginia, North Carolina and Georgia. Only as the Union Army advanced into new rebel areas after January first would slaves be emancipated.

The proclamation itself was a dry, emotionless, legalistic paper. It stated that the action being taken against slavery was a "fit and necessary war measure" for suppressing the rebellion. Never once did it condemn the slave system as morally reprehensible; never once did it express sympathy for the captive slaves. Instead, it asked black people to refrain from violence and encouraged them to work for wages in their current positions. It did say that "the people so declared to be free" would be accepted into the armed forces of the United States. In short, it was like all of Lincoln's other actions on slavery — practical, legalistic, precisely worded, and circumscribed. Lincoln's hope was that most abolitionists would be satisfied for the moment even though he had not freed all of the slaves, and that conservative and border state people would recognize that he had only acted out of necessity to save the Union.

Many abolitionists were *not* satisfied. They were angry that Lincoln had exempted a million slaves from freedom (those in Border States and conquered areas) and that he had based emancipation solely on military necessity. But William Lloyd Garrison, always aware of the dynamics of change, was overjoyed. He had grown accustomed to watching Lincoln sail the ship of state through the water mines of public opinion, always heading slowly but inexorably to a shore more morally advanced than the one he had left. The winds of war were pushing Lincoln faster than he wanted to go, but Garrison was not going to condemn the captain for trimming the sails to keep the ship balanced — as long as he kept the sails up!

As for the fact that the proclamation did not free any slaves immediately and left slaves in loyal areas still in bondage, Garrison was largely unconcerned. The Union would win the war, he was certain, and then all the slaves in the "Confederate States of America" would be free. From then on, the slave systems still functioning in Kentucky and elsewhere would be like the last remaining leaves on a dead tree. Isolated and unnourished, they would quickly wither and die.

On the afternoon of January first, Lloyd was sitting with fellow abolitionists at a concert in the Music Hall in Boston. The day had passed with no word from Washington, and there were some pessimists conjecturing that Lincoln had backed down at the last minute. Suddenly, the music was interrupted by the announcement that the signing of the Emancipation Proclamation had just come in over the wire. The crowd burst into applause that lasted for several minutes and then subsided into a general excited rumble. Someone asked for nine cheers for Abraham Lincoln, and the crowd lustily gave them. Then the crowd chanted for Garrison and Lloyd, smiling and benign as always, stood up to thunderous applause. The city that had once almost lynched him was now celebrating him! "Glory Hallelujah!" he exclaimed in *The Liberator.* (20)

CHAPTER NINE

On Common Ground at Last

1863-1865

Lincoln's responsibilities as commander-in-chief and defender of the Constitution finally meshed with Garrison's demands for black freedom. Thus, Lincoln was able to free the slaves AND save the Union. Unfortunately, the president and the abolitionist's elation over their shared victory was short-lived.

1. GARRISON TRIUMPHANT

When the Massachusetts Anti-Slavery Society met in January of 1863, Garrison was in an ebullient mood. "Thirty years ago it was midnight with the anti-slavery cause," he reminded his allies, some of whom had been with him since he began his crusade, "(but) now it is the bright noon of day, with the sun shining in its meridian splendor. Thirty years ago we were in the Arctic regions surrounded by icebergs; today we are in the tropics, with the flowers blooming and the birds singing around us." (1) Perhaps his mind wandered back to the snowy evening in 1832 when he and his twelve friends, alone against almost all of American society, stepped out into the storm after they had organized the New England Anti-Slavery Society.

In a mellow mood, Lloyd introduced resolutions calling for emancipation in the Border States expressed in language of gentle prodding — far different from the inflammatory words of Garrisonian resolutions in earlier times. Confident that Lincoln would continue moving in the right direction and that most of the North had adopted proper attitudes toward slavery, Lloyd believed the need for absolutism had passed. He was ready to co-operate with all right thinking people.

To the annual meeting of the American Anti-Slavery Society in May, Garrison invited all those who had organized the society with him thirty years before, including those who had broken with him in 1840. Many of them came and, in an atmosphere of triumphant cordiality, the society issued a call for a constitution-al amendment abolishing slavery nationwide.

Final success of emancipation, of course, depended on a Union victory over the Confederacy. In May of 1863, victory still seemed a long way off. Only a few days before the meeting of the American Anti-Slavery Society, General Hooker, Lin-coln's latest choice to lead the Army of the Potomac, suffered another defeat at the hands of Robert E. Lee. Outmaneuvered at Chancellorsville, the Union commander suffered ten thousand casualties and barely escaped annihilation. Clearly the South was far from defeated.

The Union war effort struck Lloyd's family in 1863 in a way that made him strangely sad yet proud. Since it was now a war against slavery, one of Lloyd's sons, George Thompson Garrison, chose to enlist in the Union Army. Lloyd told his son that he had hoped the young man would fight for moral principles on a high-er, non-violent plane, but if he honestly believed in using violence for a just cause, then he should be true to his convictions and fight for the slaves.

Still, Garrison was worried. George was going to join the Massachusetts 55th Regiment, one of the first black regiments organized since the Emancipation Proclamation. Lloyd was sure that, because of the racial prejudice of northern officers, the 55th would be used for dangerous duty. Moreover, he was afraid that the son of William Lloyd Garrison serving in a black regiment would be treated cruelly if he were to be captured by the Confederates. In a heavy rain, Lloyd stood on the pier watching a ship carrying the Massachusetts 55th glide out of Boston harbor on its way to the war zones. He and Helen had given their lives to the cause of emancipation; now he wondered if they were going to have to give a son.

As George Thompson Garrison went to war, the Union's fortunes dramatically improved. After his victory at Chancellorsville, Lee moved north hoping once again to win a victory on Union soil. Soon after he crossed the Pennsylvania border he encountered the Army of the Potomac under General George Meade. For three days the two great armies fought it out on the rolling hills outside the town of Gettysburg. Finally Lee, with ten thousand of his men killed or wounded and the rest exhausted, retreated back to Virginia. Meade, like McClellan the year before, did not follow up his victory with a knockout blow, but the Battle of Gettysburg served notice to the world, if not the stubborn South, that the North's overwhelming numerical advantages were taking their toll.

In November of 1863, Lincoln traveled by train to Gettysburg to say "a few words" at the ceremony dedicating the new cemetery that was being created on the battlefield. Under a slate sky, Abe paid homage to the brave men whose sacrifices gave his words and policies meaning. " . . . we cannot dedicate, we cannot consecrate, we cannot hallow this ground," he said. "The brave men living and dead who struggled here have consecrated it far beyond our poor power to add or detract." The speech was to become his most famous for its simple yet eloquent explanation of the meaning of the war – that "government of the people, by the people and for the people shall not perish from the earth." Abraham Lincoln was profoundly aware that all of his strategizing and maneuvering on the slavery issue ultimately depended on the willingness of brave men to face bullets and bayonets.

In the year 1863, William Lloyd Garrison watched his son march off to war and knelt with Helen to pray for their son's safety; Abraham Lincoln gave a moving speech as he looked out over thousands of fresh graves. Both men saw with heart-rending clarity what their ideas and causes meant to the average person.

2. THE MEETING

Meanwhile, in the West, General Grant, who had been laying siege to Vicksburg Mississippi for six months, finally forced the starving inhabitants to surrender. The town was the last Confederate stronghold on the river. Its fall meant that the Union controlled the Mississippi River all the way to the Gulf of Mexico, and the Confederacy was split in half. President Lincoln, perhaps recalling his raft voyages to New Orleans in the 1830's, rejoiced that the "father of waters" now went "unvexed to the sea." The Vicksburg and Gettysburg victories, both coming in the first week of July, 1863, meant that the war might soon be over. Sadly, another twenty months of bloody fighting still lay ahead.

As Grant occupied Vicksburg and another Union force in the west moved through Tennessee, the Emancipation Proclamation set free its first slaves. Some slaves defended their masters' plantations against the invading Union armies, but most of them ran to freedom at the first opportunity. They streamed into the Union camps and followed the troops wherever they went. Most of the "freedmen" were understandably bewildered at their new status and unable to decide what to do next.

As Lincoln thought about the black people wandering off the plantations, jobless and uneducated, he felt sympathy and pity. Yet, he was reluctant to do much to help elevate African-Americans to full equality with whites. A sudden reversal of the order of things any more severe than that already wrought by emancipation would anger white people in the South and make it particularly difficult to get the country back together again. As always, Lincoln's top priority was to restore the Union. Moreover, Lincoln believed that pushing the African-Americans toward equality too fast would build up white resentment against them. Once the period of social change ended — as surely, at some point, it must — white Southerners would let loose their pent-up feelings and possibly knock the African-Americans further down than they had been before.

Thus, Lincoln's plans for the post-war South, as he began to announce them in late 1863, were decidedly moderate towards white Southerners and mostly unmindful of the freedmen. He said that any Confederate state could return to the Union with full privileges once ten percent of its people had pledged their loyalty to the United States Government. Beyond emancipation, no state would have to do anything for the African-Americans — or even give them any rights at all — in order to be a member in good standing of the United States of America.

In March of 1864 two African-American men from Louisiana called on Lincoln at the White House. Since he had announced emancipation, Abe had received many black visitors, including Frederick Douglass, and had treated them all with dignity and respect. These callers gave him a petition asking that African-Americans in Louisiana be given the right to vote.

Abe listened to them cordially, but gave them little satisfaction. Believing that the establishment of voting requirements, under the United States Constitution, was the province of the state governments, Lincoln told his guests that he could only refer them to a state constitutional convention being organized at the time in Louisiana to bring the state back into the Union under the "Ten Percent Plan." The next day, he did write to Governor Hahn suggesting that some "Negroes" in Louisiana — those who were industrious and intelligent — be given the vote in the state's new constitution. However, when Louisiana did not adopt his suggestion, he did not object. He was pleased to have the state preparing to return to the Union. For the time being, that was enough.

William Lloyd Garrison tacitly backed Lincoln's policies toward the "freedmen." Throughout 1863, his editorials and speeches praised the Emancipation Proclamation and Lincoln's conduct of the war. They never condemned the president for not trying to give the African-Americans citizenship or the right to vote.

Taking this position, Garrison increasingly found himself at odds with some of his fellow abolitionists who continued to be as radical as he once was. At the 1864 meeting of the Massachusetts Anti-Slavery Society, Wendell Phillips spoke critically of Lincoln and introduced a resolution condemning the president for being ready to make peace with the South "in disregard of the Negro." He believed the net result of Lincoln's policies would be to free the African-American in name only, leaving him completely subject to the racist whims of white Southerners.

Garrison rose to defend Lincoln. He said he did not want so severe a resolution and opined, rather uncharacteristically, that he would "always rather err on the side of charitable judgment than of excessive condemnation." (2) Lincoln was proceeding as fast as the people would let him, said the aging firebrand, and he must be judged by his possibilities, rather than by our wishes, or by the highest abstract moral standard. Nearly gasping at this very un-Garrisonian statement, the members of the society felt that Lloyd was losing the moral absolutism and revolutionary fervor necessary to lead them, and proceeded to vote in favor of Phillips's harsh resolution.

To some members, Lloyd seemed, at least temporarily, broken. In December of 1863, Helen had suffered a stroke that had left her partially paralyzed. Lloyd's worry and tender care for her must surely have taken the edge off of his abolitionist intensity.

Between this meeting in January and the American Anti-Slavery Society meeting in May, Garrison came out firmly in support of Lincoln's re-election to the presidency. Phillips, meanwhile, played a part in organizing a movement in the Republican Party to dump Lincoln and run John C. Fremont in his place. Phillips thought Fremont was much more ready to help the freedmen than Lincoln was. At the May meeting, the gap between Garrison and Phillips opened even wider. Phillips began the meeting with a long speech contending that the Lincoln government was going to let the relationship between the races in the South continue as it had been before the war, with the African-American free in name only. The only way to prevent this, he concluded, was to deprive the whites in the South of the right to vote for twenty years, or give the black people the vote immediately.

Garrison quickly jumped to Lincoln's defense. He repeated his argument that Lincoln had advanced as far and as fast as the public would allow. Then he recounted all of the things Lincoln had already done. He had freed three million slaves when barely a small majority of Northerners favored the idea; he had asked the Border States to abolish slavery; he had stopped the foreign slave trade, and more. "I do not feel disposed," Garrison concluded,

" . . . to take this occasion, or any occasion, to say anything very harshly against Abraham Lincoln." (3)

As the time for the Republican convention drew near in June of 1864, Phillips and Garrison went separate ways — Phillips to Cleveland for a splinter convention of disaffected Republicans to nominate Fremont, Garrison to Baltimore to watch the Republican majority nominate Lincoln. On June 7th Lloyd sat in the balcony at the Republican National Convention and beamed with pleasure as the delegates voted unanimously for Abraham Lincoln. After Lincoln's nomination, the convention voted to call for a constitutional amendment to abolish slavery nationwide. "It was the first national verdict ever recorded . . . against slavery as a system," he wrote. "It was a full endorsement of all the abolition 'fanaticism' and 'incendiarism' with which I have stood branded for so many years. The time for my complete vindication had come." (4)

If Lloyd was displeased that the convention chose to dump the abolitionist vice-president, Hannibal Hamlin, in favor of Andrew Johnson of Tennessee, he did not say so. It seemed a minor point at the time, but, of course, it was to have major implications later on for Lloyd's dream of full racial equality.

Happy now to be part of the main stream of American life, Garrison went from Baltimore to Washington to accept the invitation of Senator Henry Wilson of Massachusetts to visit Abraham Lincoln at the White House. On June 9th he was ushered into Lincoln's office and the two men saw each other for the first time. Lloyd, 5'9" and bald, looked up at 6'4" Lincoln through steel rimmed glasses, his eyes full of admiration for the man whom he had once disparaged as just another politician, but whom he now revered as the man who was bringing freedom to the slaves.

William Lloyd
Garrison

Abe Lincoln

Lincoln, his chin covered with thick, wiry whiskers, his eyes full of care and sorrow, looked kindly at the man whom he had once scorned as a dangerous fanatic. Now the two men stood on common ground and felt a palpable kinship with each other.

Each man had been born into poverty. Garrison, as a young boy, had practically starved to death on the streets of Newburyport; Lincoln had spent years hacking an existence out of the wilds of Kentucky, Indiana and Illinois. Each had mostly educated himself, Abe writing with charcoal on wooden planks, Lloyd setting type as a printer's apprentice. Each had been heavily influenced by their beloved mothers who had died when they were still very young. Each had suffered the anguish of watching two beloved children die and had carried on in their lives laden with grief. Each had worked energetically and skillfully at divergent yet parallel careers. Now, they stood together in the executive mansion of the United States discussing the paths they had followed that led to this significant moment.

Abe joked with Lloyd about the Baltimore jail the abolitionist fanatic had been locked up in back in 1830 and which had long since been torn down. "Then, you could not get out of prison," the president chuckled, "now you cannot get in." Lloyd, thinking of his efforts the day before to find the old jail, smiled and nodded. The two men got along well, and Lloyd agreed to call again the next day.

When they met on June 10th, Lloyd confessed, "Mr. Lincoln, I want to tell you very frankly that for every word I have spoken in your favor, I have spoken ten in favor of General Fremont." It was very difficult, he went on, to support you when you were revoking Fremont's proclamation and saying you would save the Union, if possible, without destroying slavery. "But, Mr. President, from the hour that you issued the Emancipation Proclamation and showed your purpose to stand by it, I have given you my hearty support and confidence." (5)

Lincoln told Garrison of the difficulties under which he had labored. As president, his primary duty had been to uphold the Constitution and keep the Union together. This required the support of border state men and Democrats — none of whom favored emancipation. On the other hand, delaying a move against slavery risked losing the support of anti-slavery people in the North and left open the possibility that England would recognize and even assist the Confederacy. Timing was everything. Now, Lincoln emphasized, the goals of saving the Union and emancipating the slaves were conjoined. He was sure of his course and anxious to secure passage of a thirteenth amendment to abolish slavery altogether.

Lloyd fully understood Lincoln's descriptions of the difficulties a president faces when making major public policy. Through his abolitionist career he had recognized, and occasionally even articulated, the compromising and calculating nature of politics. He had always known that at *some* point some political leader would calculate that the abolitionist crusade had made emancipation of the slaves a wise political move. He was thrilled to have lived long enough to see it. The two men parted with a warm handshake, unaware that this would be the only time they would ever meet.

Lloyd left Lincoln's office nearly skipping with pride and delight. No longer a social outcast and pariah, he had discussed the most important issue of the century with the President of the United States. They had agreed on the slavery issue and had fully understood the role they each played in bringing about the great social revolution that was in process. Most importantly, he had discovered that Lincoln was strongly behind the Thirteenth

Amendment to abolish slavery nationwide; it was not something that was being forced upon him by the Republican Convention as some people were saying. Lloyd had deeper admiration and respect for the president than ever before.

At about this time, a member of Fremont's staff remarked that Garrison had descended from the level of a radical reformer to that of a conservative politician. Garrison responded in *The Liberator*. I have always understood the nature of politics, he asserted, but I can admire Lincoln as a politician because he has adopted many radical ideas.

> At all times I have attempted to judge him fairly, according to the possibilities of his situation and the necessities of the country. In no instance, however, have I censored him for not acting on the highest abstract principles of justice and humanity, and disregarding his constitutional obligations. His freedom to follow his convictions of duty as an individual is one thing — as the President of the United States, it is limited by the functions of his office, for the people do not elect a president to play the part of a reformer or philanthropist, nor to force upon the nation his own peculiar ethical or humanitarian ideas, without regard to his oath or their will. (6)

Garrison even defended Lincoln's refusal to insist on black voting rights. It was not the president's constitutional right to tell the states what voting requirements they must have, he said. Moreover, Garrison quite presciently predicted, white Southerners would make a mockery of the enforcement of voting rights for black people. They would submit to African-American voting rights as a necessity at first, while the Union Army was still in their midst. But, once left to manage their own affairs, they would unquestionably alter the franchise in accordance with their own prejudices.

Garrison had once scorned excuses based on practicalities such as these. Now, he seemed to be embracing them.

3. FULL EMANCIPATION

Through the summer of 1864, Garrison avidly called for the re-election of Abraham Lincoln as the way to defeat the South, ensure passage of the Thirteenth Amendment, and bring about restored harmony in the land. The Democrats nominated General McClellan, who had never been enthusiastic about fighting for emancipation, a fact that might have been the basis of his major fault as a military leader — a tendency to have "the slows," as Lincoln succinctly put it. The Democratic platform called for peace with the South at any price. It was evident that, if elected, McClellan would undo much of what had been done for the African-Americans by the Lincoln administration.

Garrison was confident that Lincoln would win but, as the hot summer dragged on, Republican hopes began to dim. The war was not going well. Lincoln had called General Grant from the West in March to be the seventh commander of the Army of the Potomac. Impressed with Grant's willingness to fight (a quality very lacking in other Union officers), Lincoln had told the grizzled, cigar smoking general to press Lee and not let him escape as the other commanders had done. More than happy to oblige, Grant engaged Lee's army in battle after battle near Richmond, vowing at one point to "fight it out on this line if it takes all summer." On smoke choked battlefields, thousands of bodies lay for days as Grant's army barely paused to bury its dead, and went right on to grapple with the Confederates again. Casualty lists with hundreds of names on them were being posted in northern cities every week. People began to fear the slaughter would never end unless the South was let go. There was a great deal of talk that Lincoln should be voted out of office.

In the White House and at the telegraph in the War Department, Lincoln waited anxiously for each piece of news about Grant's grapple with Lee. The number of young men dying in Virginia sickened him and caused his face to grow more careworn and aged. His tales and jokes came less often, and when they did, they were so obviously meant to ease the terrible strain that it was difficult for anyone to laugh. He began to believe, as Garrison did, that the war was God's punishment of Americans for their sin of allowing slavery to exist. Lincoln was sure the people could take the punishment no longer, and they would defeat him in November.

Suddenly, after months of torment, news flashed across the North that caused a sea change in people's thinking. "Atlanta is ours and fairly won," was the simple message from General Sherman. William Tecumseh Sherman, the relentless commander of the Army of Tennessee, had bludgeoned his way into Georgia, had laid siege to Atlanta, and had finally driven the Confederate defenders out. The retreating Confederate soldiers set fires in warehouses that quickly engulfed the city in flames. The fall of this important city meant that at last the South was coming to its knees. Even Grant's battles with Lee in Virginia no longer seemed so hopeless. At least this Union general was keeping the pressure on and not scurrying back to Washington as all his predecessors had.

Lincoln became more confident that he would win re-election. He used every available means of collecting money for his campaign, including assessing "fees" from each member of the government who wished to keep his job. He urged local Republicans to use any means they could to discredit Democrats. (The Democrats, of course, were reciprocating.) Finally, he asked all Union commanders to issue passes to as many men as they could spare so the men could go home to vote.

With the North's spirits lifted by the capture of Atlanta, and with the federal bureaucracy and army on his side, Lincoln easily defeated McClellan. The president received 2,203,831 votes to the general's 1,797,019, and carried every state but Kentucky, Delaware and New Jersey. The victory meant that Lincoln would be able to see the war through to its conclusion.

As the year ended, Union victory became virtually assured. In September, General Sherman left Atlanta and marched his army across Georgia toward the seaport city of Savannah. Along the way, his soldiers burned almost every plantation house and cotton bale they came to; they tore up railroad tracks and bent the rails around trees; they left a three hundred mile swath of destruction and Southern resentment. Intoning "War is hell," Sherman was determined to break Southern morale and will to fight.

He also broke the slave system in Georgia. Behind the soldiers straggled a procession of African-Americans that grew longer every day. Freed by the Emancipation Proclamation, they instinctively followed their liberators. Contrary to the tale told in Gone With the Wind and other popular fiction, very few slaves in Georgia stayed on the plantations and remained loyal to their masters.

Three days before Christmas, Sherman telegraphed Lincoln, "I beg to present you as a Christmas gift the city of Savannah, with one hundred and fifty guns and plenty of ammunition; also about 25,000 bales of cotton." (7) With its slave system, its cities, its land and its economy in ruins, the South was dying.

In Petersburg, a suburb of Richmond, Grant soon had Lee cornered. Union spies and deserters from the Confederate Army were saying that Lee's men were hungry, without adequate clothing, and poorly armed. Jefferson Davis and his government in Richmond, almost isolated from the rest of the world, were holding joyless Christmas celebrations, wistfully thinking that Lee might yet save the capital as he had before. Secretly, many people were preparing to flee the city once Grant's troops closed in.

With victory imminent, Lincoln's problem of what to do with the "freedmen" was becoming more urgent. He was sticking to his view that the federal government should guarantee only their freedom, at least until the southern states were back in the Union and white Southerners were ready to accept a change in race relations. His days of living amongst the people in Kentucky, and even Indiana and Illinois, made him very aware that an attitudinal change of that magnitude would be a long time coming and very difficult to achieve.

As 1865 began, even complete emancipation was not yet accomplished. One would think that two years after the Emancipation Proclamation, and after the liberation of hundreds of thousands of African-Americans in the South, that freeing *all* the slaves would be almost a formality. But that was not so. In January, the Thirteenth Amendment freeing *every* slave in the United States came before the House of Representatives. Since the House had defeated the amendment the year before (after the Senate had passed it), Lincoln moved vigorously to line up enough votes to secure its passage. He asked Congressman James Ashley of Ohio, the House Majority floor manager, to talk with two or three Democratic congressmen who might be persuaded to vote "yes." He promised a New York congressman a federal appointment for his brother in return for a favorable vote. (A post office in exchange for freedom for four million people made sense, Lincoln believed.) He called Congressman James Rollins of Missouri to the White House and gently pressured him, as an "old Whig friend," to vote for the amendment. When Rollins agreed, Abe asked him to sound out other Border State congressmen for their support. Before the vote was taken, Lincoln pushed

Congress to admit Nevada to the Union as a state knowing the Nevada representatives were for the amendment.

On January 31st, the morning of the vote, a rumor circulated that threatened to send the amendment down to defeat yet again. Peace commissioners from the Confederate States of America were said to be in the city prepared to talk peace. The few Democrats in the House who were tentatively prepared to vote for the emancipation bill might back down for fear that passage of the amendment to abolish slavery would scuttle the chances for an immediate peace and an end to the war. There were, in fact, three representatives from the Confederacy on their way to nearby Fort Monroe, but Lincoln evaded that fact with a note to the House that would do credit to an obfuscating teenager. "As far as I know," he wrote, "there are no peace commissioners in the city, or likely to be in it." (8) The devil was in the word "in," of course – they were not exactly "in" the city — but the president's note snuffed out the rumor long enough for the vote to be taken.

In the days and hours before the vote that would change the nation forever, the role of the consummate politician, Abraham Lincoln, was critical. Even at this final moment, as Garrison well knew, the entire crusade depended on the skills of the political leaders. As Lincoln put it, "We are like whalers who have been long on a chase. We have at last got the harpoon into the monster, but we must now look how we steer, or with one 'flop' of his tail he will send us all into eternity." (9)

As the congressmen filed into the chamber for the vote, the galleries were packed with nervous and excited spectators. The clerk of the House read each name in a roll call vote, and as each "aye" was recorded a cheer went up. But, the crowd was restless when "nays" were recorded because a two-thirds vote was necessary for passage. When, at last, the final vote was announced it was 119 "ayes" to 56 "nays," with 8 abstentions. The amendment to end slavery had passed with but four votes to spare.

When the vote was announced, the House chamber was quiet for a few seconds and then burst into pandemonium. Dignified congressmen sat weeping at their desks or danced in the aisles. Hats and papers filled the air. It was a moment of jubilation that everyone present would always remember.

The next day, a happy parade of citizens marched up to the Executive Mansion accompanied by a band. They called for the president, and Lincoln came to a window to address them. Smiling wearily, he thanked Congress for passing the Thirteenth Amendment and told the people he was confident that the required three quarters of the states would quickly ratify it. Already, he was proud to say, his own state of Illinois had ratified, and so had Maryland, a former slave state.

Privately, Lincoln may have noted the irony of the Thirteenth Amendment. When he took office in 1861, he had tried to set the mind of the South at ease by announcing his willingness to support a thirteenth amendment to the Constitution guaranteeing slavery forever. The South, refusing to accept his sincerity, had chosen secession and civil war. Now he was supporting a thirteenth amendment that *abolished* slavery forever!

In Boston, William Lloyd Garrison basked in the adulation of friends and admirers. As he went about the city, people hailed him to offer their congratulations. Previous celebrations after the Emancipation Proclamation had been shadowed for Garrison by the need for the Union to win the war and the fact that the proclamation left vestiges of slavery in the Border States and Union occupied areas of the South. Now, there were no shadows at all; slavery was completely and forever abolished!!

A "Grand Jubilee" meeting took place in the Music Hall on February 4th. Garrison, his face aglow, stood before his abolitionist friends and spoke:

> At last, after eighty years of wandering and darkness — of cruelty and oppression on a colossal scale, toward a helpless and unoffending race . . . the nation, rising in the majesty of its moral power and political sovereignty, has decreed that LIBERTY shall be PROCLAIMED THROUGHOUT THE LAND, TO ALL THE INHABITANTS THEREOF," and that henceforth no such anomalous character as a slaveholder or slave shall exist beneath the "stars and stripes," within the domain of the republic. (10)

Then, in a paean to the man he had once disparaged but had come to love, he went on:

> And to whom is this country more immediately indebted for this vital and saving amendment of the constitution than, perhaps, to any other man? I believe I may confidently answer — to the humble rail-splitter of Illinois — to the presidential chain-breaker for millions of the oppressed — to Abraham Lincoln. (11)

The audience cheered wildly for several minutes as Garrison basked in their approval. The warm glow of victory felt wonderful. He would surely have felt even more fulfilled if he had known that President Lincoln was said to have remarked to General Daniel Chamberlain, that he was "only an instrument" in the struggle against slavery. "The logic and moral power of Garrison and the anti-slavery people of the country and the army," the president continued, "have done it all." (22)

4. BITTERSWEET VICTORY

On March 4, 1865, Abraham Lincoln stood once more on the steps of the Capitol building to take the oath of office. Symbolically, the dome that had been only half constructed in 1861 when the Union was dividing was now complete and topped by a bronze woman in robes called the "Statue of Freedom." Appropriate, also, was the new Chief Justice who was to administer the oath. Old Roger B. Taney, a slave owner and author of the Dred Scott Decision, had died in 1864. Lincoln had replaced him with his treasury secretary, Salmon P. Chase, an abolitionist.

As Lincoln stepped forward, the crowd cheered and then settled down to listen. The president put on his spectacles, then produced a short manuscript from his pocket. "Fellow country-men," he began, "at this second appearing to take the oath of the presidential office, there is less occasion for an extended address than there was at the first." He hoped that the progress of the war was encouraging to all, and he felt no need to comment on what they all knew.

Neither side expected the war to last as long as it has or to be as terrible as it is, he went on. Then he ventured his explanation for why it had been such an ordeal:

> Fondly do we hope – fervently do we pray – that this mighty scourge of war may speedily pass away. Yet, if God wills that it continue until all the wealth piled by the bondman's two hundred and fifty years of unrequited toil shall be sunk, and until every drop of blood drawn with the lash shall be paid by another drawn with the sword, as was said three thousand years ago, so still it must be said, "The judgments of the Lord are true and righteous altogether."

In closing, Lincoln delivered one of the most eloquent and poetic paragraphs ever delivered by a public speaker. It was more than just beautiful words; it was Lincoln's heart-felt sentiment that the divisions of the country be laid to rest as quickly as possible. He said:

> With malice toward none, with charity for all, with firmness in the right as God gives us to see the right, let us strive on to finish the work we are in, to bind up the nation's wounds, to care for him who shall have borne the battle, and for his widow and his orphan, to do all which may achieve a just and lasting peace among ourselves and with all nations. (13)

To achieve this binding of the nation's wounds with "malice toward none," Lincoln was continuing with his policy of bringing white Southerners back to United States citizenship with full voting rights. As for the newly freed African-Americans, Lincoln had always felt that their ability to make their way in the world after freedom came would be one of the major concerns of immediate and complete emancipation. As a first step, he signed a bill proposed by Senator Sumner creating the "Freedmen's Bureau," an agency of the U.S. Army, to assist them in finding work, getting educated, and dealing with the hostility that was sure to come from the whites all around them. Predictably, restoring whites to power at the same time that their former slaves were just trying to make a beginning as free and equal members of society was going to be problematic, to say the least. How Lincoln would handle the friction that was bound to occur was a major question as the war ground to a close.

Increasingly, Lincoln was finding himself at odds with some abolitionists and with a number of radicals within his party. Men such as Thaddeus Stevens in the House and Charles Sumner in the Senate were urging harsh punishment of the South for its treason, and demanding vigorous efforts to uplift the "freedmen." Whether these Republicans were just vindictive and eager to make the Republican Party dominant in the South by giving

African-Americans the right to vote, or whether they were truly interested in black equality, Lincoln could not tell. He only knew that when the war ended, he would have to work out policies with the "Radical Republicans."

The war ended quickly in the spring of 1865. On the night of April 1st, Lee abandoned his positions in Petersburg, leaving Richmond defenseless. Confederate government officials escaped, but most people in Richmond remained to watch in horror as Grant's soldiers, some of them black, marched through the streets. Half of the city was burned by the Confederates, so Union soldiers mostly saw buildings gutted by fire. They walked through the bricks and glass that littered the streets and smelled the pungent stench of burning cotton. Richmond, like the Confederacy, was in ruins.

The day after they occupied Richmond, Union soldiers stood aghast at what they saw. Ambling down the street in his stovepipe hat and carrying his coat in the warm sun came President Lincoln. He had been visiting General Grant at army headquarters and had decided to inspect the Confederate capital. White citizens of Richmond peered at the spectacle from behind closed curtains, but African-Americans in the streets clustered joyously around the president. Here was "Father Abraham," the man who had set them free. They walked excitedly behind him and beside him, and ran ahead to proclaim his coming to others. Lincoln had met with small groups of black people at the White House — usually people who had been free a long time, such as Frederick Douglass, or people who had never been enslaved — but this was his first contact with the masses of black people that his Emancipation Proclamation and Thirteenth Amendment had freed. Lincoln kept no diary, but he must have been touched by the freedmen's joy as he walked slowly, accompanied by his son, Tad, and a cordon of army officers.

To the Christian freedmen the scene must have been reminiscent of the entry of Jesus into Jerusalem; if they had palm branches, they would have spread them across Lincoln's path. They could not have known, of course, that in two week's time, the analogy would be horribly complete.

After he returned to Washington, the good news Lincoln had been awaiting finally arrived. "General Lee surrendered the Army of Northern Virginia this morning on terms proposed by myself," Grant telegrammed on April 9th. The terms, as Lincoln had outlined them earlier, were that Lee and his men would be paroled and free to go home, that the men would be allowed to keep their horses for spring plowing, and the officers allowed to keep their side arms.

As the news spread, all Washington fell into a dither of celebration. Cannon boomed, firecrackers snapped, and bells peeled. On the night of April 11th an excited crowd gathered before the White House because the president had promised to make a speech. Every lamp in the house was aglow behind Abe as he stepped out onto the balcony. He began reading from several pages in his hands and, as he dropped them, Tad scurried around on the floor below him to scoop them up. He told the people how weary he was and how glad he was to have the chance to give up war and reunite the country in peace. He chose to believe that the southern states had never left the Union — that they were merely out of their proper relationship to it — and that all that needed to be done was to assure Southerners that they were safely home. It was not a triumphant speech; it was not the hard-hitting proclamation of victory the people were in a mood to hear. Before it was over, some of them walked away to do their celebrating elsewhere.

The speech did not sit well with the "Radical Republicans" in Congress, either. They saw it as another sign that Lincoln was going to go easy on the rebels and abandon the African-Americans. They made further plans to achieve their own brand of post-war reconstruction.

Whether Lincoln was planning to gradually compromise with the Radicals and grant equal citizenship to the freedmen as time went on, or whether he actually planned to forget the African-Americans and let Southerners handle the race issue as they pleased in order to secure their loyalty to the Union, we will never know. The record shows that during the war he moved toward emancipation in response to radical pressure and according to his perceptions of what conservatives would be willing to tolerate. Perhaps he was planning to do the same thing with black equality.

William Lloyd Garrison had complete faith that the African-Americans were in good hands with President Abraham Lincoln. But he was so busy celebrating his triumph over slavery that he seemed almost unconcerned with the "freedmen." In *The Liberator* he wrote that equality could not be given to the freedmen by laws, anyway. "(Emancipation will) open the way for ultimate social, civil and political equality," he said, "but this through industrial and educational development, and not by arbitrary mandate." (14)

This argument anticipated the position of the black educator Booker T. Washington who, thirty years later, was to make similar statements. And just as Washington was to have severe critics, so did Garrison. He received a stern rebuke for his complacency (and naivety) from some of his old friends. "O Garrison, this is not abolition," said the Boston *Commonwealth*. "The black men may well rejoice that they have got, out of our military necessity, a certain installment of liberty. . . . But for a prophet to say they may well be content with this . . . is of the madness that goes before ruin." (15) Wendell Phillips continued to insist that further moral agitation was needed to support the Radicals in Congress against the morally obtuse president. But Garrison, exhausted and mellow with the feeling of victory, ignored them all and went right on supporting Lincoln and celebrating emancipation.

In early April, 1865, Lloyd received an invitation from the United States Government to be an honored guest at the ceremonial raising of the U.S. flag in Fort Sumter on the fourth anniversary of its fall. To witness the symbolic victory of freedom over the slave power was an opportunity he could not refuse. Furthermore, Secretary of War Edwin Stanton telegrammed that George Thompson Garrison would be in Charleston on special leave from the army to meet his father.

On April 14th (Good Friday), on a specially erected platform in the shattered fort, Garrison watched General Anderson deliver a short but moving remembrance of his fight there exactly four years before. Then, with the help of the honored guests, he raised the same tattered flag he had lowered in defeat in 1861. "When the flag reached the apex," Garrison wrote later, "the whole bay thundered with . . . a volley of cannon from ship and shore. . . . Then we grasped hands, shouted, embraced, and wept for joy." (16)

That evening Garrison and the others were entertained at a dinner given in their honor at the Charleston Hotel. When it was his turn to speak, Garrison remarked on the irony of how he had been mobbed in Boston (in 1835), and now he was being cheered and feted in Charleston in 1865. Even Lincoln has been converted, he added. "Either he has become a Garrisonian abolitionist, or I have become a Lincoln emancipationist, for I know that we blend together like kindred drops, into one, and his brave heart beats for human freedom everywhere." (17)

As Garrison and his appreciative listeners pictured the president in their minds, none could have imagined what was taking place that very evening in Washington.

Exhausted from the war and the problems of post-war reconstruction, Abraham Lincoln was seeking an evening of relaxation with Mary at Ford's Theater. At 10:15, as he sat watching the comedy *Our American Cousin* in the presidential box above and to the right of the stage, an actor and southern sympathizer, John Wilkes Booth, slipped into the box behind him, pointed a derringer pistol at the back of his head, and fired. As he leapt from the box onto the stage to make his escape he shouted "Sic Semper Tyrannis" ("thus always to tyrants"). Abraham Lincoln's struggle to keep the Union together amidst drastic social upheaval was over. The savior of the nation and the emancipator of four million souls, had been killed on Easter week-end. Millions of Americans, at least in the North, fully appreciated the irony.

Lloyd and his party received the news of Lincoln's assassination on the boat back from Charleston. For Lloyd, personally, it was a stunning and devastating blow. He had come to regard Abraham Lincoln as the greatest man in America. He had watched Lincoln grow into "The Great Emancipator" who skillfully maneuvered the abolition of slavery through the maze of civil war. He had come to love Lincoln as the man who had crowned his thirty years of abolitionist exertion with success.

Even with Lincoln gone, however, Garrison still believed that any further work for the African-American could be done through the political — rather than the agitation — process. Indeed, he felt the need for an abolitionist organization and an abolitionist newspaper had passed.

At the American Anti-Slavery Society meeting a month later, Garrison proposed that the society disband since its work was completed. He reminded the members that they were an *antislav-*

ery society, that their work on behalf of free African-Americans was, and always had been, incidental to their main objective which was to free the slaves. Slavery is destroyed, he said, therefore "it is ludicrous for us, a mere handful of people, with little means, with no agents in the field, no longer separate, and swallowed up in the great ocean of popular feeling against slavery, to assume that we are of special importance, and that we ought not to dissolve our association, under such circumstances, lest the nation should go to ruin? I will not be guilty of any such absurdity." (18)

It is not recorded that anyone reminded Lloyd of the little speech he gave his "Apostolic Twelve" followers that night in the snow after they organized the New England Anti-Slavery Society: "Our numbers are few and our influence limited; but mark my prediction, Faneuil Hall shall ere long echo with the principles we have set forth. We shall shake the nation with their mighty power."

Wendell Phillips and the majority of the members emphatically did not agree with their leader. After a debate lasting two days, the society voted 118 to 48 to continue. The nominating committee put forth Garrison's name to be president for the twenty-fifth year in a row, but he declined. The members then chose Phillips to lead them.

Lacking the power to end the society he had founded, Garrison still controlled *The Liberator*. He decided that 1865 should be its last year; the Thirteenth Amendment was ratified by December, slavery was officially dead; there was, he felt, no further need for an anti-slavery paper. On December 31st, he printed the last edition, personally setting the type for his valedictory editorial just as he had set the "I will be heard!" editorial thirty-five years before. To those who questioned his closing of his anti-slavery shop, he gave answers.

He was aware, he told his readers, of what was happening to the black people in the South. White Southerners, back in control under the lenient reconstruction policies of President Andrew Johnson, were denying the freedmen their rights and making them second-class citizens with laws known as "black codes." But the work for the African-American needed to be carried on in ways other than radical agitation. He would stand by the black people as he always had, but there was no need, now that public sentiment toward the African-Americans had changed so much, to be a man apart. His work for the oppressed would now be within the system.

American racial attitudes, of course, had not changed as much as Garrison thought they had — or at all, for that matter. The vast majority of white Americans, north and south, still viewed the African-Americans as an inferior race. Garrison was looking for signs of improvement because he was weary — weary of fighting for abolition for thirty-five years and weary of being a social outcast. He wanted to hail the "year of jubilee." The most significant sentence in the valedictory editorial was this one: "Most happy am I to be no longer in conflict with the mass of my fellow countrymen on the subject of slavery." (19)

In 1865, Abraham Lincoln's great political voice was silenced forever and William Lloyd Garrison retired from radical agitation. The work of changing America into a land of racial equality was left in the hands of others. Andrew Johnson, a southern racist to the core, attempted to carry out Lincoln's moderate reconstruction, but he was a failure. He was incapable of compromising with the Radical Republicans in Congress and he ended up standing with the white Southerners against them. The Radicals pushed through the Fourteenth and Fifteen Amendments to the United States Constitution to give citizenship, equal rights and the vote to black Americans. But gradually, after 1870, several of the leading radicals died and the rest lost interest in the African-Americans and ignored the fact that white Southerners were devising clever ways to nullify both amendments.

It is sad to contemplate how things might have been different if the Republican Party had nominated abolitionist Hannibal Hamlin to continue as President Lincoln's vice-president for a second term. With Hamlin occupying the White House after the assassination, the Radical Republicans in Congress would have had a chief executive who not only favored racial equality, but would enforce it in his role as commander-in-chief. The alliance between the executive branch and the legislative branch might also have bestowed some degree of economic independence upon the freedmen that could have given them a fighting chance at equality. Payment to African-Americans (reparations) — taken from the traitorous Confederate landowners — was a better idea in 1869 than it would be 150 years later.

In the years that followed the war, William Lloyd Garrison wrote letters and guest editorials and spoke occasionally in support of the Radical Republicans and other causes such as women's rights, but never with the vigor and willingness to stand alone that he had shown in his younger days. Certainly he had *earned* a restful retirement, and he had Helen to look after. Frail and depressed since her stroke, she died in 1876. Lloyd died in 1879. On his final day, surrounded by his children and singing hymns, he departed this world at ease in the knowledge that his name would always be linked with the abolition of American slavery.

Summary and Conclusion

William Lloyd Garrison and Abraham Lincoln played central roles in one of the greatest social and political revolutions in history. Because of their efforts — and the efforts of other radical agitators and politicians and the slaves themselves — four million black Americans were freed from bondage, and the aristocratic southern plantation owners who had dominated American politics for eighty years were stripped of their power.

This book could have focused on other radical abolitionists such as Frederick Douglass, Theodore Dwight Weld, Angelina and Sarah Grimke or Wendell Phillips. Yet, while Garrison is not regarded by some historians as the most significant abolitionist, it was he who lifted the anti-slavery movement off the ground, and it was he who staked out the most extreme and uncompromising anti-slavery position. Thus, it was he who set the ultimate anti-slavery standard — the magnetic pole toward which all

Americans with any humanitarian impulses were drawn, and the standard by which all anti-slavery efforts were measured. It was certainly he who caused the most extreme conservative backlash against abolitionism.

Everyone agrees that Abraham Lincoln was the most consummate politician of his time. Although vilified by radicals and conservatives through most of his presidency, and thought by many to be incompetent, his skills, in the end, were indisputable. He managed people, guided the ship of state through the narrow shoals between extremes, and timed the important changes in policy in such a way that the Union was saved and the slaves were freed. Through it all, his eloquence clarified the struggle and inspired millions of people to support his goals.

The people who lived through the years 1830 to 1865 could not see the pattern of change as it was forming, although Garrison was amazingly prescient and insightful. But, looking back on those years, *we* can now see the process that was taking place.

In 1831, the abolitionists who gathered around Garrison were a pitiable minority, ridiculed and scorned by "normal" society and far more "unreasonable" and extreme than any of the previous anti-slavery advocates had ever been. Garrison and his friends handed out *The Liberator* and spoke energetically to uninterested and often hostile people, gathering converts by ones and twos. Theirs was an embryonic movement, likely to die within a few years when its leaders grew tired or married and decided to "settle down." To be sure, Garrison was proclaiming "I will be heard," but other fanatics before and since have said much the same thing and then promptly disappeared.

Then came the conservative response to the radical abolitionists — the banning of *The Liberator* in the South, the threats from southern newspapers and state legislatures, the mobbing of Garrison in Boston, the murder of the abolitionist Elijah P. Lovejoy in Alton, Illinois, and the passage of the "Gag Rule" in Congress. Suddenly Garrison and his followers had the attention of the American people; they had the sympathy of those who, while not abolitionists, wanted to defend the right of all Americans to enjoy freedom of speech, press and assembly. In the years after 1835, Garrison's greatest allies were not his fellow abolitionists but rather conservatives — slave owners and businessmen –- who overreacted to him and his tiny movement.

Time after time, in their efforts to protect the slave system and justify slavery as a "positive good," Southerners alienated many people in the North. The South demanded and got Texas's admission to the Union as a state, even though this risked war with Mexico. Then, when war with Mexico occurred, the South demanded that all of the territory taken from Mexico be open to slavery. As their price for giving up the right to bring their slaves into California, the South demanded and got a strong fugitive slave law that would force Northerners to return runaway slaves to bondage. Finally, in the mid-1850's, the South demanded that territories that had been previously closed to slavery by mutual agreement be open to slavery once again on the basis of "popular sovereignty."

All of these actions backed up the abolitionists' contention that the Union was dominated by the "slave power." Garrison's solution was northern withdrawal from the Union, depriving the South of the major prop of its system — the northern economy — and leaving the North free from the moral curse of slavery. Most Northerners were not prepared to go that far, but they increasingly felt a sense of northern unity against a southern threat. This unity became very strong when, in the 1850's, northern politicians began to speak of the "slave power conspiracy's" threat to the northern way of life.

Moderate politicians believed strongly in order and the rule of law. These men began to see that if the South continued to have its way, particularly in the western territories, northern interests would suffer and slavery would continue to thrive, perpetuating the North's complicity in an immoral institution and threatening the North's free labor system. These moderates began to believe that slavery should at least be confined to its existing area even though it should not, and legally *could* not, be dismantled by the federal government. In 1858, during his debates with Stephen Douglas, Abraham Lincoln became the most articulate spokesman for this point of view.

Better than most members of the Republican Party that sprang up in the 1850s to oppose slavery in the territories, Lincoln was able to wrap moral opposition to slavery, the economic needs of the North, and observance of the law and the Constitution into one tidy package. He could prove effectively that the legal confinement of slavery was the intention of the founding fathers; he could convince northern workingmen that restriction of slavery would open lands in the West to settlement by free white people who, incidentally, would not have to live side-by-side with black people; he could convince northern businessmen that restriction of slavery would weaken the South's voting power and open the way to high tariffs, internal improvements and other laws favorable to the growth of industry; and he could argue strongly for those who believed as he did that slavery was a moral wrong, that restriction of it would lead to its eventual demise.

Although the argument between the North and the South was more heated by the mid 1850s, the situation in America was not revolutionary. There was hope, especially in the minds of men such as Lincoln, that the issue could be settled with a reasonable compromise that would allow slavery to die a gradual and natural death, unaccompanied by any violent agonies that would tear society apart. But the South, close to a state of paranoiac frenzy after thirty years of abolitionist agitation, was not ready to accept *any* restrictions on slavery. The North, aware of the economic interests at stake and convinced that slavery should, indeed, be on the "road to ultimate extinction," was unwilling to retreat either. The area for compromise quickly shrank.

The killings in Kansas and John Brown's raid on Harper's Ferry enabled the violent, uncompromising men in the South to convince other Southerners that their system was in imminent danger from the North. John Brown, the argument went, was more than a mad man, he was a manifestation of the Republican Party. Thus, although Lincoln was truly a moderate man, Southerners perceived him as a fanatic — another John Brown, another William Lloyd Garrison — and when he was elected president, they left the Union.

When Lincoln took office and seven slave states were out of the Union, the situation in the North was still not truly revolutionary. People were not ready to make the drastic change of abolishing slavery. The government, and most of the people in the North, would have been happy to have the South return to the Union with slavery still intact. Even after the Confederates fired on Fort Sumter and war began, Lincoln and the North were not in a revolutionary frame of mind. The sole goal of the northern war effort was to restore the Union. But, when the war dragged on, increasing steadily in its cost to the North, even Lincoln began to see that the crisis required extreme action. The underlying cause of the war had to be removed and a major prop of the Confederacy had to be eliminated. The South, because of its warped view of Lincoln and its own paranoia, had made its ultimate over-reaction to the abolitionists and brought about the very change it was so desperately seeking to avoid.

Although he finally accepted the need for emancipation, Lincoln took every opportunity he could to make it gradual and to minimize the social disruption he was sure would result. He delayed as long as he could so that the Border States could be secured and so no one could accuse him of acting rashly; he gave the South time to come back into the Union without emancipation; he tried to arrange compensation for slave owners; he even tried to find a suitable plan for deporting as many African-Americans as possible.

Through all of this, William Lloyd Garrison was amazingly tolerant. To be sure, he chastised Lincoln for even thinking of compensation and colonization, and he wrung his hands over the delays. But he repeatedly defended Lincoln before his impatient followers. After Lincoln signed the Emancipation Proclamation, Garrison linked up with the president so closely that in 1865 he was able to say that it was not clear whether Lincoln had become a Garrisonian abolitionist or he, Garrison, had become a moderate politician. Garrison was convinced that the need for radical agitation was over, that public opinion was now on the side of the African-American, and that all friends of the African-Americans could work within the political system.

Some abolitionists followed Garrison and Lincoln and, after Lincoln's death, worked through the "Radical Republicans" in Congress for black advancement. But Wendell Phillips and other "super radicals" continued to stand apart from politics and demand, in uncompromising terms, equality for the African-Americans. The result was that the status of the black people was bought and bartered in the political arena and finally deserted by the "Radical Republicans" who moved on to another cause — the industrial growth of the United States.

A revolution in American society starts with very slim chances of success. If a revolutionist is dedicated and is fortunate enough to have a skilled politician respond to the rising revolutionary tide, the cause might follow the pattern that Garrison's did. But, very few radicals are capable of presenting their program with the eloquence and powerful moral force that Garrison did; most radicals do not have the perseverance and clear conception of their role that Garrison had. Very few politicians have Lincoln's touch with the common people, his reasoning power, his clarity of speech and, above all, his ability to have strong moral convictions yet hold them in check until the time is right to act on them. William Lloyd Garrison was the ultimate agitator; Abraham Lincoln was the ultimate politician. Their story serves as a guide for those of us who wish to understand how the greatest social, political and economic change in American history came to pass.

Critical Documents

PRELIMINARY EMANCIPATION PROCLAMATION
SEPT. 22, 1862

I, Abraham Lincoln, President of the United States of America, and Commander-in-Chief of the Army and Navy thereof, do hereby proclaim and declare that hereafter, as heretofore, the war will be prosecuted for the object of practically restoring the constitutional relation between the United States, and each of the states, and the people thereof, in which states that relation is, or may be, suspended or disturbed.

That it is my purpose, upon the next meeting of Congress, to again recommend the adoption of a practical measure tendering pecuniary aid to the free acceptance of rejection of all slave states, so called, the people thereof may not than be in rebellion against the United States and which states may then have voluntarily adopted, of thereafter may voluntarily adopt, immediate or gradual abolishment of slavery within their respective limits; and that the effort to colonize persons of African descent, with their consent, upon this continent, or elsewhere, with the previously obtained consent of the governments existing there, will be continued.

That on the first day of January in the year of our Lord one thousand eight hundred and sixty-three, all persons held as slaves within any state, or designated part of a state, the people whereof shall then be in rebellion against the United States shall be then, thenceforward, and forever free; and the executive government of the United States, including the military and naval authority thereof, will recognize and maintain the freedom of such persons, and will do no act or acts to repress such persons, or any of them, in any efforts they may make for their actual freedom.

EMANCIPATION PROCLAMATION
JANUARY 1, 1863

Whereas, on the twenty-second day of September, in the year of our Lord one thousand eight hundred and sixty-two, a proclamation was issued by the President of the United States, containing, among other things, the following, to wit:

"That on the first day of January, in the year of our Lord one thousand eight hundred and sixty-three, all persons held as slaves within any state or designated part of a state, the people whereof shall then be in rebellion against the United States, shall be then, thenceforward, and forever free; and the Executive Government of the United States, including the military and naval authority thereof, will recognize and maintain the freedom of such persons, and will do no act or acts to repress such persons, or any of them, in any efforts they may make for their actual freedom.

"That the Executive will, on the first day of January aforesaid, by proclamation, designate the states or parts of states, if any, in which the people thereof, respectively, shall than be in rebellion against the United States; and the fact that any state, or the people thereof, shall on that day be, in good faith, represented in the Congress of the United States by members chosen thereto at elections wherein a majority of the qualified voters of such state shall have participated, shall, in the absence of strong countervailing testimony, be deemed conclusive evidence that such state, and the people thereof, are not then in rebellion against the United States.

Now, therefore I, Abraham Lincoln, President of the United States, by virtue of the power in me vested as Commander-in-Chief, of the Army and Navy of the United States in time of actual armed rebellion against the authority and government of the United States, and as a fit and necessary war measure for suppressing said rebellion, do, on this first day of January, in the year of our Lord one thousand eight hundred and sixty-three, and in accordance with my purpose so to do publicly proclaimed for the full period of one hundred days, from the day first above mentioned, order and designate as the States and parts of States wherein the people thereof respectively are this day in rebellion against the United States the following, to wit:

Arkansas, Texas, Louisiana, (except the parishes of St. Bernard, Plaquemines, Jefferson, St. John, St. Charles, St. James Ascension, Assumption, Terrebonne, Lafourche, St. Mary, St. Martin, and Orleans, including the City of New Orleans), Mississippi, Alabama, Florida, Georgia, South Carolina, and Virginia (except the forty-eight counties designated as West Virginia, and also the counties of Berkley, Accomac, Northampton, Elizabeth City. York, Princess Ann, and Norfolk, including the cities of Norfolk and Portsmouth), and which excepted parts, are for the present, left precisely as if this proclamation were not issued.

And by virtue of the power, and for the purposes aforesaid, I do order and declare that all persons held as slaves within said designated states and parts of states are, and henceforward shall be free; and that the Executive government of the United States, including the military and naval authorities thereof, will recognize and maintain the freedom of said persons.

And I hereby enjoin upon the people so declared to be free to abstain from all violence, unless in necessary self-defense; and I recommend to them that, in all cases when allowed, they labor faithfully for reasonably wages.

And I further declare and make known, that such persons of suitable condition, will be received into the armed service of the United States to garrison forts, positions, stations, and other places, and to man vessels of all sorts in said service.

And upon this act, sincerely believed to be an act of justice, warranted by the Constitution, upon military necessity, I invoke the considered judgment of mankind, and the gracious favor of Almighty God.

In witness whereof, I have hereunto set my hand and caused the seal of the United States to be affixed.

Done at the City of Washington, this first day of January, in the year of our Lord one thousand eight hundred and sixty-three and of the independence of the United States of America the eighty-seventh.

By the President: ABRAHAM LINCOLN
WILLIAM H. SEWARD, Secretary of State

THIRTEENTH AMENDMENT TO THE UNITED STATES CONSTITUTION

Section I

Neither slavery nor involuntary servitude, except as a punishment for crime whereof the party shall have been duly convicted, shall exist within the United States, or any place subject to their jurisdiction.

Section II

Congress shall have power to enforce this article by appropriate legislation.

Notes

CHAPTER I: TWO YOUNG AMERICANS, 1831

1. Beveridge, Albert J., *Abraham Lincoln, 1809-1865, Vol.I,* Houghton Mifflin, Boston, 107.

2. Garrison, Wendell Phillips, and Garrison, Frederick Jackson. *The Life of William Lloyd Garrison Told By His Children.* 4 Vols. New York: The Century Company, 1889. Vol. I, 94. (hereafter referred to as *Life)*

3. *Life I, 87.*

4. *Life I, 118-119.*

5. *Life I, 119.*

6. *Life I, 121.*

7. *Life I, 125.*

8. *Life I, 133-134.*

9. *Life I, 134.*

10. *Life I, 140.*

11. *Life I, 151.*

12. *Life I, 166.*

13. *Life I, 183.*

14. *Life I, 200.*
15. *Life I, 209.*
16. *Life I, 214.*
17. *Liberator,* January 1, 1831.
18. *Liberator,* January 1, 1831

CHAPTER II: THE PRAIRIE POLITICIAN, 1831-1844

1. Van Doren Stern, Philip, *The Life and Writings of Abraham Lincoln,* New York: Modern Library, 1940. 221-224.
2. Sandburg, Carl, *Abraham Lincoln; The Prairie Years, 2 vols.* (New York: Harcourt, Brace and Co., 1940), Vol. I, 64. (Herein referred to as Sandburg, *Prairie Years*)
3. Sandburg, *The Prairie Years, I,* 137.
4. Sandburg, *The Prairie Years, I,* 155.
5. Thomas, Benjamin, *Abraham Lincoln, A Biography* (New York: Alfred Knopf, 1952), 49.
6. Sandburg, *The Prairie Years, I,* 195.
7. Sandburg, *The Prairie Years, I,* 211-212.
8. Van Doren Stern, 237.
9. Van Doren Stern, 263
10. Sandburg, *The Prairie Years, I,* 243.
11. Sandburg, Carl, *The Prairie Years, I,* 234.
12. Sandburg, *The Prairie Years, I,* 281-285.
13. Sandburg, Carl, *Abraham Lincoln; The Prairie Years and the War Years,* New York: Harcourt, Brace and Co., 1954), (Herein referred to as: Sandburg, *Prairie Years and War Years),* 65.
14. Van Doren Stern, 279.
15. Sandburg, *The Prairie Years, I,* 343.
16. Sandburg, *Prairie Years and War Years,* 81.
17. Van Doren Stern, 268.
18. Donald, David, *Lincoln,* (London: Jonathan Cape, 1995), (Herein referred to as Donald), 90.
19. Van Doren Stern, 269.
20. Sandburg, *The Prairie Years, I, 475.*
21. Sandburg, *The Prairie Years, I,* 307-308.

CHAPTER III: THE RADICAL AGITATOR, 1831-1844

1. Mayer, Henry, *All on Fire, William Lloyd Garrison and the Abolition of Slavery*, New York, St. Martins Press, 1998. 69.
2. *Life, I, 43.*
3. *Life I, 58.*
4. Life I, 100.
5. *Life I, 173.*
6. Mayer, *120.*
7. *Life I, 259.*
8. *Life I, 229-230.*
9. Mayer, 121-123.
10. *Life I, 280.*
11. *Life I, 301.*
12. *Life I, 351.*
13. Merrill, Walter M., *Against Wind and Tide, A Biography of William Lloyd Garrison*, Cambridge: Harvard University Press, 1963. 71-72.
14. *Life I, 385.*
15. *Life I, 385*
16. *Life I, 396.*
17. Alonzo, Harriet Hyman, *Growing Up Abolitionist, The Story of the Garrison Children* (Boston: Univ. of Mass. Press, 2002), 30.
18. Alonso, 32-33.
19. *Life I, 426-427.*
20. *Life I, 447.*
21. *Life I, 501.*
22. *Life I, 511.*
23. *Life I, 519.*
24. Life I, 521.
25. *Life, Vol. II, 16.*
26. Mayer, 206.
27. *Life II, 50.*
28. *Life II, 124.*
29. *Life II, 78.*
30. *Life II, 140.*

31. *Life II, 166.*
32. *Liberator,* December 15, 1837.
33. *Life II, 349.*
34. *Life II, 355.*
35. *Life III, 18.*
36. *Life II, 216.*
37. *Life III, 88.*
38. *Life III, 100.*

CHAPTER IV: GARRISON AND LINCOLN IN 1845
NO NOTES

CHAPTER V: BY THE FRUIT THE TREE IS TO BE KNOWN 1845–1850

1. Craven, Avery, *The Coming of the Civil War*, Chicago: University of Chicago Press, 1966. 192.
2. Van Doren Stern, 284-286.
3. Merrill, 210.
4. *Life III, 143.*
5. Van Doren Stern, 286.
6. Wikipedia: "United States Declaration of War Upon Mexico."
7. Merrill, 211.
8. McPherson, James, *Battle Cry of Freedom; The Civil War Era* (New York, Oxford University Press, 1988), 51.
9. Donald, 123.
10. Donald, 126.
11. *Life III, 232.*
12. *Life III, 231.*
13. *Life III, 231.*
14. *Collected Works of Abraham Lincoln, 9 vols. Vol. I: 452.*
15. *Donald, 126.*
16. *Collected Works, I, 503-505.*
17. Sandburg, *The Prairie Years and the War Years, 102*
18. Thomas, John, *The Liberator, William Lloyd Garrison, A Biography.* Boston: Little, Brown and Co., 1963. 399.

19. *Life III, 19.*
20. *Life III, 193.*
21. *Life III,* 194.
22. *Life III,* 195.
23. *Life III, 199.*
24. *Life III, 205.*
25. *Life III,* 230.
26. Mayer, 400-401.
27. *Life III,* 283.
28. *Life III,* 288-300.

CHAPTER VI: THE SLAVE POWER CONSPIRACY, 1850–1859

1. *Life III, 323.*
2. *Life III, 324.*
3. *Life III, 324.*
4. Thomas, John, 382.
5. *Life III, 367-368.*
6. *Life III, 360-362.*
7. Thomas, John, 386.
8. *Life III, 409.*
9. *Life III, 412.*
10. *Van Doren Stern, 348-349.*
11. Van Doren Stern, 370.
12. Van Doren Stern, 372.
13. Van Doren, Stern, 374.
14. Sandburg, *The Prairie Years, II,* 167.
15. Van Doren Stern, 390.
16. Van Doren Stern, 392.
17. Van Doren Stern, 395.
18. Freehling, William, *Becoming Lincoln,* Charlottesville, Univ. of Virginia Press, 2018, 187.
19. Sandburg, *The Prairie Years II, 85.*
20. Van Doren Stern, 413.
21. *Liberator,* December 24, 1854.
22. *Life III, 437-439.*

23. *Life III, 441.*

24. *Life III, 443.*

25. *Life III, 443-444.*

26. *Life III, 448-464.*

27. *Life III, 470-473.*

28. Van Doren Stern, 427.

29. Sandburg, *The Prairie Years, II, 103.*

30. Van Doren Stern, 438-439.

31. Van Doren Stern, 537.

32. Sandburg, *The Prairie Years II,* 169.

CHAPTER VII: RADICALISM BREEDS WAR 1859-1861

1. Thomas, John, 397.

2. Reynolds, David S., *John Brown, Abolitionist (New York: Alfred Knopf, 2005),* 395.

3. *Life III, 486.*

4. Merrill, 273.

5. Van Doren Stern, 555.

6. Van Doren Stern, 561.

7. Van Doren Stern, 569-591.

8. Van Doren Stern, 592.

9. Van Doren Stern, 594-595.

10. Thomas, Benjamin, 210.

11. *Life, III, 485.*

12. *Liberator,* February 16, 1860.

13. *Liberator,* June 1, 1860.

14. *Liberator,* July 20, 1860

15. *Liberator,* January 20, 1860.

16. Merrill, 274.

17. *Life, III, 504-509.*

18. *Life, III, 504-509.*

19. Mayer, 516.

20. Van Doren Stern, 631.

21. Van Doren Stern, 626.

22. Van Doren Stern, 626-627.

23. Van Doren Stern, 646-657.

24. *Life, IV, 18-19.*
25. Thomas, Benjamin, 254.
26. Donald, 296.
27. *Life, IV, 40-41.*
28. *Life, IV, 21.*
29. *Life, IV, 30-32.*
30. *Liberator,* June 14, 1861.

CHAPTER VIII: SLAVERY AND THE TACTICS OF WAR 1861-1863

1. Van Doren Stern, 681-683.
2. Van Doren Stern, 681-683
3. Sandburg, *The Prairie Years and the War Years,* 267.
4. *Life, IV, 33.*
5. *Life, IV, 34.*
6. *Life, IV, 35.*
7. *Life IV, 44-45.*
8. Quarles, Benjamin, *Lincoln and the Negro,* Oxford, 1962, *104.*
9. *Life, IV, 49.*
10. *Life IV, 51.*
11. *Life, IV, 53.*
12. Donald, 368-369.
13. McPherson, James, *The Struggle for Equality: Abolitionists and the Negro in the Civil War and Reconstruction,* Princeton University Press, Princeton, New Jersey,1964. 117.
14. McPherson, 534.
15. *Life, IV, 62.*
16. *Liberator,* December 26, 1862.
17. Sandburg, *The War Years, II, 14.*
18. Quarles, 113.
19. Quarles, 132-133.
20. *Life, IV, 70.*

CHAPTER IX: ON COMMON GROUND AT LAST 1863–1865

1. *Life IV, 71.*
2. *Life, IV, 95.*
3. *Life, IV, 104-110.*
4. *Life, IV, 113.*
5. Thomas, John, 426.
6. *Life, IV, 119-120.*
7. McPherson, 811.
8. Goodwin, Doris Kearns, *Team of Rivals, The Political Genius of Abraham Lincoln,* New York: Simon and Schuster, 2005, 688.
9. Goodwin, 688.
10. *Life, IV, 128-130.*
11. Goodwin, Doris Kearns, *Leadership in Turbulent Times* (New York: Simon and Schuster, 2018), 241.
12. Mayer, 568.
13. Van Doren Stern, 840-845.
14. McPherson, 297.
15. McPherson, 295.
16. Merrill, 296.
17. Merrill, 297.
18. *Life, IV, 158-159.*
19. Merrill, 303.

Index

WA